Sleeping Between the Rails

Sleeping Between the Rails

A WOMAN'S ODYSSEY

Carroll Devine

Some names have been changed to protect the innocent, as well as the not-so-innocent.

ISBN: 0692576479
ISBN 13: 9780692576472
Library of Congress Control Number: 2015957984
Rabbit Hole, Mandeville, LA

This book is dedicated to
the memory of my beautiful mother Alice
who always inspired and encouraged me to travel,
both inwardly and abroad, to learn and to live an uncommon life.
Her continual prayers and concern covered me as I did.

With many thanks to my husband Louie, and other close family
and friends whose love and patience have helped
to make this book a reality.

Prologue

By all rights I should be dead. No. By all *wrongs* I should be dead. All I wanted was the world. I didn't know it would cost so much to get it.

I didn't know it would cost me my innocence, my pride, my dignity, and a great measure of sanity. I didn't know it would almost cost me my life, more than once, or more importantly, my faith in everything.

But I *had to* go.

Some irresistible unseen force was at work drawing me across the ocean, leaving behind my family and all I knew of my safe, provincial, Catholic life in New Orleans. The Universe in collaboration with this force arranged pathways and opened doors behind the scenes, and despite all the obstacles, made sure it happened. Otherwise the improbable pieces would never have come together.

When I was twenty, I fell in love, or fell in *whatever,* with one of the editors of the college newspaper for which I was writing. Alex was assigned to show me the ropes. On dates as we sat in dark, uncomfortable booths in the college haunt and drank cheap beer, which I hated, he made me cry, browbeating me because I was so ignorant of the world. I had no answer for my roommate's logical question: "Why do you keep dating him?"

Alex had a fine intellect and world curiosity, and he provoked and challenged me as no one else had. I didn't realize then that he possibly saw something beneath this ingenuous Pollyanna coed's exterior that looked a lot like daring and a hunger to know what made the world tick.

He also made me laugh and introduced me to a foreign world in my own New Orleans hometown. He took me to unorthodox, interesting places, like the seedy riverfront bar where Greek sailors worked themselves into collective ebullience as they connected arms to shoulders in one long snaky dance. We drank *cervezas* at an overcrowded Latino bar where the seductive, hip-shaking rhythms plucked the strings in the deepest part of my musical soul. We ended the nights with greasy fried rice in the Chinese café next door. This new kind of life intrigued me.

Fate arranged it that the day before Alex moved to California for his long planned transfer to another college, he would hand me a copy of *A Coney Island of the Mind* by Lawrence Ferlinghetti. "Look inside," he said. I did.

"To Carroll who hasn't been to the circus yet." His inscription was both an affront to my nice little life and a thrown gauntlet. I knew from that moment I *must* go to the world circus, although I didn't know how or when or with whom.

Almost two years would intervene before it all came together, while at the same time the world I knew would begin to fall apart. My life would become a perilous, vagabonding, world odyssey of five and a half years.

CHAPTER 1

Seafaring

When we presently got underway … I became a new being and the subject of my own admiration. I was a traveler! A word had never tasted so good in my mouth before. I had an exultant sense of being bound for mysterious lands and distant climes.
—Mark Twain, "Life on the Mississippi"

"Come to Spain and I'll write poetry on your breast," he wrote in a fervent letter from Madrid.

I was a few weeks away from leaving for Chicago for airline stewardess training–in 1967 still a glamorous, sought after position–when the fateful letter arrived. Alex's words burned into my romantic soul. Would the poetry be *about* my breast or *on* my actual breast? I didn't care. It sounded like a marriage proposal to me, which is what I told my parents. How could I *not* go?

Never mind that I barely knew Alex or that my parents had seen him only twice, and didn't trust what they saw.

Never mind that after I scraped together the two hundred thirty-two dollars for the two-week passage on the Spanish freighter, I would sail away with only a couple of hundred dollars in my pocket. My parents, with five other children, had nothing to spare.

"Are you sure you won't change your mind, honey?" Mama asked for the hundredth time, her tears nearly choking out her words as she drove me to the New Orleans Robin Street Wharf.

It was too late. I was a projectile already launched. In fact, once the decision was made to sail into a wide unknown, everything fell into place so quickly that neither my family nor I fully comprehended what was happening.

We parked in a narrow off-street spot adjacent to my port of embarkation–a heavy wood and concrete wharf, separated from the street by dark, squat warehouses. It was only one in a procession of identical colorless wharves lining the east bank of the Mississippi in this seedy part of town. A nuts and bolts farewell point, this was where sweating longshoremen daily loaded and offloaded the raw stuff of commerce.

Tightly moored with its gangplank down, my ship, the *Mar Egeo*, looked equally unpretentious. While I'm sure it had its distinguishing features, they weren't obvious to me. What's more, I didn't care. This bulky, grey metal vessel was seaworthy, I presumed. All I cared about at that moment was that it would transport me across the Atlantic to an exciting new life, one that would begin with my reconnecting in Europe with my erstwhile boyfriend.

Don't misunderstand. It wasn't that my old life was bad. It wasn't bad at all. I had a very loving, supportive family and good friends, and I was armed with a sunny outlook and a recently earned college degree. Prospects for a beautiful life hovered, but something was missing. To find out what that was, I had to run away from home–in this case, *sail* away.

One of the ship's officers stood on its no-frills deck, eyed his soon-to-be passenger, and waved. I was obviously overdressed to board a freighter, wearing a black and white striped, fully-lined organdy sundress I had made especially for the occasion. I waved back. Two of my sisters, my young brother, my godmother and her son were all in my farewell entourage.

My mother wasn't ready for me to board. She kept fidgeting and stalling by attempts at conversation. She picked up a fly-away piece of my hair and parked it behind my ear. "Hold your shoulders up," she said.

Daddy wasn't there yet. Ordinarily he was a man who couldn't be rushed, but his second oldest daughter's departure brought him urgency. I knew he would come as fast as he could after work today, rushing from the Ninth Ward across town. Where *was* he?

The ship strained against the ropes and groaned against the dock's rubber bumpers. When it was time, it would sail, no matter who was missing.

Stalling in her own way, my godmother was taking pictures of everyone on the dock with her Polaroid camera. After each one was taken, we waited the required minute or so for the stiff paper to slide out and the black and white images to gradually appear. Precious minutes evaporated.

Mama tried to smile, but the tears now streaming down her cheeks gave away her distress. She had cried the night before, almost begging me not to go, but finally resigning herself to it. "Just don't let him bring you down," she urged me before she went to bed. This was especially hard for her because she knew I was going to be living with a man to whom I wasn't yet married. In those very early days of the so-called sexual revolution, decent people didn't do that, especially not good Catholic girls. She had raised me as a good Catholic, and I don't think she could accept that her firstborn was no longer a follower.

If truth be told, my mother was in large part responsible for my yearning for the world, for romance, and love of adventure. "You can do anything you want," she had whispered into my childish ear many nights as she put me to bed. "Don't just be a housewife."

Alice was a bright, talented woman and mother of six whose own dreams of career and travel had been short-circuited by her circumstances–taking care of her ailing parents right out of high school, then at age twenty-two, marrying my father who already had a young daughter.

While growing up I tried to give my mother what made her happy–academic success and involvement in extra-curricular activities. While it turned out that these things also made *me* happy and fulfilled, my mother reveled in them and always encouraged me to do what she hadn't been able to do.

"Wait a minute," Mama might have said, "I didn't mean something *this* different." Although she didn't say so, I knew a large part of her heart now regretted her original advice. Now, although I would be the traveler she couldn't be, I was embarking on a voyage of thousands of miles with no defined time or geographical boundaries, and no inkling of how I would live or support myself.

But my fire was ignited, and so were the ship's engines. Their rumble announced it wouldn't be long. When Mama couldn't delay the inevitability of my boarding any longer, I made my rounds, hugging and kissing everyone before walking up the gangplank with my mother close behind. A ship officer greeted us, motioning for us to follow two crew members who lugged my grossly over-stuffed bags to a closet-sized cabin.

Mama looked around, sized up the accommodations and helped me find space to stash the bags. The dejection in her eyes told me she still hoped I would change my mind and not go. *Just one more kiss.* Her loving arms clutched me tightly, then, reluctantly released their hold. Before disembarking to join the others, she gave me a parting bottle of sherry, a box of Fig Newtons, and a peignoir set for my presumed wedding night.

Just as crewmen pulled up the gangplank, my father appeared and ran up to the edge of the wharf. He and I held hands through the railing for the few remaining moments. Always a man of few words, he was even more at a loss now. "Be careful, you hear?" was all he could say, though I knew he loved me dearly.

The engines now roaring, two crewmen unlashed the heavy ropes and the freighter was loosed from its moorings. I was ready.

"I promise I'll write," I called to my family. Standing on the deck with the only other two passengers and two Spanish stewards, I was too wrapped up in the excitement of the moment to pay much attention to the sadness in my parents' eyes as we pulled away. My family waved furiously. I waved too, clinging to the railing. I watched this small group of people who had been my life's anchors until tears and distance obliterated them from my sight.

I was still misty-eyed when the freighter took us downriver past the area of the Battle of New Orleans site and its tall obelisk monument. I was hoping my family had made it to the levee there by then and I could have one more glimpse of them waving, but the Barcelona-bound ship hurried with the swift Mississippi towards the Gulf of Mexico.

CHAPTER 2

A Wide Berth

Throw your dreams into space like a kite, and
you do not know what it will bring back,
a new life, a new friend, a new love, a new country.
–ANAIS NIN

MANUEL, A STEWARD, GENTLY TAPPED me on the shoulder. "*Por favor, senorita, puedo ayudarle?*"

Consulting the pocket-sized Spanish English dictionary in my shoulder bag, I found out that he was asking if he could help me.

Help? I didn't need any help. Not yet anyway.

No one on board spoke more than a few words of English, including the other passengers, Olga and Ricardo, but with my dictionary and the fourteen days of total immersion sailing ahead of me, I felt up to the challenge. It was exciting. Besides, I had a place to sleep, my food was provided, and presumably the captain was a skilled sailor. What did I have to worry about?

Olga and Ricardo, young newlyweds from Chile, were bound for the University of Madrid. Ricardo, tall and lean with wavy black hair, had the exuberance of a man on a mission. Olga was quietly attractive. She had shoulder length, light brown hair and a winsome, but careful, smile.

The three of us stayed up late into the first night talking, taking considerable time to exchange even basic information. Since necessity compelled us to drop the common communication barrier of self-consciousness, we also did a lot of gesturing and acting out. It surprised me how much could be communicated without words. But when Ricardo asked, "*Porque viajas sola?*" Why are you traveling alone? I had to rummage longer through the dictionary.

I managed that *mi novio* was waiting for me, but it was even more difficult, linguistically and practically, to answer the question of what work *mi novio* did or would do. Ricardo didn't understand how we would live.

Honestly, I hadn't given it much thought myself. I had blind faith, the kind that comes from living in the United States at this time of its development. I believed—if I even gave it much thought—that the hardest times were behind us as a country. We still had some social injustices to correct, but economically, the Great Depression was far behind us and beyond our ken and concern. My generation grew up expecting anything was possible. Follow your dreams, we were told, so I did. Somehow the Universe would take care of me. I jumped into this adventure heart first. I didn't want to be sobered by details.

Undoubtedly, even as I stepped brazenly into a new world, my soul clung to the fresh memory of home and the faces on the dock I loved so well. Manuel, a diminutive balding middle-aged man, offered me solace in a cassette tape he had recorded in America.

We clumsily sang along with *Michael Rowed the Boat Ashore*, and then listened to a cut of Elvis Presley's deep velvet voice singing *Love Me Tender.*

Elvis, crooning under the stars on the deck of a quiet ship, gliding smoothly over silken waters. How good could it get? Well, maybe if I had a man's arms wrapped around me, my man's arms, it would be better. But I could wait. I could be content now with being in love with the feeling. For the first time in my life, I was enjoying being completely on my own.

I went to bed in my tiny inside cabin, tired from the emotional strain of the day, but eager for the next sunrise. I awoke before dawn. During the darkest time of the night, our ship sailed into the mouth of the Mississippi where its fast-flowing waters clash and rumble with the bigger-bodied Gulf of Mexico. The ship's rolling and pitching tossed me around my bunk until I tumbled out of it, staggered on rubber legs to the head, and heaved. As bad as I felt, I was laughing at myself—me, seasick. I had never been seasick before.

Growing up two blocks from the Mississippi River and the tall levees that restrained it, I used to watch massive seagoing vessels floating high above the streets, and I would listen to their foghorns as I fell asleep at night. In the small Creole cottage where I shared a twin bed with one sister and the bedroom with two more, I dreamed of being on one of those ships one day, but seasickness was not a part of that picture.

Thankfully, the "*mareo*" never returned throughout the rest of the voyage, and waters remained as calm as a rocking chair's rocking, so calm an outside observer might have thought the long voyage boring. For me it provided a mercifully gradual acclimatization to a new world—a world of living with strangers, different customs, ever-changing places, and of deep water, of whose nature I knew little, but on whose substance I must count to sustain me.

The days of this transition period I spent mostly on the scrupulously clean deck studying my Spanish dictionary, reading, and writing. As the sun gradually deepened the color of my skin, the sweet, pungent, provocative aroma of olive oil from the galley and the salty sea essence seeped into my nostrils and imagination. I never tired of gazing at the ocean spread out before me, watching for any interruption on its surface or changes on the horizon.

Changes were rare. Once, we watched dolphins, showing off nearby, and on a few occasions saw a ship in the far distance. Two days out of New Orleans, we picked up a Miami radio station, but we didn't sight land until the eighth day, when we passed near the Canary Islands. Manuel knocked early that morning so I could see the comforting outline of mountains and houses.

We ate most of our meals with the ship's officers. Small continental breakfasts gave way to four and five-course lunches and two and three-course suppers. A soup, salad or plate of beans, was followed by fish, then some type of meat and potatoes, and a dessert of fruit or flan. Meals were always accompanied by wine, a fact that prompted me to learn quickly how to say I had had enough. "*Basta*," I repeated, careful to pronounce it clearly. Nodding his head in recognition, Manuel smiled, ignored my pleas, and filled my glass again.

Playing cards became a nightly ritual. Olga and Ricardo taught me a couple of Spanish games, along with a growing Spanish vocabulary, and I taught them Rummy.

After the first night, I switched cabins to an outside one because I found some of the crew peeping into my quarters. This outside cabin gave me the luxury of a view of the sea through the porthole, and the privacy made me feel more secure, that is, until one late night about a week into the voyage when I heard a knock at my door.

It was Ricardo. He came, so he said, to give me some information about Spain we had discussed earlier in the day. I let him in and we talked. We spread out a map of Spain on my bunk and sat down beside it because there wasn't any other place to sit. Before long I noticed that Ricardo's attention had left the map. I felt his intense gaze on me. What was the true purpose of his visit? Had he planned to seduce me or was the simmering passion on both sides coincidental to the circumstances? Young, dashing, virile Latino meets attractive, totally vulnerable blonde. *Ouch*!

The electricity bounced back and forth between us and finally overwhelmed us. I didn't mean to let him touch me. I didn't mean to let him put his long arms around me and kiss me, but I did. Those eyes—I don't know. It felt like a drug-induced fantasy world. I was swept along with the tide of events with no will of my own. Was I losing my mind? Why was it so unbearably hot in here? So hot, I couldn't think. So hot, I could barely breathe.

Out of the still cabin air and my tumultuous mind came a clear voice commanding me to stop. *What about Olga? What about Alex? What about my self-respect? Who was I anyway? This was not me.* The temperature in the cabin spiraled before the fever finally broke.

Breathe. I collected myself and pulled away before things went too far. Catholic girls were good at that, or bad, depending on your perspective. Not that it was in the least bit easy for me, but "*Por favor, vaya te,*" I told Ricardo, "Please go away."

He left. His leaving prompted the vanishing of what had just happened. For the rest of our time together, the three of us were fast friends, carrying on with our nightly card games, talks, and an occasional songfest. In the closeness we shared, I started seeing how happy and compatible Olga and Ricardo were, how considerate of each other and of everyone else. One night they said that if anything were to happen, if Alex didn't meet me in Barcelona, I would be welcome to stay with them. The steward Antonio, who had become a friend too, offered me a place with him and his family. That night I went to bed feeling especially content. They were both generous offers, but I didn't expect to take advantage of either one. Really, what could go wrong?

I slept like a swaddled newborn during the clear, starry nights, as the gentle arms of the dark sea rocked me to sleep. What a beautiful, restful, meditative experience! The many days and nights gave me enough time to expand my vision of myself from that of a young woman in a predictable pedestrian life into one who was ready for the unplanned, unexpected, and unconventional. I was free to adopt a whole new personality and make up my life as I went along—a rare opportunity. Normally, change comes hard. Even when we decide to change ourselves, there's always someone who knows us who won't allow us to change or who won't accept that we *have* changed.

But on board this ship in the middle of the Atlantic Ocean, my feet not having touched land since the New Orleans dock, I felt nothing tying me to my home or my old self except memories. I could have been Amelia Earhart, realizing my dream.

One day we *passajeros* were mostly confined to our quarters as the routine deck painting got underway. It was a small inconvenience at worst and a reminder that this wasn't a passenger ship. That evening, with alcohol loosening his tongue, Manuel spoke more English than I had ever heard him speak. Serving our supper, he was red-eyed, smelling strongly of wine, and unsure on his feet. He pleaded with me, "You no tell the *capitan* I *borraccio*."

Though we laughed about it, Manuel was no doubt feeling lonely from spending so much time at sea, away from his family. He combatted it, the way so many do, with music. Pulling a harmonica from his pocket, he serenaded us with a melancholy tune as we had supper.

The night we passed through the Strait of Gibraltar was momentous. Stopping our card game early, we began seeing a number of small fishing boats clustering and a few large ships just ahead. Along with them, our ship was entering the Strait with welcoming lighthouses flanking the passageway. My heart beat faster when I understood we were sailing between two vastly different continents at a point where they seem to reach for each other.

A couple of miles to the north stood the Rock of Gibraltar, forming the tip of the Iberian Peninsula, and a half dozen or so miles to the south was Morocco. Because of the darkness, I could see only the enormous silhouetted hump of the Rock rising from the water, and lights rimming the bottom of this minor British colony.

Though Gibraltar had long been an object of contention between Spain and the United Kingdom, its people were determined to keep their identity separate from Spain. Unmoved by the controversy, Gibraltar stood with its chest out to welcome or warn voyagers. For me, passing so near it and through these continental portals was passing through a birth canal.

Antonio, sensing our excitement, brought out a wine bottle we had just emptied and suggested we put a note into it. After we scribbled our names, destinations, and notes on a piece of paper, Antonio then stuffed and re-corked the bottle. He ceremoniously kissed it. When he tossed it overboard, we could see the bottle briefly as it drifted toward the lights of the Dark Continent. What a thrill! My name was being carried into a new world. How far would the bottle go, and who would find it?

Now officially a part of the larger world, I felt my new life beginning. Stretching out on my bunk that night, I wasn't homesick. Already I could sense a subtle transformation in me, evolving as smoothly as each shade of blue in the daytime sky gave way to the next.

The African coast slipped away during the night. The last full day on board I awoke earlier than usual and hurried to the deck. Watching the new-born sun penetrate the haze, I studied the hunchbacked mountains outlining this new land. What wonderment lay beyond them? When Manuel's radio picked up a Valencia station, the air pulsated with the insistent, sexy strains of a flamenco guitar accompanying the fiercely exotic voice of Peret. Although I couldn't see the country behind the mountains, I could hear it. I was standing, invitation in hand, outside a closed door waiting for it to open.

The door opened for me the next day when the *Mar Egeo* pulled into the busy Barcelona harbor. In the brand new morning, I awoke to the sounds of subdued, deep-throated fog horns and slowed engines, like a mother tip-toeing ever-so-gently to awaken her sleeping child. There was no need for tiptoeing. Like a child at Christmas, I jumped out of my bunk, ready for surprises.

Throwing on my clothes, I hurried to the deck to watch the ship negotiate the lanes leading to the wharf. Centuries-old, ornate gray stone buildings stood facing the port from across the street.

A tall bronze statue of Christopher Columbus stood on top of a column about five times his height. As far as I could tell, his outstretched finger was pointing eastward, not westward as many people believed. He commanded the harbor at the spot to which this explorer returned from his first trip to the Americas. I felt an immediate kinship with this man called *Cristobal Colon* and knew he could not have been any more excited about arriving in his new world than I was at arriving in mine.

My happy seagoing home now eased through the harbor and nuzzled up to the concrete wharf. Crewmen threw heavy ropes around creosoted moorings, and the engines were cut. My heart pounded at the prospect of stepping onto foreign soil and of meeting the man I had come to meet. He would be waiting for me to start this new life together.

Or would he?

Expectantly, my eyes scanned and re-scanned the dock and harbor. Meanwhile my friends helped me look and look again. Alex was nowhere to be seen. *No, he had to be here. Look again.* It was a wide open wharf, unlike the one in New Orleans hemmed by dark warehouses. *My eyes are playing tricks on me.* "Okay, wake up," I said to myself. "Focus." The seasickness came back, my mind and heart in turmoil. Thoughts in my head, like frightened animals in a cage, bumped into each other as they struggled for their freedom.

How could Alex do this to me? What would I do now? How could I live? I didn't know the language, didn't have a job or place to live, and had very little money. I had no plan and no way to find Alex. I was plain scared and felt like a fool.

Maybe my parents were right about him. Alex, who had a sharp wit and sharper tongue, was rebellious. He had no religion, hadn't finished college, had no visible means of support, and came from a world very different from mine. His parents were worldly. Alex had spent six of his young years in Venezuela where his father was port captain. As a merchant marine captain who spent long stints at sea, Alex's father was as emotionally distant from his children as he was geographically. He eventually abandoned them and his wife.

My father Wilfred was far removed from Alex's father in all aspects. He had finished only eighth grade in school and had never lived anywhere else but New Orleans. He was a talented auto mechanic. For years, he worked at one garage or another, and often brought cars home to work on at night. Sometimes he and my mother would dance the foxtrot in the den to music on the radio. Sometimes he danced with me standing on his feet. Although Wilfred was no saint, he was a family man who grew up in the big small town of New Orleans, a place where family was everything.

All these differences between our backgrounds aside, perhaps Alex's worst offense in my parents' eyes was his insinuating himself into their daughter's life, stealing her away, and causing her to flagrantly break their rules.

I was a college graduate who would make something of myself and make the family proud. But not now. This confounded them. Why would I throw away my college education and forsake the possibility of a teaching career, in order to do—what? As far as I was concerned, whatever we did would be the adventure I craved.

Alex was in the land of the Alhambra, flamenco music, tapas and good Spanish wine. I was the one still bound, to my conventional life, to my longing for the world, and to Alex. Apart from vague fantasies, I certainly didn't know what I would do, beyond meeting him here. And now he wasn't here. How did I wind up in this predicament? Maybe, I had gone wrong from the start.

During the semester after Alex moved to California, we shared many tearful long-distance phone calls. Tears on my end. I missed him and how he made me feel, perhaps also because he had troubled my quiet waters and made me think.

Although I started to date others again, the dates were typical of small-town college life in the sixties: mindless fun in an extended childhood. Date-talk skirted risky political, social or religious issues, as if meaty mental explorations were none of our business.

By the end of my junior year, I was looking forward to the excitement of a summer job I had been hired for in Yellowstone National Park.

On one of our many phone calls, Alex persuaded me to change my ticket and stop in San Francisco on my way to Yellowstone. It would be just a short detour, I thought. When I boarded the plane for my first flight ever, I was dressed in high heels and a smart, crisp, green and white paisley suit, a small-town-girl-meets-the-big-city look. Within days of my landing in San Francisco, I ditched the suit in favor of purple flowered bellbottoms. Within a week of my arrival in this land of blossoming flower children, my Yellowstone plans were derailed.

"Why don't you just stay here for the summer?" Alex urged. It was an agonizing decision. Yellowstone, home to some of the country's most awe-inspiring wilderness, was a huge draw, but Alex was a great persuader and I dearly loved San Francisco. I adored everything about it—the ocean air, hilly streets, outrageously bold flowers, smell of eucalyptus, cosmopolitan atmosphere, and the freedom to be a new me. How could I not stay, even if it was in the rundown neighborhood of Haight-Ashbury? I was young and naïve enough to believe there would be other opportunities for Yellowstone and everything else in the nebulous future.

No matter what's been *officially* said since then, for me and many others, 1966 was the real "*summer of love.*" It was before the media and commercialism co-opted what was really happening in the Haight. Sure, there were some hard drugs on the streets, but there was more innocent pot smoking and LSD experimentation. The "protesting" was mostly passive objection to the establishment by way of the poetry of Bob Dylan, abandonment of conventional dress codes, and taking art into the streets. We watched free performances of Moliere's plays in Golden Gate Park, and friendly games of Frisbee often broke out in the grassy Panhandle. The Yellow Submarine was open for business. I bought a ticket to ride.

Alex, his sister, Miranda, and I rented a funky three-bedroom flat on Haight Street above a shop owned by a sour old Jewish man who sold broken candy at a discount. We rented it along with a quirky acquaintance named Mary and all her itinerant friends. *Everybody* was her friend.

Appropriating the living room as her bedroom, Mary draped the bay window overlooking Haight Street with thin blue and green Indian cotton bedspreads and an obligatory mattress on the floor. A constant stream of people passed through or stayed—people whom she felt compelled to "help." Music continually played, mostly Dylan or Donovan, interspersed with the Beatles, Baez, and the Rolling Stones. The air was charged with fragrant patchouli or sandalwood incense, candle wax, and marijuana smoke. I had my first brief encounter with weed, coached by a pot veteran, "Take a deep, long draw." I broke out in a coughing fit. "That's good," he said, "The coughing helps your high." Finally, I got a little buzz, but ultimately it only made me sleepy. For the most part, I left marijuana and the itinerant population of the house alone; I was still the responsible one.

I soon found a part-time job typing for a stock market reporting company in the financial district. Its extreme tediousness was offset by the excitement of being in the heart of one of the most intoxicatingly beautiful cities in the world.

A few days after I was hired, Alex found a job too. The job he found, through the influence of his merchant marine Captain father, was on a cargo ship to Vietnam. Consequently, we spent most of that summer apart after all. He returned a couple of weeks before I went back to Louisiana, mostly at my mother's insistence, to finish my senior year of college. In between, I blossomed in this new soil.

On board Alex's ship to Vietnam, an adventurer named David befriended him and persuaded him to go to Spain. As I flew home, Alex and his forever-footloose sister Miranda flew to Madrid. I had not seen him since. A year ago now, he found a girlfriend in Spain within months, and I found a boyfriend in Louisiana.

"*Pues, donde esta, senorita*?" Manuel wondered aloud to me, interrupting my ruminations. Where is he? It was hard to swallow back the tears welling up inside.

Even though Olga and Ricardo were anxious to leave the ship, they wouldn't leave me. After half an hour, Ricardo suggested we check our luggage at the train station, then we would think about the next step.

CHAPTER 3

Las Ramblas and Beyond

All of the art of life lies in a fine mingling
of letting go and holding on.
—Havelock Ellis

We three took a taxi to the train station, found rental lockers, and stuffed in our things. The *Mar Egeo* rested at the dock only a few blocks away, but even without the luggage, the walk back to her was long and heavy. Disheartened and frightened, I didn't know what to do.

As we neared the ship though, I saw the profile of a man with thick, wavy, brown hair and a short beard. He was talking with Manuel on the dock. What a relief!

Manuel nodded in our direction. Alex turned. He ran to me and wrapped a bear hug around my excited body. "Hey Kiddo. I thought you'd never get here. What took you so long?" he teased.

"What took *me* so long? Where were *you*?"

Alex said he had been at the dock a couple of times earlier. "Your ship was late, so I sat on top of *Montjuich* watching for you." He pointed to a landmark mountain that once guarded the Barcelona harbor, now home to a museum and a park.

"Never mind. You made it, and we have a lot to do. *Vamanos.*"

Smiling, Antonio got off the ship. Manuel stood by like a proud Papa delivering his daughter to her groom. "*Cuidado,*" he instructed Alex. "Careful."

"*Gracias*, Manuel. *Gracias*, Antonio," I said, practicing a word now very familiar to me. "*Gracias por todo.*"

I introduced my Chilean friends to Alex. They exchanged a few polite words while sizing up each other. Ricardo gave me an address where they might be reached—just in case. We three hugged and then Alex grabbed my hand, spiriting me swiftly along the wharf on the Costa Brava. I was breathless.

"*Vaya con Dios*," Manuel called after us.

"*Adios*," I called back.

Finally, I'm safe now. I didn't know what was next, but I didn't need a plan because I believed Alex had one. He made me feel daring and alive. What else mattered?

At that moment, I surrendered myself on the altar of adventure, but I deposited my life and destiny into someone else's hands, a thing no human being should ever do.

We crossed the street and I met what would become another love of my life. The *Ramblas* is a magical thoroughfare forever for me the heart and soul of this Catalonian city. Tree-lined and vibrant, this wide promenade is populated with street vendors of all kinds, selling flowers, newspapers, magazines, pets, and cups of coffee. The *Ramblas* separates two narrow and opposite lanes of traffic, adding to the noisy mix with the rumble and clatter of the diesel engines of the cars and taxis.

The *Ramblas* is a place to *be*. Life flows in an exciting, always changing mélange. You could take a seat and watch the whole world go by at one end, or you could walk half a mile on it to the *Plaza Catalunya* and do so there.

We walked to the Plaza and joined old men smelling of black tobacco and smart-looking working people perusing *La Vanguardia*, the local newspaper. Friends, cousins, and mothers sat on benches, chatting and alternately feeding insatiable pigeons and shooing the children who chased them.

Something about the scene reminded me of the simpler, pre-air conditioning days of my childhood. Neighbors sat outside on their stoops on hot, invariably muggy summer evenings, revisiting the news of one another's lives, telling stories, and watching their kids play ball in the streets.

Some evenings, with little else to do or money with which to do it, my dad would pile us all into the car, roll down the windows, and take us for a breezy ride. With gas about twenty cents a gallon, it was the best way to cool off. My sisters and I argued over the coveted seats next to the windows seeking the breeze on our faces, and we went absolutely no place in particular.

"Just for a ride!" Daddy would always frustratingly answer when we asked him for the umpteenth time, "But where to?" Finally, no answer came, only frustrated sighs.

Here in Barcelona, families go for walks instead. They go window shopping, stopping to gaze appreciatively, and even longingly, at the artful displays of food in the store windows. I envisioned myself in the days and months ahead becoming one of the strollers in this *Ramblas* world. Today, as we doubled back, Alex stopped at a flower stall, bought a long-stemmed red rose, handed it to me and kissed me. Holding it close as we strolled, I deeply breathed in its fragrance, trying to inhale the whole city, the whole day, this whole new world, and this love.

Eventually, we crossed the street to an old graying building which housed a cheap pension, *our* pension for a few days. Alex already had a room on the third floor. There was no elevator, so we walked up the narrow, dimly lit stairs into our narrow, dimly lit room. A small wooden crucifix hung on the otherwise bare walls. An uncomfortable full-sized iron bed dressed in plain white sheets and a thin, colorless wool blanket dominated the room. A plain nightstand sat beside it. A metal shower stall stood in the corner of the room, but the WC was a shared one, and down the hall. The room's one saving grace was its single window overlooking the *Ramblas.*

Eager to be refreshed, I stepped into the tiny shower and had my first taste of a different standard of living. I couldn't cajole any hot water from the faucet. In this chilly room, it would be only chilly showers.

My most pressing business was to send word to my worried parents. The telegram, addressed to my father, said simply and economically, "*AM FINE. ARRIVED A.M. ALEX MET. LOVE*"

The following day under the clearest blue October sky, we went to the modern, airy, Barcelona zoo. It was not something I would have expected to do in a foreign land, especially not at first. Already I was impressed by Alex's knack for finding interesting, extemporaneous, and affordable things to do. He made fun happen. It was part of his charm.

This zoo was cleaner and more accommodating to animals than my old childhood zoo in New Orleans, and nicer than many U.S. zoos where most of the animals were kept in cramped cages.

Here I connected with the eyes of the formerly wild creatures. I hand-fed a giraffe whose head and neck extended up to the raised walkway we were crossing. Barcelona was ahead of its time, at least, in this way. Zoo animals were more or less liberated. Not so the people who were, since 1936, still under the tight dictatorship of *Generalissimo* Francisco Franco—the same Franco who had dissolved the Spanish Parliament and helped Nazi Germany and Fascist Italy in their efforts against the Soviet Union. The gray-uniformed *Guardia Civil,* who made their presence apparent in the streets, was an easy reminder of Franco's past. His regime kept crime in check in the streets, if not in the upper echelons of power.

Two days later, we arose with the sun and rode the bus to the train station where I re-deposited my duffle bag and suitcases, keeping with me only a few changes of clothes. Donning our Army surplus style knapsacks, we bought tickets for a few pesetas each and caught a train west out of Barcelona.

Although many of the traveling *campesinos* had their food supplies with them, tied up in cloths and baskets, the train car was comfortable and clean. Some *campesinos* brought live chickens, while a few had wine, which they generously passed around.

The slow local train stopped in one small dusty town after another. We hadn't yet eaten breakfast. At one of the stops, Alex stood up and said, "Listen, you hold down the fort while I go grab something for us to eat." Before I could say anything, he jumped off the train. In a few minutes, he was back with a loaf of bread and a hunk of cheese, but after he handed them to me, he quickly turned away and said, "I'll be right back." I assumed he was getting off the train again to buy something else.

In a few minutes, the train started moving slowly down the tracks and I didn't see Alex. Alarmed, I stood up and anxiously looked out the window.

Some of the other passengers took notice and joined in my looking. I didn't know the name of the town we were leaving and couldn't ask what it was. In my panic, all my Spanish, hard-learned aboard the *Mar Egeo* disappeared.

Again I had put myself into the vulnerable position of being totally dependent on someone else for my whereabouts and well-being. *What a big baby I am*, I thought. *Why didn't I pay more attention to things, like names of train stops? Why hadn't I bought the tickets, or even bought the food? When will I learn? When will I start living my life as if I mattered, as if I could take control of my own destination and destiny?*

While it was true I hadn't been to the circus yet, I had taken some major steps towards it. I expected that Alex would stay with me and hold my hand at the circus he so wanted to show me. I didn't think he meant to take me to it and drop me off.

Stop. Just stop. One part of my mind reprimanded the other. *This is getting blown way out of proportion. Everything's going to be fine.*

Tears welled up inside, but before they reached my eyes, Alex appeared in the doorway and saw my alarm. I heard sighs of relief from passengers around me, some grinning, even laughing aloud. "I'm so glad you made it. I was worried!" The words fell out of my mouth before I could stop them.

Alex grinned. "Hey, no problem, Kiddo. I was on the train, just in the head in another car."

"Did you do that on purpose—to scare me?" I suggested.

But he dismissed my implication. "Why would I do that?"

It's hard to say. Why would he, or why would I believe he had done it on purpose? Was I being unduly anxious, or being intuitive? In an attempt to reassure myself and my parents, in my next letter home, I described what happened and explained that otherwise, Alex had been taking very good care of me—because he really *was*. "Sometimes I think he worries about me almost as much as you do, Mom," I wrote.

We de-boarded the train at Lerida, stood by the side of the road, and stuck out our thumbs—another first for me. After a few minutes, I confessed it felt really odd, to stand on a roadside and beg strangers for a ride. I didn't know anybody who had ever hitchhiked.

Alex was quick to reassure me. "Nothing to it. Don't worry; you'll get used to it." In the last year he had become a veteran of this mode of travel.

I was wearing a just-above-the-knee-length dress, and in no time, a small car pulled over. The driver, named Alfonso, motioned us in, and we were on our way to Madrid.

The car, a *Deux Chevaux,* was one of the homeliest vehicles ever made and probably one of the slowest. The name itself gave a clue, "two horses." Its body resembled a misshapen, corrugated, sardine can. We squeezed in, with Alex in the front to chat up the driver and me in the back. Because Alex could speak Spanish so well, we would try to "pay" for our ride by engaging in conversation with the driver. Why else would people give hitchhikers a ride? Even if the drivers were just good-hearted souls who wanted to help us out, they had a right to expect something in return.

This became our usual pattern. I didn't mind, because holding even an elementary conversation in Spanish required much effort on my part. Happily relaxed, I sat back, adding an occasional word or two, whenever the drivers turned around to include me, which was frequently.

While Barcelona hugs the Costa Brava on the northeastern ledge of Spain, Madrid is smack in the middle of the country, about five hundred kilometers away. It took the entire day to get to Madrid, not only because of the slow pace of the ride, but also because our driver stopped to have the main meal of the day, a full lunch which is always accompanied by wine.

One of the loveliest customs in Spain was the way mealtimes were honored, even if the meal was only cheese and bread or a bowl of beans. A meal was not something to be rushed, but was a time for kicking back, for conversation and for getting to know one another, a major factor in the enjoyment of life. And why not? What could be more important than breaking bread together? Meanwhile in the States we were busy dishonoring mealtimes with dinners on TV trays.

Because there is no minimum drinking age in Spain, families customarily send a child to the neighborhood *bodega* to pick up a bottle of table wine to accompany lunch. Midday wine might have had a bearing on the creation of the custom of siesta or maybe the siesta allowed time for a glass or two with lunch. No matter which came first, the result is a midday, slow-down to sanity. On this travel day we certainly had no reason to hurry, and being at the mercy of the driver, we adopted the relaxed rhythm too.

The roads we traveled, predominantly two-lane and rural, wound up, over, or around hills, and finally across the plains of central Spain heading toward Madrid. Well after dark, we arrived in the capital city and our *muy simpatico* Alfonso dropped us in the center of town, near the great plaza. With the last "*muchas gracias*," we were out of the car.

Half a block away we encountered the impressive, enormous seventeenth century *Plaza Mayor* surrounded by uniform, three-story buildings. We entered through one of the nine arched passageways. Alex relished showing this marvel to me.

Facing us was the building known as the *Casa Panaderia*. Two symmetrical towers stood in the center, while a large bronze King Philip III commanded from his mount. The Plaza was floored in cobblestones. The two hundred or so balconies facing the Plaza were bathed in a soft ethereal glow that seemed magical to me, as if an image stolen from the centuries.

We found a reasonable pension near the plaza, checked our knapsacks, and spotted an inviting café nearby. The hearty *sopa de judias*, crusty bread, and flan made a perfect end to a long, satisfying day.

In the morning, after exploring narrow streets and small shops, Alex took me to a *bodega* and introduced me to one of the bartenders.

"*Hola, Miguel, que tal*?" Alex launched into a conversation in his best Castilian accent. Most of the conversation was lost on me, although I pretended to understand. We stayed a while, drinking *vino tinto* and indulging in the free *tapas,* part of the Madrid bar tradition.

We spent part of one day visiting the Prado. As we wandered through its cavernous halls, staring at the works of the old masters, I felt as strongly that I was in a cathedral as I had ever felt before. Struck by the exquisite faces in paintings of artists like El Greco and Goya, I was certain the artists' hands had been divinely led.

Then we stumbled upon a piece by the Dutch painter Hieronymus Bosch, the *Garden of Earthly Delights.* It had none of the elements of the classical old works—no faces with fine features, no serene countenances, no hints of underlying pain, no enduring depth of spirit. What I saw instead was a brightly colored carnival reflecting a mind exploded by drugs. It was chaos. I didn't like the sarcasm, irreverence, and darkness it suggested to me. When I mentioned I thought the old classicists were straightforward and easy to understand, Alex reminded me they could be just as dark.

"You think because they painted faces to look like real faces, you get what's behind them?" he nudged.

A thought-provoking question. So what was it really? Why did it bother me that Bosch had painted a picture full of cavorting nudes in a frenzy of pleasure, depicted in every conceivable position, some picking and eating fruit from a tree, some with human legs protruding from broken eggshells and clamshells? The nudes were nightmarish and disturbing. Why was it especially uncomfortable for me to look at the hell depicted in the third panel of the painting? Why was Alex more attracted to this painting than to the Old Masters paintings? Why did I cling to the more classical? For me the painting was more politics than art. It provoked me much like *A Coney Island of the Mind* had two years before. I didn't like dark messages mixed with art. It seemed as unappetizing as swallowing a spoonful of bitter medicine with a sumptuous dessert. Why couldn't it just be beautiful? I didn't want to see the underbelly of life; I just wanted to appreciate the eye and skill of the artist.

I had never trifled in irreverence before, but now, as I stood staring at this painting, I felt an emotional, even visceral conversion inside. I began listening to the long-ignored voice inside, urging me to let go of the old standards, to release my preconceived ideas—about art and how it should be and yes, about life and how it *should* be.

"Hey, let's get out of here," Alex said, breaking my trance. "Let's go find a café in the sun and drink some wine." A good idea. He took my hand and we left.

CHAPTER 4

Serendipity Rides

Sometimes I've believed as many as six
impossible things before breakfast.
—Alice from Lewis Carroll's "Through a Looking Glass"

Leaving Madrid, we headed northwesterly, two hundred kilometers to Salamanca. The road stretched on endlessly, across flat, sallow plains, interrupted here and there by small, impoverished villages, defined by rudimentary houses clustered around a centuries-old, imposing symbol of their faith.

Our driver stopped at one village so we could look around. I was struck by the contrast between the wealth of the church and the poverty of its faithful, wondering about its fairness. Then I realized, all logic aside, and for better or worse, our human tendency is to invest our wealth and the care of our souls in something or someone we see as outside of and greater than ourselves.

As we drove deeper into the heart of this country, I began to sense its increasing age. In my adolescent *Vieux Carre* stomping grounds, I mistakenly thought I knew old; I didn't.

We Americans seem to lack a sense of continuity, connection to, and respect for the long past shared by most Europeans and Asians. Many of our ancestors severed their umbilical cords to start completely new lives thousands of miles from their ancestral homes. The buildings in which these pioneers lived and worked were ones they built themselves. Even St. Augustine, our oldest city, was not founded until the middle of the sixteenth century.

Although some of the buildings in Barcelona were of the same age and architectural style as ones in the New Orleans French Quarter, many were much older. Approaching Salamanca, a city founded in pre-Roman times, I recognized a deeper past.

Finally, there it was, appearing suddenly, like a found jewel shining on the plains.

On the opposite side of the *Tormes* River, an assortment of homes and buildings with red-tiled roofs clustered and climbed the rocky sides of the elevated land. A cathedral with a tall bell tower stood watch over it all. An ancient Roman stone bridge, built on a dozen arches stretched across the river.

We arrived in the late afternoon, just in time to watch the honey-colored sunset melting over Salamanca's sandstone buildings, an old gold spectacle.

The *Casa de las Conchas* especially beguiled me. Four hundred stone conch shells were affixed to its façade, arranged in exact equidistant order. I believed the age-old legend that a treasure is hidden under one of them. Why not? Don't we all believe what we choose to believe?

Suddenly, as if the old stone buildings talked to me, I had an overwhelming sense of belonging not only to my own history, but also the history of all of Europe. The buildings seemed to have muscled upward from the ground itself, and stayed as unbroken connections in the chain of history, for anyone who cared to listen. As Alex and I made our way through the stone-lined streets, walking through the great arched doorways of the ancient buildings, hearing the echoes of time, I tried to eavesdrop on conversations that must have taken place here.

At the University of Salamanca, we walked through hallways where Cortes, Cervantes, and even Columbus had once walked—names that awed me as a young schoolgirl. Columbus, in fact, had been so persistent in his campaign to convince King Ferdinand and Queen Isabella to underwrite his mission to the New World that, for a time he followed them to wherever they traveled, including this place.

"Salamanca casts a spell on all those who have enjoyed its peacefulness," Cervantes, a former student, had written.

Although I had just arrived, I felt the pull from every building, an invitation to discover stories and legends of the centuries. Every street, a seductress for a trip back in time. A person could relinquish an entire lifetime to walk in the footsteps of others, but I had more places to go and my own footsteps to leave.

We came to Salamanca to visit some friends Alex made the year before when he studied briefly at the university. I met John, an American student, and Andrew, a classy British artist, both instantly likeable. We joined them in an evening *chateo* at their favorite watering holes.

The next day Alex insisted we visit Carmen, the Puerto Rican who was his girlfriend during the year we were estranged. She was petite, pretty, and tan-skinned. Unlike her, I was tall, blond, and except for what was left of my shipboard tan, fair-skinned.

Carmen was in bed with the flu. Although the prospect of meeting her caused me angst because I wondered if Alex still cared for her, I did go. It was an extremely awkward and uncomfortable situation for me, but Alex didn't seem to notice or care. I was completely superfluous to the conversation they held in Spanish and understood little of it. He may have wanted to show her off to me, or to show me off to her. He may have been trying to prove something. Although it didn't make much sense, I got through it fairly unruffled, at least to all outward appearances. In the end, I decided if I were keeping score, this would have counted as some major points against my partner and major points for me because I had been such a trooper. Okay, so I *was* keeping score.

On the third morning in Salamanca we hit the road westward towards Portugal. In short order, a bright and personable Portuguese couple picked us up. They bought us lunch at a little café in the town of Coimbra where he was an architect and professor at the University.

Not in any rush, they went out of their way to drive us on a grand tour of the area. First we stopped by a twelfth century monastery, then the unique, beautiful, out-of-the-way fishing village of Nazare on the Atlantic coast.

No imposing monuments or architectural wonders beckoned us in Nazare, but only small unpretentious stone houses dotting the landscape. The wonders were the people and the old traditions. Young and old men drove mule and ox-pulled carts loaded with hay or grapes, or other goods. Narrow, brightly-painted wooden boats with graceful curved prows, after their day's labor, sat resting on the sand. Before walking away, a leather-skinned fisherman with eyes permanently squinting against the sun, patted one as he would a prized horse.

In an age old habit of watching for their men to return home, a few women dressed in seven colorful layers of long skirts carrying bundles on their heads as they walked, kept an eye out to the sea. Conflicting stories explained the skirt layers. Did they represent the colors of the rainbow, or the seven days of a week of waiting for their men's return? Most of the stories had their origins in superstition, in attempts to influence good luck.

In this place, we had stepped back in time. While Nazare may not have been an easy life, to me, the air smelled of the beauty and contentment of an uncomplicated life. I wasn't yet ready for such a simple life, but my soul connected with contentment and hoped for some distant future of simplicity.

Our Portuguese hosts left us to spend a night in a town I liked especially for its musical name, *Bombarral.* The next morning, we traveled to Lisbon.

When I first laid eyes on this city, I was stunned that it reminded me so much of San Francisco, especially because of its suspension bridge, the *Ponte Salazar.* Like the Golden Gate, it is strung across a mile span over the Tagus River, its feet on either side planted on high ground.

The day we arrived was superbly beautiful. The sky couldn't have been bluer and the perfect temperature confirmed my belief that October was the best month for romantics to travel almost anywhere. Yet no matter the weather, the romance of this place could not be diminished. Neither of us spoke Portuguese, but we managed with the Spanish and French we knew.

Walking up and down hilly cobblestone streets, we soon discovered a friendly, old-world restaurant named *Ena Pai.* Sitting at an outside table, we laughed and lingered for hours over a meal of fish and buttery potatoes, and drinking a bottle of dark red wine. We made love and slept in a soft, warm bed in a small hotel. Our brief stay in Lisbon felt as a honeymoon must feel.

Never mind we hadn't had a wedding yet. There would be time for that later. We were in love, starting our life as a couple, and this might be the most romantic time we would have.

I was still waiting though, for the poetry on my breast.

Serendipity laughed out loud as we hitchhiked outside of Lisbon. It was a cool, non-descript morning as we situated ourselves on the roadside, expecting nothing unusual. Within minutes, a young Peruvian man, driving a bulky, pale gray German Ford, Taunus, with an Italian license plate, entered our line of sight. He was, in fact, looking for someone to pick up. Judging by his speed, he was in a hurry, but when he spotted us he made an abrupt stop.

"*Buenos dias*," he said, sizing us up. "*A donde van*?" Where are you going?

We gave him a quick once-over, although our tendency was to trust. "Well, that depends on where *you're* going," Alex answered quickly.

That settled that. We were easy. Our man removed a briefcase from the front seat. We got in and he pressed hard on the accelerator. After we engaged in only a few minutes of small talk, he popped the question.

"I have to leave the country today. The truth is I'm on my way to the airport right now." He told us he was flying to Canada and hadn't had time to sell his car.

"How would you like to buy it?"

What a stupid question, I thought. *If we had the money to buy a car, why would we be hitchhiking?*

"*Mira*," Look, he said, "just give me ten American dollars and I will give you the keys. You can take me to the airport."

Hmmm. Alex and I looked at each other with raised eyebrows and similar thoughts running through our minds. It was an interesting proposition. Were we crazy enough to take this stranger up on the deal? We didn't know anything about him or the car. Although he looked harmless enough, tall and well-groomed in a dark blue business suit, maybe he was some kind of international criminal. Why was he willing to part with the car for next to nothing? It was running smoothly now, but as the daughter of a mechanic I knew hidden problems might manifest in days or even weeks. Who knew what trouble we might have?

But wait a minute. This is only ten dollars we're talking about, no great fortune. So what if it was stolen? So what if the car had problems and stopped running tomorrow? We could always just leave it on the side of the road and start hitchhiking again. We weren't very concerned about any possible negative consequences because, although neither of us consciously admitted it, we felt invincible, and we leaned on each other.

We needed to make the decision quickly. Simultaneously, the light switched on for us both. Alex and I grinned at each other.

"Well, okay, we'll take it," Alex said to our sudden sugar daddy. "*Porque no?*" Here was a gift straight from the heavens.

We solidified our agreement with handshakes and a drive to the airport. Once the Peruvian disappeared into the terminal, Alex and I stood for a moment, disbelieving what had just happened. Searching through the car, we were surprised to find some legal-looking papers. These were inconsequential for us because we would never make our ownership legal, a step that would no doubt be too complicated and costly to take, and ownership would somehow tether us.

The trunk held an old suitcase filled with an assortment of pharmaceutical bottles, mostly empty. Dumping them into a trash bin, we headed down the road in "our car."

It was built like a tank and had a manual transmission. Luckily we could both drive a stick, but soon a challenge of a different nature surfaced. The car had no working reverse gear. *So there's the catch.* This might not be such a good deal after all.

Remembering to park so we didn't need reverse gear was tricky, and a few times when we forgot, we both had to get out of the car and push it backwards. Stopping for gas one day, we were chagrined to discover from the friendly attendant that the reverse gear did work. The secret was to push down the gearshift before trying to move it into reverse. After that, we drove happily, counting ourselves lucky. We were never stopped and questioned about anything.

I once heard someone say, "You're lucky if you think you are." We did and we were. We drove the Taunus to the south coast of Portugal, crossing into Spain again at Jerez de la Frontera.

Continuing south and eastward we stopped in Cadiz, then Malaga, and Torremolinos on the Costa del Sol. They were all sleepy towns with quiet beaches, an admirable number of bars, and especially friendly, hospitable residents. I liked the Sun Coast area immediately. If job prospects had been brighter, we might have stayed, but for now, Alex and I agreed our chances for work would be much better in Barcelona.

In the meantime, we were still on a vacation or honeymoon, of sorts, so we took a detour slightly northward to Granada in eastern Andalusia, at the foot of the Sierra Nevadas. How magical these names sounded to me. Even more magical was our destination in Granada, the Alhambra, the region's jewel. We approached it by climbing the steep, narrow street leading to the entrance of the hilltop complex. At first glimpse, my feet wanted to dance.

Despite the Alhambra's tumultuous military and political history and its abuse and neglect, it was magnificent. Once a palace for kings and a small *medina*, it had finally been lovingly restored to its fairy tale beauty.

Intricately beautiful, Arabic-inscribed horseshoe arches were perched on top of round columns on every side of the courtyard. Everywhere I looked, stunning form and color met my gaze—the explosions of blue and gold and white mosaic tile work, medallions, stars and circles, arabesques, and inscriptions. For me the Alhambra feels like what great art accomplishes and should be—the jumping out joy of existence, the height of creative expression, music set in stone, or as Ralph Waldo Emerson called it, "the illusion of a loftier reality."

The scene sent electric sparks of imagination through my whole body. I heard breezes of Arabian intrigue blowing through the porticos. I was the woman of *Scheherezade* who wove elaborate tales for a thousand nights to save her life.

The Alhambra was at the same time another tie to my country's past. Here in its largest hall, the *Salon de los Embajadores*, King Ferdinand and Queen Isabella finally gave their support to Christopher Columbus to sail to the New World.

Alex and I had this magnificent place almost to ourselves. As the sun dropped slowly behind the hills, so did the temperature. After a last look around, we went into the town of Granada where our body heat kept each other warm all night, in an uncomfortably drafty old hotel.

CHAPTER 5
The Right Clothes

Music expresses that which cannot be put into words and that which cannot remain silent.
—Victor Hugo

Being in Andalusia in Southern Spain nourished me. Was it the nearness of the sea on the Costa del Sol, or the palpable passion that permeated the air? This land birthed, and lives with, the fiery song, dance, and guitar of flamenco. As one watches the dance and hears this insistent music, it is impossible to be unresponsive in some way.

Genuine music, born as a natural and necessary expression of a people, takes on a life of its own. Music lingers in the environment, resides in walls and roads and trees, stays as long as someone is listening, and feeling it. I was listening and feeling the music, not just in the small bars where it was performed live, but in the atmosphere of the streets and marketplaces where it dictated both the pace and the priorities of daily life. I recognized that pace and those priorities because I came from a place where, natural-born, heart-baring, soul-stirring music was always high on the list of the necessities of life, inseparable from daily existence, and as ubiquitous as the humidity. Like most native New Orleanians, I counted jazz, soul, blues, and downhome funky rock and roll as my birthright.

From the time I arrived on the Iberian Peninsula, I was in love with the history that enveloped me, the architecture and art, the new landscapes, the Mediterranean, and my new life. I was especially taken by the friendly people in Andalusia. They seemed to work through their days to music, and Alex and I easily moved with it too.

The flamenco that so pervades the region originated in the souls of the *Gitano,* the gypsies, a people whose rhythms inspire and sustain their lives. Their music has supported their stubborn independence even in the face of a life of rootlessness and material deprivation. Were they my kindred souls or was that only in my imagination? When we crossed paths with one of their shanty-town encampments near Granada and spoke to a couple of *gitanos,* I believed them to be kindred souls. Yet, if I chose, I could have abandoned my vagabond life and returned to a middle-class American situation with a home, a job and three square meals a day. How many *gitanos* could or would make such a trade?

In my childhood, when I first heard about these vibrant people, I was smitten by the romanticized version of their lifestyle. I believed they were footloose and happy, so happy that they wore colorful clothes and dangly jewelry, played music and danced all the time. I wondered now if my romanticized view of gypsies was not unlike the romanticized view of the lives of slaves, from Roman times to modern days.

Gypsies have been in Spain since the Middle Ages, but Spain had not yet recognized them as citizens. In fact, for a few hundred years, *gitanos* were on the list of people to be either assimilated or driven out of the country. Under Franco's regime they were harassed and persecuted. Gypsy settlements were destroyed. They were denied their language and their rituals. As a permanently submerged underclass, they were feared and distrusted. It would be a number of years before gypsies would be appreciated for themselves and their place in the Spanish culture. But Alex appreciated them and made relating to them seem easy and natural.

Tracing Andalusia through its eastern side, Alex and I made a brief stop in Almeria where he had worked as a translator on a movie set the year before. Maybe we could find jobs there now, but the people he had worked with, Director Bob Parrish, and actors James Coburn and James Mason, had left for other movies. There was a lull in, if not the death of, the Spaghetti Western industry in Spain.

We left too, traveling along the country's mountainous east coast. Not long ago I had been on the other side of those mountains. Aboard the *Mar Egeo*, the intense beat of flamenco and the wail of Peret beckoned to me.

Continuing north, we passed Valencia and reached the southern end of the *Costa Dorada* in the province of Tarragona. We needed a rest and so did our car.

We landed in Amposta, a quiet town at the mouth of the Ebro River, about one hundred sixty kilometers south of Barcelona. With dust-colored houses, squat buildings, and unpaved, narrow streets, the town was as unpretentious as its name. If Amposta were a girl at a dance, she would be the last wallflower. Although there were no obvious signs of prosperity or even much mirth, the town did claim a history. Its medieval origins included a castle and a fourteenth century tower, still standing guard at the entrance of the river.

Nothing inspired or excited me about the surroundings. Still it seemed odd that even ancient architectural wonders could be so taken for granted that the townspeople no longer noticed them, like a lover who, due to familiarity, loses sight of the wonders of his beloved.

It was late afternoon, past the long lunch and siesta time, but just in time, and always in time for, a glass of wine at a neighborhood bar. We didn't have to look far for a watering hole. In Spain, the center of social life is the *bodega*, a place you could get a small glass of wine for three or four pesetas—a few American cents. We happened into a bar owned by a tall, thirtyish, fair-skinned Englishman named David. He grinned when we spoke.

"Ah, *Americanos*," he said to no one in particular. Though he looked out of place next to his much shorter, darker customers, he seemed quite comfortable in his adopted home. His mastery of Spanish, especially of the local dialect, was impressive.

"Yes, I've been here for five years," he said, pronouncing "been" as we do the legume.

"How did you happen to land in Amposta?" I wanted to know.

"Well, that's a rather long story that I don't want to delve into at the moment, but if you stick around a bit, perhaps we could trade stories."

David looked somberly at me. When he said that he had no desire to go home—this was his home now, I guessed his story involved a woman.

Our new friend seemed happy for an opportunity to speak in his mother tongue, even if it was *American* English. We welcomed the conversation as much as he did, but we were road-weary, and after a couple of glasses of *vino tinto*, it didn't matter which language was spoken.

"Look, if you're not in any great hurry, why not stay here for a bit? I could use some help in the bar," David said. After studying us a while, he aimed the invitation at me. "I mean, I couldn't pay you much, but you would have a place to stay." He included Alex in the invitation, but *I* would be the 'help' in the bar.

"Well, why not?" Alex concluded, noting it might give us a chance to figure out what we were doing next.

"The thing is, my Spanish isn't great," I offered, "and I've never worked in a bar before."

"Absolutely no problem," David assured me. "I have lots of regular customers. Everybody knows everybody and they won't mind if you don't understand everything they say. In fact, they'll probably like that better." He winked. "At any rate, they usually order the same thing all the time. *Carajillo.* That's a strong black coffee with a bit of cognac in it."

The logical decision was made to stay a few weeks, and David showed us to his extra room. I started work the next morning.

It was easy enough to pour the morning *carajillos*, and it wasn't often that anyone ordered anything different. The regular customers, all men, usually came in around eight and sat at the bar in their regular seats. Most of them were older, or possibly the leather look of their faces made them seem older.

I learned the regulars' names and occupations, and after some days I was able to make small talk, *really* small talk. My speaking was improving, although my Spanish comprehension was light years ahead of my expressive ability. This was somewhat of an advantage. I could listen to what the men were saying about me without their knowledge. They were flirts, but sweet and harmless flirts, and the job was pleasant enough.

Our extended stop gave us an opportunity to learn more about the town. When I wasn't working, we took long walks. I learned to appreciate some of Amposta's subtle, finer features. In the eyes of this beholder, the town had grown in beauty.

One thing this little job did for me was to break the ice. As I understood more of the language, I began to feel more like a resident and less like a visitor in Spain. In addition to being fun, the job increased my confidence in my adaptability. As the men ogled and flirted, I was emboldened to explore yet another person lurking inside of me.

The boss flirted too, but we also became friends. After the last customer left on the day before Alex and I departed, David and I were talking about the direction of our lives and what I would be doing after we left Amposta.

He became silent after a bit, then looked squarely into my eyes said, "You know, if you had the right clothes, you'd look like a princess."

The right clothes, yeah. Not much chance of that. David's estimation was at the same time both complimentary and disturbing. I was not on a princess path.

The next morning we got into our Taunus and drove to Barcelona.

CHAPTER 6

Days of Wine and Roses

When we are no longer able to change a situation,
we are challenged to change ourselves.
—Viktor Frankl

Getting back to Barcelona was like coming home again, but after retrieving all of my luggage from the train station, it was decision time. Not considering the lifestyle I would be leading, I had brought much too much with me from the States. It hadn't occurred to me I would be an itinerant without even a home base where I might store my possessions.

I handled the difficult question of what to keep and what to jettison via a fashion show. I modeled many of the dresses I had made myself, some just for this trip. Alex was the judge, giving delighted nods to some. By the end of the show I had whittled down my new wardrobe to only a few pieces of clothes chosen by their weight, packability, and multi-functionality. Kissing the rest of my things good-bye, I shipped them to my parents' home in my hard-backed Samsonite suitcases. I had no choice. Unbeknown to me, the Zen part of my education had begun with this first lesson in non-attachment.

Alex and I set up housekeeping in a one-room space in a pension a block off the *Ramblas,* on *Calle Puertaferrisa*, a narrow street within easy walking distance to the harbor.

With taller buildings surrounding ours, there were only a few minutes when sunlight was shining through our small window. It often felt grim. What made it bearable were the chimes from an imposing Catholic church down the block. The bell would chime on the hour and every quarter hour, beginning a musical sentence at the first quarter, adding a phrase each additional quarter until the sentence and the hour were complete. A full, sonorous chime, it reverberated in the stones of the steeple and the pavestones of the street, beautifully filling my expectant ears and connecting me to the centuries.

The managers of this pension were an odd couple. Although they were both short, she was very round and he was thin, like Jack Sprat and his wife. He was meek and she was loud. They argued often and loudly, or rather *she* argued loudly and would call her husband a clown. "*Otro paiso, tu!*" she would scream, insultingly. As she did her daily housework, I often heard her singing at the top of her lungs, "*Me llaman abandonada.*" They call me abandoned. I laughed because no one would question why, but, secretly I wondered, *How must that feel?* I didn't want to know.

Many pensions included one meal a day in the cost of the room, but ours didn't. Consequently, we had coffee for breakfast with some kind of bread or roll from a nearby *panaderia* or café. For lunch, in Spain the main meal of the day, we usually improvised. I should say, *I,* improvised.

Often I made a salad with vegetables from the giant covered market a few blocks away, usually adding garbanzos or other cooked beans. Sometimes I bought vegetables and pasta or potatoes, and concocted a dish that could be cooked in our one pot. We had a little electric burner we hid in the room. Cooking in the room was *prohibido*, but we took our chances.

Besides being an economical way to eat, this "cooking" also provided the backdrop and occasion for something that Alex rarely did, which was to compliment me. "You can make a home out of any place," he said. Small potatoes, as far as compliments go, but I put it into my treasure box.

Alex took a job teaching English at the Berlitz School of Languages, a short walk away. Because I wasn't fluent in Spanish, and I was reluctant to even apply, he suggested a job he thought I could do. Alex took me to an unpretentious bar just off the *Ramblas* and introduced me to the boss. I was hired on the spot to be a B-drinker. I didn't know what a B-drinker was until that night.

I guessed I could handle it because in New Orleans we learned how to drink when we were still in high school. Sometimes my friends and I got into Bourbon Street clubs or other bars without IDs. In those days, nobody cared. The drinking age was eighteen, but managers and bouncers tended to look the other way.

For this bar job, in Barcelona's Gothic Quarter, I didn't have to say much, but just smile, pretend to understand what the customers said, and pour more drinks. I found out later, the customer would pay for the drink, then the barmaids would either surreptitiously fill their own glasses with something non-alcoholic or find a way to dump their drinks as the customer continued to drink and buy. I hadn't figured out a way to do either, so I drank and drank and drank until the night was over.

I don't recall how I got back to the pension from five blocks away at 2 A.M., but somehow I did. Atrociously drunk and sick, I threw up until there was nothing else to vomit except the lining of my stomach. I thought I would turn inside out and die. Alex slept through it all. So began and ended my B-drinking career.

The next week I found my courage and asked for a job at the school where Alex was already working. Fluency in Spanish wasn't a requirement because translation was never used in any of the dozens of languages taught in Berlitz classes worldwide. From the first lesson students begin the process of speaking and thinking in English.

The classes were thoroughly enjoyable, and our routine began to feel comfortable. We taught classes in the morning, broke for two hours for lunch and siesta, and returned to school for several hours. In the evenings, we had supper at a nearby, unpretentious, family-owned restaurant. The restaurant had no name, but only a "*Comidas*" sign outside to indicate that it was a place to eat. Many evenings Alex and I ordered plates of down-home bean*s,* or we had vegetable soup. Sometimes we ate *arroz a la Cubana,* an interesting dish consisting of rice, topped with a banana, red sauce, and a fried egg. Yes, interesting, rather tasty, and very cheap.

We lived like lower income Spaniards and had a spare existence. It wasn't bad, but as we settled more into our routine, something happened that interrupted the flow. One afternoon Alex received a telegram from his sister Miranda. Taking a deep breath, he opened it.

There were the words in clipped, unvarnished truth. His mother had passed away. While it wasn't totally unexpected for Helen, no matter when it comes for our loved ones, death's knock at the door is never one we want to answer.

What little I knew of Alex's mother, I admired. I also felt deeply sorry for her. Devastated by her life's circumstances, she fell ill. I had met her during the summer I spent in San Francisco when she was already sickly and frail and her youngest son Malcolm was living with her. She had a good mind and, I believe, a good heart, but one which had been trampled, leaving her broken and demoralized.

Helen was in the hospital when she became comatose. Although the doctors could only guess at her remaining time, she went quickly. Alex wasn't prepared for that news. He threw himself across the bed in the pension and cried. I had never seen him cry. I never knew him to be so emotional. Often, when Alex spoke of his mother, he regretfully recalled the hard time he and his sister had given her when they were young. He had mentioned though, what a good catch his mother had been for his father when they first met.

Within a few minutes of getting the news, wordlessly, Alex ran from the pension, into the street, and disappeared. I knew he needed to be alone, but I was worried about him. Eventually, I searched for him, but after checking our usual haunts, I gave up. After several hours, he returned.

Whatever his feelings were, I didn't know what to say to comfort him. I had never lost anyone close to me, except for my grandfather. When he died I was too young to understand what happened. It wasn't something I had to "handle." My mother and aunts comforted me.

However else Alex's mother's death affected our relationship, rightfully or not, it strengthened my resolve to give him a family. He had never had a family like mine. In my family, we weathered our differences and spats, our pettiness and inconsideration, but we were close. Like many New Orleans area families, we knew we could count on one another for help when we needed it. Our parents were our parents forever and we were forever their children.

Eventually our lives in Barcelona continued as they were. Time and distance, especially distance, separated Alex from his grief.

We tried massaging the pain through various means. Some days we played tourists, visiting grand cathedrals, the art museums of Miro and Picasso, and the fort, museum, and *Parque Guell* at *Montjuich.* At *Parque Guell,* with its curved and flowing mosaic-tiled benches, I first appreciated the genius of their creator Antonio Gaudi. When I stood beside Gaudi's *Sagrada Familia,* towering, and after many decades still unfinished, I knew that great art, like life, is never really a finished product.

Comfort came in other forms too. Sound heals, at least for me it did. The heavy church bells punctuating the day and night were a sign of solidity and permanence echoing through the cobblestone streets and gaining strength from the thick-walled buildings.

Nightly I anticipated the last sound of the evening, the concierge dropping the huge corrugated metal doors down to the sidewalk, securing the building.

One day I went with Alex to see my first bullfight. Although bullfight season was already over, this one was for a charity. It was a beautiful spectacle—at first. The young, slim, handsome *torero* in his tight pants was striking as he lifted his chin, arched his back, and gracefully swung the red cape outward and to his side to attract *el toro.* The bull snorted and charged as the *torero* whipped the cape away and as in a tango, turned and stepped elegantly aside. The passionate dance moves were repeated, over and again, until the crowd yelled for blood. Closer and closer the torero brought the bull. When the time and angle were right, with one quick flourish the sword went into the bull's thick neck, already weakened by the two sharp pics of the *picador.* The once fierce bull dropped to the ground. A clean kill and it was over. The judge ruled the bullfighter had earned one ear for his smooth work.

A beautiful, yet barbaric spectacle, it was more art than sport, mainly because the bull didn't stand a chance. The bull's only options were to die gracefully and artfully or clumsily. Some people speculated the bull was usually drugged first. Regardless of the truth of the allegation, I decided to sit out future man-bull tangos.

Barcelona's climate was similar to that of New Orleans, a little colder in winter maybe, but still humid. In December, it was fun to walk down the *Ramblas* and smell the wonderful aroma of chestnuts roasting on the street vendors' open fires. A couple of times I bought a bag of roasted chestnuts and tried to like them, but, for me at least, they were better smelled than eaten.

Because Alex was lonely for a pet, we bought a soft, furry, light brown, guinea pig from a street vendor. Marvin, who was just like a tiny-eared rabbit, lived illicitly in our room, sleeping at the foot of our bed. Each day when I went to the covered farmer's market, I would find some discarded lettuce leaves and bring them home for him. When he heard me coming with his lunch, he would squeal. I thought it remarkable, as Pavlov discovered, how easily animals and people are conditioned to act in certain ways. I also recognized the way to lessen concern about your own troubles, is to take care of someone, or something, else.

That winter, in the wake of the devaluation of the British pound, Spain devalued the peseta, and all our American money increased in value. Dollars that had previously fetched us sixty pesetas apiece now brought seventy. We hurried to exchange our remaining money in case the American dollar went down suddenly, and we felt rich.

Our classes went well. The students, all adults, truly wanted to learn. They had the motivation to be attentive, even enthusiastic. What more could a teacher ask?

On afternoons when I didn't have class, I scouted the local *tiendas* on the narrow streets and *El Corte Ingles*, one of the few big department stores. Usually I could only afford to window-shop.

I loved stopping in front of the pastry shop. The window was always beautifully, artistically and intricately dressed, with seasonal chocolate sculptures. I loved buying a hot loaf of bread, fresh from the bread shop oven. I loved deciding which kind of sausage to buy from the outstanding variety in the *charcuteria*.

Shopping was an adventure, and serendipity lurked around every corner. Walking down the streets I often heard calls from a little distance away. "*Rubia*!" the men sang. Blondie! They didn't mean any offense in this innocent pastime and I didn't take any. I didn't turn around, but enjoyed the flavor of the day, smiled to myself, and went into the next shop, thinking how nice it was to be appreciated, even in this small way.

Around Christmas we drove our Taunus back to Salamanca to visit Alex's friends. It was a good trip and my first "White" Christmas. After Christmas, we used the car for a day trip to the French border town of Perpignan.

We left Barcelona in the early morning, driving north through quiet towns nestled in the foothills of the Pyrenees. In one town we stopped and watched a bunch of shivering kids in shorts playing *futbol* on a grassy field in the cold mountain air. In another spot we stopped and climbed a hill, reaching the abandoned ruins of an old castle. From the extremely windy top we had a magnificent view of everything for miles around.

Finally, we drove straight through Port Bou, a charming town that hugged the Spanish border on the Mediterranean. Realizing we were missing the papers for the car, we stopped. Wanting to play it safe, we left the car just outside of France in order to avoid being questioned, leaving or returning. It was *almost* a good plan.

We walked across the border and took a bus to Perpignan, a small, pretty town with a wealth of enticing pastry shops that I would defy anyone to ignore. Alex and I strolled around, taking in the sights and sampling ambrosial pastries, and I used some of my almost forgotten French along the way. Eventually, we found a café and sat in the sun sipping coffee and exchanging stories about childhood times. Overall, it was a good day.

Just before nightfall, when we returned to the car, the flaw in our plan became apparent. We had actually driven out of Spain. We were in a no-man's land between the two countries. To return, we had to cross the Spanish border.

"*Buenos tardes*," the border official snapped as we stopped and he asked for our papers. When we didn't produce any papers, he was perturbed. Alex kicked into high gear his best Spanish language skills.

He led the officer through a maze that included stolen papers, a German-made car, a Peruvian in Portugal traveling to Canada, an Italian license plate, and two poor naïve victimized American teachers. He blew quite a smoke screen.

"Never mind," the confused officer finally barked. "Go, but don't come back again."

Breathing huge sighs of relief, we wasted no time taking advantage of his confusion and his generosity. We counted ourselves lucky once more and laughed about it later.

CHAPTER 7

What's a Haggis?

In all people I see myself; none more and not one a barley-corn less,
And the good or bad I say of myself I say of them.
—Walt Whitman, "Song of Myself"

Lenny, from a small coal-mining town in Scotland, was a tall, lanky young man with extraordinarily blue eyes that barely hid a tendency to good-natured mischief. A gentle soul, he was soft-spoken with a more than musical Scottish lilt. He was a guitar-player without aspirations to rock stardom. His talent was drawing people into intimate circles and entertaining them for hours, affirming that this was indeed what life was all about. Alex met Lenny the year before when he was working in Almeria.

Lenny had a sharp, inquisitive mind and, like Alex and me, an unquenchable need to experience the world through adventure. Yet this need was not simply for adventure's sake, or for the adrenaline rush coming from danger, whether climbing mountains or going deep sea diving. Risk-induced rushes I found to be a by-product of something deeper. We were seekers questing not only to find ourselves. We sought not only the answers to life's great questions, but also the great questions themselves—the great mysteries.

Alex and I shared a passion for challenging our assumptions and ourselves. We were both inspired by meeting and engaging with people from different cultures. I loved being awed by it all.

In 1845 Henry David Thoreau built his own simple shelter in the woods near Walden Pond where he would begin his exploration of life. Providentially, during my college days I resonated with Thoreau through *Walden,* the book that was a reflection of his days. He said he went to the woods because "I wished to live deliberately, to front only the essential facts of life, and see if I could learn what it had to teach, and not, when I came to die, discover that I had not lived…I wanted to live deep and suck out all the marrow of life…"

And so did I. The reason I had always been involved in so many activities as a student was that I had interest and curiosity about them all. This prompted my high school journalism teacher to autograph my yearbook only with the head-scratching question, "*Quo vadis*?"

Confronting life was the shared passion that drew Alex and me together, directing our odyssey. Seeing this same passion in Lenny, Alex was attracted to him, and the two plotted to travel together.

While we were teaching and saving our pesetas in Barcelona, Lenny and his American girlfriend Jean were amassing their travel fortunes in London. Satisfied they had what they needed, they then went to Lanarkshire in Scotland to visit Lenny's family. The plan was for us to meet and spend a little time there before hitchhiking together across Europe.

In the meantime, I was keeping in touch with some members of my family. Of the four sisters, Wendy and I were the closest in nature. Just over two and a half years younger than I, Wendy was engaged to be married to Jack, her high school sweetheart. I was against the marriage. I thought it was premature. Although Wendy was very bright and attractive, I doubt she thought of herself in those terms. She lacked the confidence to let her light shine, to claim her rightful throne. An avid reader, possessed of an inquisitive mind and an adventurous soul, like my mother, she was stifled by circumstances. I felt that Wendy was settling before she experienced the wonders of the world, before she explored or mined her own talents and dreams. I wanted to help her explore.

I wished I could dissuade Wendy from marrying now, and from marrying Jack. I didn't think he was right for her. At the very least, I wanted to be able to show her what I was seeing, and possibly infect her with the desire to explore herself. Through letters I began to work on her in earnest, trying to convince her to come join us. "You could come see the world with us," I urged, "or at least some of Europe."

"I'll think about it," she wrote back. I could in my mind's eye see her struggling to choose between two seemingly exclusive options. She always found it difficult to say no, even when it was to something she really didn't want to do. I was convinced that somewhere deep down, she wanted to break whatever emotional or psychological shackles holding her back and to jump into the wide world. Whether she consciously knew it or not, I believed she longed to take control of her life, as I *imagined* I had done.

Always conscientious and hard-working, in the end, Wendy would do what was most responsible. Since high school graduation, she held a secretarial job. Valued and respected, she didn't want to jeopardize her job, but she was due two weeks of vacation time, so she booked a flight and planned to meet us in Scotland. I was thrilled.

My exhilaration would soon be overshadowed by sadness, frustration, worry, and even shame.

The weeks passed quickly. In early May, we were scheduled to leave Barcelona. After we quit our teaching jobs, we had one last night out in the *Barrio Gotico* with our teacher friends. We drank *vino tinto* in a small bar while strains of guitar-thumping Flamenco music nearly drowned out our conversations.

Because of lack of papers, we couldn't sell or take with us our ten-dollar Taunus. We gave it to an Australian colleague. Strings cut, we hit the road north.

There's something about cutting ties and disposing of superfluous baggage that is liberating and exciting, almost addictive. You have the illusion you leave all your mistakes behind. It's a chance for a do-over, a time to get on the road with nearly empty bags, to find new experiences with new people in new places, to collect as you go, to refill the bags.

I say *nearly* empty because we always kept the essential parts of ourselves—the core of who we were. Our zebraic stripes bore our strengths and weaknesses, both hereditary and experiential. In my case, I wished so hard to lose my weak stripes, to be a new me that I often forgot to appreciate the strong ones. I forgot I could draw on their strength to give me courage to act as I knew I should.

Stripes intact, we traveled smoothly north through Girona and Figueres, then into France from Perpignan. In high school and college, I studied and became infatuated with French language and culture. My choice at this point was to spend some time exploring this romantic place, visiting the famous landmarks, but I was learning my choice didn't matter. Alex didn't know the language, and I believed he was uncomfortable having to depend on me. Besides, Lenny and Jean were waiting for us, so we sped through the whole of France, pausing to eat and sleep. In Paris though, we did walk along the Seine, browse some book stalls, and find a pastry shop that satisfied at least one longing of mine.

We ferried across the English Channel, caught a train to London, and thumbed rides to the Galways' home in Lanarkshire.

The home was small and working-class, but cozy and comfortable. Lenny's parents and his sister Meg made us feel welcome. Even though I didn't find Scottish food to be the tastiest, Mrs. Galway was a more than a decent cook and I watched as she did her magic.

A little on the grumpy side, Mr. Galway was a coal miner, and a man of very few words. I attributed his disposition to a hard life. Alex and I were young and foolish enough to believe because we had broken loose from a mundane existence, anyone was capable of doing the same. It was hardly a compassionate position.

One day we took a trip to *Loch Ness*. We didn't spot the monster, but we did see some interesting long-haired cows grazing on hillsides. Along the way, we were on the lookout for a haggis, that elusive animal found in the ever-popular haggis stew. We didn't see one, so we asked about it, receiving what we later discovered to be the standard tongue-in-cheek answer for tourists.

"It's a little wild beast that lives in the Highlands," Lenny explained. "It has two legs on one side shorter than the two on the other side so he can run around the slants better."

In truth, haggis is a dish, not an animal. It is traditionally made by stuffing a sheep's stomach with liver, heart, lung, oatmeal, suet, stock, onions and spices. I was happy I didn't have to come face to face with this dish at our hosts' table. How could I have found a way to politely refuse it?

One day our explorations took us several miles to the city of Edinburgh to see one of Scotland's most famous landmarks. Edinburgh Castle was a magnificent building in a spectacular location. More than a thousand years old, it sits atop a tall, volcanic rock, seemingly emerging from it. Almost any vantage point allowed a commanding panoramic view of the area. This day the view was obscured by gray skies, but it was still remarkable.

We walked part of the Royal Mile ramping to the massive entryway. The castle was both majestic and forbidding in its stone coldness. I wondered how centuries ago people living in such a place were ever warm.

How must it have felt to be a member of the royalty living there, immaculately nursed, coddled, and elaborately dressed, making this same trip in a horse-drawn, servant-driven carriage? The noble lifestyle held little appeal for me because my preference was always having the freedom of a simple life. While it is easy to feel trapped in any kind of existence, judging others for their choices or birthrights is a mistake. This kind of mistake was responsible for altering our plans and causing much pain and anguish for some of us—for the Galways, for me, and for Wendy, who was almost on her way to Europe.

On early mornings and during the times we didn't have any particular plans, Alex would write, filling notebooks with his observations, wordsmithing his way around the realities of daily life. One day while we were out, he had left a notebook lying in the Galways' living room. Unfortunately, Mrs. Galway picked it up. Possibly she didn't mean to thumb through the pages, but her curiosity got the better of her. Soon she was as sorry as I was.

Alex could be astute and insightful at times, but he could also be merciless and uncharitable, using razor-sharp words to describe his observations. In his notebook, not intending for anyone else to see it, he had written the cutting words: "In Lanarkshire, death is a forty-year process."

How did it feel to this wife and mother to have her life denigrated in such cavalier terms? How could she possibly deal kindly with the person who has stuck a knife so deeply into her psyche? Although she didn't confront Alex directly, Mrs. Galway let us know through Lenny she was hurt and terribly angry. I didn't blame her. Here we were, accepting their gracious hospitality, and Alex might as well have slapped our hosts in the face.

So it was that our applecart was upset. The Galways didn't ask us to leave, but let Lenny know we were no longer welcome. Lenny and Alex then started hatching plans to start our trip through Europe as soon as possible. They didn't want to wait around Scotland anymore.

In the meantime, here came Wendy. I tried to get Alex to wait so we could show her a good time while she was in Europe, but he and the others were unmoved. I felt bad and cried. Alex said she could come with us, but I knew she had neither the time nor the inclination to do that. I had invited Wendy and agreed to be with her. She wouldn't have come if I hadn't extended the invitation. I felt tortured way down to my soul. This wasn't right, but still I was torn. I had faulted Wendy for not being more adventurous, but I lacked the confidence to stand up to Alex and tell him I would stay even if they left. I couldn't do that because I thought it would mean the end of my life with him and the end of my life abroad. Strains of the old fifties era song *Sisters* ran through my head… "Lord help the Mister who comes between me and my sister, and lord help the Sister who comes between me and my man." I told myself the decision was out of my hands.

When Wendy arrived, we met her in London, spending the day with her, showing her a few sights, and hanging out in Kensington Park. I was so happy she had come. It was good to have her there, but it was also awkward. We had arranged for her to meet Lenny's sister Meg and stay with her for the duration. They would tour together in England while we went on our way.

The shame of my decision haunted me. I couldn't imagine my mother would ever forgive me. I couldn't forgive myself, but I hoped that big-hearted Wendy eventually would.

Leaving the British Isles and the botched situation, my heart hurt for what I had done to Wendy. I felt guilty. I worried about her. Part of me stayed behind as we began a journey that would take us around the cradle of civilization.

Without a destination or time constraints, we had been sitting on the launch pad for a time. Now, in spite of the mess we were leaving, it was lift-off, whether I was ready or not.

CHAPTER 8

Rocking the Cradle of Civilization

A good traveler has no fixed plans and is not intent on arriving.
—Lao Tzu

A FERRY BOAT DEPOSITED US in Ostend, Belgium. Quickly we made our way to the Netherlands—the fabled land of windmills, tulips, and sabots. Somewhere in my memory, I see an image of myself costumed for Mardi Gras in a little Dutch girl outfit made by my mother, complete with white starched organdy pinafore and some facsimile of inflexible wooden shoes. That image, captured in an old black and white photograph, long since lost, was Holland for me—more make believe than real.

While the Holland of my imagination may have been at odds with reality, one aspect of the place with which I immediately felt a kinship was its geography. Amsterdam, like much of New Orleans, was flat marshland, several feet below sea-level, but the Dutch were careful planners. In Amsterdam's Golden Age in the seventeenth century, canals were created as fortifications, running in four concentric rings around the city. Consequently, the city is composed of a number of small islands connected by hundreds of bridges. Amsterdam has successfully waged centuries of battles against the incursion of the sea and has prevailed through its ingenious and strategically engineered system.

Amsterdam is a practical place, comfortable in its own skin, unashamed of its red light district and its *laissez-faire* attitude towards marijuana. I hoped one day I would be as comfortable with myself.

During the few days we stayed here, I learned more about practical accommodations, preparing for the European trek ahead. At this jumping-off point, we stayed in the first of many youth hostels with their gender-separated dormitory rooms. We explored on foot, by bicycle, and by riverboat, sampled the local fare, and generally stretched our physical, mental, and psychic muscles.

Alex and I said *adios* to Lenny and Jen, promising we would all meet up somehow at loosely planned destinations. Standing by the side of the road once more, I was a veteran, and my thumb knew what to do.

Because we were hitchhiking, we had little control over our routes, stops, or schedules. We would spend more time in Germany than I wanted to, and stayed in emotionally uncomfortable places like Nuremberg. Our drivers gave us more history lessons than I wanted.

I didn't want to be reminded of Hitler's insidious rise to dictatorial power or his savagery. I didn't want to reflect on the legions in his service, otherwise good people, and how they were so easily fooled until no one could stop the catastrophe. My mind hit a wall pondering how to prevent despotism from happening again and again. The silent response in my mind was deafening. I listened to silence echo through the walls of the former-castle-turned-youth-hostel where we spent the night. I didn't have an easy sleep. But life goes on, always with new opportunities to learn and to do right.

Our next stopover at Innsbruck, Austria was much more pleasant. Although the town had suffered bombing after bombing by Allied Forces between 1943 and1945, it was still spectacularly beautiful.

Situated in the Inn Valley in the lee of some magnanimous mountains, Innsbruck gave me a completely new perspective—that in spite of man's atrocities, nature would prevail. Nature could overcome, could overshadow any actions by a feeble and sometimes dishonorable mankind.

Innsbruck hosted the Winter Olympics a few years before our visit. Some of the athletes who competed stayed in the very same lovely, cozy hotel where we spent the night on a marshmallowy feather bed. The panoramic view from our window was even lovelier. Buildings stood tall like nobility, against a background of taller mountains, glinting with the sun, drawing my eyes upward to the heavens. How could anyone remain depressed seeing a sight like this?

We spent one night and part of the next day in Innsbruck. Exchanging heights for speed, we hitched a ride to Italy with a daredevil driver in a Ferrari. Because there were no speed limits on these roads, he wasn't breaking any laws when he flew around mountain roads, ignoring the fact that he couldn't see anything coming from the opposite direction. He took the curves as quickly as an alligator flips its tail. I had to admit it was exhilarating, but my heart stayed in my mouth until he landed that car. We got out, wobbly-legged.

Our next ride, a little saner, took us to Venice. With its arms open wide, indeed, practically its whole body, open to the Adriatic Sea, the difficulty is telling where the city ends and the sea begins. How could anyone not love Venice? Part of what makes Venice so captivating is that its art and architecture embrace another era, watery to the point of being unearthly. I was convinced it sat in a fifth dimension, an Atlantis, between visible and invisible incarnations. Many of its city blocks are islands, and young people learn to handle a boat before they learn to drive a car. I half expected the citizenry to sport gills.

The constantly sinking buildings reminded me the fingers of the watery realm are forever pulling Venice and all of its treasures farther beneath the sea. While there is no way to stop the progression, its inhabitants struggle, clinging to the topside of the earth. I felt as if I were going down with Venice. I hoped it would land in a place the Beatles had called an "octopus's garden in the sea."

I was so intrigued I didn't even mind the omnipresent pigeons' droppings throughout St. Mark's Piazza or the fact I was denied entrance to St. Mark's Cathedral because of my mini-skirt. In my youthful oblivion, it didn't occur to me exposing so much of my legs would be disrespectful.

During the day we walked miles, passing canals glowing with a bright, green fluorescence. This was 1968, a year Italian students were always protesting something. They had dumped green dye into the water as a sign of their discontent.

Occasionally, we ran into groups of students in the streets, carrying red flags and bursting into their revolutionary song like a spontaneous opera, all emotionally charged as if they understood what they were protesting for and against. "*Avanti populo, alla riscossa,... bandiera rossa triomfera...,*" they chanted. Forward people to the rescue...the red flag will triumph.

As young and impressionable as they were, I suppose I was too. I didn't comprehend that this most famous Italian labor movement song, glorifying the red flag, was a rallying cry for socialism and communism.

Leaving the drama of Venice for more solid ground, we hitchhiked to Rome, playing tourists in a tourist heaven.

In the Vatican's Sistine Chapel, I was awestruck. The magnificent art competed with nature itself, and I wondered how such art was humanly possible. Only the blind would not be astonished at Michelangelo's *Creation.* I could feel electricity coming through the depiction of God's hand as it nearly touched the finger of Adam.

All of Rome begged to be appreciated. We did what we could, and only scratched the surface. Among the ruins, I visualized earlier days, philosophers in the Forum and sea battles in the Coliseum. We tossed coins into fountains, making wishes, and ate lunch on the Spanish steps.

I loved the prevailing lust-for-life attitude in the streets of Rome, witnessing firsthand how Italy gained its reputation as a land of flirtation. This atmosphere enhanced my feeling that in some ways we had the ultimate romantic life, love being an adventure with endless possibilities and breathless anticipation. Our relationship fed on adventure and the unknown, but one unknown to us then was our growing co-dependency.

After a week of playing in Rome, we were ready for new unknowns. From Ancona on the Adriatic side of Italy, we hopped on a cheap steamer to a place we knew nothing about.

First sight of Tito's Yugoslavia at the port of Zadar didn't impress me much. We were greeted by sad, graying buildings with no names or obvious functions, some with boarded windows. In the early morning hours, the streets were colorless and quiet, not with contentment, but with the resignation that comes after days of hard work, yielding little but an aching back and no promise of better times. I could smell the poverty and hopelessness in the air. I witnessed the country's growing alcoholism in the number of men lying drunk in the streets.

As Alex and I tried to move on southward to cheerier locales, we also discovered the difficulty of finding rides. Because cars were few and far between, we were on the road much longer than we had hoped. I believed I could extract something of value from any kind of situation. This belief was justified when we finally arrived in the town of Split and entered a small public office, looking for directions to an affordable hotel.

We bumped into a middle-aged, American expatriate couple from California. Dolph, semi-retired from a professorship, and Rose, from an art career, were looking to escape the inanities of modern life. They did so in a rented cottage on the Dalmatian Riviera, tucked into the hillside on the peninsula facing the waters of the Dalmatian Coast. Riviera here didn't mean resorts and the moneyed crowd, as it did in France. What it did have was a Mediterranean climate, some sandy beaches and beautiful, swimmable water, ideal for Dolph and Jean.

After only a brief conversation, they made us an offer we couldn't refuse; they invited us to be their guests. We could stay as long as we liked, they said. As long as we liked turned out to be two weeks, not because we didn't thoroughly enjoy their company and the beautiful spot nestled in a stand of lush evergreens, but because we were anxious to meet Lenny and Jen in Greece.

Our hosts were not only hospitable, but also bright and witty. It was good to spend days with them engaging in lively conversation or reading quietly, sharing fresh, healthful meals and wine together, unencumbered by urgency.

Leaving forced us to again face the realities of hitchhiking in a country where the population was poorer, the roads rougher, and the men gruffer than in Western Europe. Hitchhiking wasn't easy or safe here. We waited for hours alongside dusty, unkempt roads. The vehicles that did stop were usually lumbering old trucks going only short distances. We were headed for Athens Greece and at our current pace it could take a very long time.

A few of the drivers were friendly or curious enough to stop. A couple of others were neither curious nor friendly, but decided they would extract a price from us—or rather from *me*.

If we were picked up in a truck, I would usually get in first and sit next to the driver, Alex to my right. We knew I was the main reason some drivers stopped at all. At one point, Alex decided the only way we would get more rides would be to use me as bait. A couple of times he hid behind a sign not far from where I stood with my thumb out. When the driver pulled over, Alex emerged and jumped into the car too. It was a dirty trick and it was a wonder none of the drivers became really angry or violent.

One particular incident caused a re-evaluation of our tactic. We were riding with one driver for a longer distance than most. When we stopped for lunch at a crude café, he downed a couple of glasses of liquid courage, and then insisted on paying for our food. Soon after we got back on the road, the driver nonchalantly reached over and put his hand on my leg. I immediately removed his hand. He tried again, possibly thinking I didn't understand the price of the ride and the meal. When I threw his hand away the second time, he understood. Game over. Abruptly he pulled over, stepped on the brakes, and put us out.

CHAPTER 9

The Resiliency of a Face

If we do not deal with our troubles, they are sure to deal with us.
—Anne Morrow Lindbergh

What now? On the shoulder of another desolate, hot, parched road we alternately stood and sat on the ground for what felt like days. For a time, Hope, that elusive bird, seemed to have flown to friendlier fields. Tasting the grit of dust in my teeth, our hopes rose and fell with each lone-passing car. One good ride was all we needed to get to Athens, Greece and then to its legendary islands.

Wait. Here's one. Maybe it would be the ticket to get us out of Southern Yugoslavia. No. Not yet.

Counting the passing cars took hours to tick off the fingers of even one hand. A couple of cars slowed but didn't stop. Once I saw a head shake "*tsk-tsk*" as the driver looked us up and down, and drove away.

On slow stretches, Alex and I often passed the time playing mindless games. The notebooks we always carried were handy for drawing them. The game of Squares consisted of drawing dots to form multiple squares within a larger one. Each player in turn drew a line connecting two or more of the dots. The object was for each player to make as many squares as possible while preventing the other player from doing the same.

Alex usually won. Winning was more important for him to win so he focused more on the game's logistics. Only peripherally engaged, I was competitive until I became bored, or knew I was losing. Were they one and the same? Possibly. Although I wasn't serious about the games, they did help make long waits bearable.

On this particular morning, our game wasn't quite over when we saw a fast approaching Taunus—very much like the one we had bought in Portugal. Fate was clearly at work here. Hurriedly Alex stashed the notebooks as I held out the scrawled, cardboard "Athens" sign. Standing with our best "Please-give-us-a-ride-we-won't-harm-you" looks on our faces, I tried to catch the driver's eye. Done.

The driver made a quick appraisal and, *hallelujah,* came to an abrupt halt. We hopped in. I got into the front seat and Alex into the back. Again we would try to somehow compensate a driver for picking us up, but this driver didn't need any recompense. I couldn't believe our luck. The driver wasn't a poor Yugoslavian farmer, but a young Greek college student on break and on his way home from Italy. He would be driving all the way to Athens. *Fantastic!* Between his few words of English, and our smattering of Italian, we were able to engage him in some rudimentary dialogue.

Aigidios, whose parents were anxiously waiting for him in Athens, started his trip later than expected, so he was driving at a good clip. This was good news for us—at first.

As scenery flew by in the opposite direction, I was disturbed to learn the driver had been at a raucous, late-night party the night before and had had no sleep. I tried to dismiss this information. After all, we had been in some fast cars before and lived to tell the tale, like the Italian speedster in the Ferrari who whipped around the curvy mountainous roads. One difference was *that* driver had been awake and alert.

In his state of diminished consciousness and rush to get home, our new friend Aigidios was driving well beyond the speed of reason. His driving became increasingly erratic. When we asked him to slow down, he initially complied, but as if he had been dozing, he intermittently sped up, slowed down, and sped up again. When Alex asked him if one of us could drive, he refused. Maybe our luck wasn't so good after all.

My better judgment urging me to demand that we be let out of the car was counter-balanced by thoughts of another long wait on the side of the road.

If we just held on we would be all right. *Surely we'll be all right.* As the odds against a safe outcome spiraled, we tried futilely to convince Aigidios to let one of us drive.

As we pressed our luck, the driver pressed on. I gripped the door handle, bracing myself at each of his erratic moves. More kilometers passed swiftly, slowly, and swiftly again. *It's going to be okay*, I thought. *Just a while longer.*

Just a while longer wasn't soon enough. In the Greek village of Lamia, the dreaded thing happened. The road suddenly curved, winding through town and around olive orchards. Aigidios didn't slow down, and instead of taking the sharp curve, the curve took him, and us. We bounced off the road into an orchard. With my fingers squeezing the door handle, I was looking straight at the olive tree directly in our path when the Taunus slammed into it, coming to a thunderous halt.

The abrupt force shattered the windshield, sending a storm of glass shards flying into my face. Just *my* face. Neither our driver nor Alex was hurt, but my face was cut. I didn't know if I had hit my head, but I could feel the blood running down my cheeks onto the front of my shirt.

Shaken into the realization of what had just happened, I sat stunned for a moment. As I turned to look at Alex, his face paled. He saw blood all over my face. There was no quick way to tell the source of all the blood. Alex removed me from the car, sat me on the ground, and assessed the damage, but he didn't say much.

Apart from the shattered windshield, the tank-like car had little other damage, but Aigidios, suddenly fully awake, went into panic mode. Because it was his father's car, he worried about the damage, the cost, and the personal consequences. Never mind me and my bloody face. He didn't ask how I was. His father would be so angry, he blurted, as he walked up and down, flailing his arms.

A small curious crowd gathered there in the orchard. Shortly, one of the more charitable residents drove us to a six-bed clinic and deposited us there. Aigidios barely acknowledged our leaving and we never saw or heard from him again.

At the clinic, a sympathetic nurse cleaned the blood while a staff member telephoned the physician on call, likely the *only* doctor. After assessing the damage, he determined most of the cuts on my face were superficial. *Most,* he said. One on my nose went a little deeper, and one at the corner of my mouth would require stitches. *Oh God, no*! The elderly doctor went to work. I don't know which was worse as he stitched—the physical or emotional pain.

When I saw the final results on my face, I wondered what kind of doctor he really was. The horse stitches he made left long pieces sticking out like cat whiskers. I was devastated. When Alex sat beside me on the hospital bed, I couldn't stop crying. "I'm going to be scarred and disfigured and ugly for the rest of my life," I worried aloud between my sobs.

"No you're not," he said, attempting nonchalance. "You're going to be fine." I wasn't convinced and the concerned look on his face told me that he wasn't either.

He held my hand and brushed a few strands of hair from my forehead trying as best he could to comfort me. In his own inimitable way, Alex's attempt at solace sounded like that of the coach of a losing team. "Don't worry," he said. "You'd be amazed at the resiliency of a face."

Easy for him to say. It wasn't his face.

Whether my face would prove resilient or not and whether I liked it or not, I had to deal with the new situation. It was what it was. I couldn't undo anything. I couldn't just stay in Lamia and bury myself. The only option was to move forward. The next day we collected our things, checked out of the clinic, and got back on the road, Alex, me, and my cat whiskers.

CHAPTER 10

The Sandalmaker

The first casualty, when war comes, is truth.
—Hiram Johnson, California governor

Word was the go-to place to get great handmade leather sandals at a good price was the small shop of A. Kazarian on Adrianou Street in Athens. Alex and I were each fitted with a durable, attractive, comfortable pair that would be our only footwear for many months.

Mr. Kazarian was a white-haired, wizened, heavy-set man who also sold goatskin and sheepskin rugs. He was popular with our fellow travelers not only because he was an expert at his shoe craft, but also because he was an English speaking teller of tales.

Storytelling and listening, a major element of our vagabonding entertainment, also provided emotional and spiritual nourishment for us. We became part of the lives of strangers in strange lands and they became part of ours. This was our education too. We learned history from those who had lived it. We studied other cultures by eating their food, walking their back streets, riding on local, often inadequate, transportation, visiting their homes, and sharing some of their concerns.

Mr. Kazarian's face was deeply lined, engulfing eyes holding unfathomable sadness. Yet, his robustness and love of life made me want to listen to his stories. Part of his shop was beneath a roof with no walls. The salty air no doubt contributed to the old man's vigor, and, for me, an added enticement to linger.

Our short-term plan—and we had no long-term one—was to find passage on a boat to the island of Santorini in a few days, and later visit other Greek islands. In the meantime, we could explore Athens and sit and listen to stories for as long as we felt so inclined.

Unfortunately, some of Mr. Kazarian's stories were sad, even horrific tales, memories of the "conflict" between the Ottoman Turks and his people, the Armenians, particularly in the years between 1915 when Turkey entered World War I and 1918.

Like many other descendants of Armenians who had survived the ordeal, Mr. Kazarian felt obliged to repeat the stories because some groups, which he said included the Turkish government, had tried to deny the undeniable. As heartbreaking as it was for him to recount it, the world needed to know the truth. The truth was something I had never heard before. This "conflict" was tantamount to genocide, he said. Although it affected some Greeks and other Christians too, the atrocities were inflicted mostly on the Armenians who had lived in this part of Caucasus for thousands of years.

As he told it, the Armenians were industrious, prosperous, and peaceable. Because some were Russian sympathizers, the Ottoman regime and the Young Turks took the opportunity of the 'cover' of the war to drive them all out.

Told they were being moved for their own safety, Armenians were robbed of their homes and possessions by the Turkish government, and some were deported. Even as they served as soldiers, they were stripped of all their guns. Some were butchered in their homes or in the streets. They were rounded up and taken on death marches through the Syrian dessert, starved, beaten, raped, forced to die of thirst, and many of their bodies simply thrown by the sides of the roads. When their Christian leaders were beheaded, their heads became trophies for the Turks.

Numbers of witnesses told of the atrocities. Henry Morganthau, the U.S. ambassador to the Ottoman Empire from 1913-1916 sent a cable in 1915 to the U.S. State Department that read, "Deportation of and excesses against peaceful Armenians is increasing, and from harrowing reports of eye witnesses, it appears that a campaign of race extermination is in progress under a pretext of reprisal against rebellion."

Before that moment in the shoe shop, I had never imagined that all through the ages and all across the world, so many men have been and still are, abominable in their treatment of other human beings. Mr. Kazarian's stories—whether I wanted them to or not—opened my eyes.

One and a half million Armenians were killed in this tragedy. When we paint war and its atrocities with a broad brush, citing thousands, even millions of casualties, it's easy to miss the human side. One story the sandal maker told made the war personal.

"The Turks, they were barbaric," he said. "One day two of them who were drunk and laughing saw an Armenian woman, a pregnant woman, walking down the street. They made a bet about her baby, if it was a boy or a girl. One of them grabbed the poor woman, drew his long knife, and said, 'Let's see.' Without a blink, he slashed open her abdomen and found out."

That image, indelibly imprinted on my mind, has remained a part of the burden and responsibility I bear for all mankind. If one of us is capable of a thing, then aren't we all?

At the time, I didn't want to believe what I was hearing. When Mr. Kazarian had finished his story he took a deep breath and let out a long sigh. He was silent for a moment, and so were we.

Finally, he said, "You go," with a nod of his head, blinking back tears. "Go and enjoy the islands. Maybe you will tell the truth to someone else. I hope you remember."

How could I forget?

The next day, newly shod, Alex and I roamed the streets of the oldest city of Europe. For hours, we sought Athens' historical and architectural treasures, confronted at every turn by the evidence of a civilization that was clearly intellectually, philosophically, and architecturally advanced. I was utterly awed by what the ancients could and did achieve in their engineering and construction. Without the help of cranes or computers, they determined how to erect formidable structures that lasted through centuries.

What sort of people were our Greek and Roman ancestors anyway? Among the ancients, the lines between supernatural and human were somewhat blurred. The gods had human failings and humans achieved godlike feats.

After putting a lot of mileage on our new sandals, around monuments, past relics, in and out of small shops, Alex and I succumbed to our human appetites when we spotted cafe after cafe with tall vertical rotisseries just outside their doors. The rotisseries held enormous chunks of lamb, turning slowly and dripping fragrant juices into a pan below. I was about to discover an irresistible gastronomic delight, a *souflaki.*

Overcome by the sweet aroma, we stopped for lunch in one of the cafes, sitting at a table near the aroma's source. With artistic flair, the cook swiped his large sharp knife down the sides of the meat, slicing thin pieces and laying them on pita bread. My mouth watered as he added onions, tomatoes, and a creamy white cucumber-yogurt-garlic sauce called *sadziki.* He rolled it up and handed one of these delights to each of us. It was without a doubt one of the tastiest, juiciest sandwiches I had ever put into my mouth.

Newly energized from lunch, we continued our walk, stepping on old ground—the ground of the remains of the Roman Agora and the magnificent temples. The most impressive of all the sites was the one most obvious. The marble Parthenon, surrounded by stately columns, sits atop the flat rock of the Acropolis, almost five hundred feet above sea level. Seeing this symbol of the birthplace of Western civilization for the first time filled me with pride. As much as I had been ashamed of the human race upon hearing of its atrocities, I stood in awe of the same race that could produce such a marvel.

When it was built, the temple was dedicated by the Athenians to their patron goddess, Athena Parthenon. The gold and ivory statue of the warrior-armored but peaceful-visaged goddess that had once commanded the site had been lost, but apparently the grace remained.

The Acropolis is as much a part of daily life in Athens as it is iconic. When I heard I might catch a sound-and-light performance of *Prometheus Bound* on its hillside, I immediately wanted to witness it.

In college I was fascinated by the Greek tragedies, due in large part to the efforts of a silver-haired, erudite professor. His love of great literature and language was heard in every word he spoke, and was traced on every line of his face. Because of his wealth of knowledge and his imposing presence, this professor was truly intimidating to me, but he caused me to love literature more than I ever had and to appreciate the Greeks. I was completely enamored.

Sadly, we didn't go to the performance at the Acropolis because Alex voted against it. I guessed he didn't see the point in spending our small funds for tickets, and I went along. In retrospect, I should have insisted and gone anyway. I regretted missing the opportunity, but I justified the decision by recalling the sandalmaker's stories, and I concluded I had probably heard all the tragedy I could handle for the moment. Three days later, we took Mr. Kazarian's advice and boarded a ferry to the fabled island of Santorini.

CHAPTER 11

Perfect Stranger

There are two tragedies in life. One is to lose your heart's desire. The other is to gain it.
—George Bernard Shaw

From the port of Piraeus, the ferry took us southeast one hundred twenty miles from the mainland to the southernmost island of the Cyclades group, the stunning, otherworldly beautiful Santorini. Even the name is lovely.

The island itself is the remains of a volcanic cone that blew its top about thirty-five hundred years ago in one of the largest eruptions in recorded history. Speculation is that this eruption was responsible for the massive tsunamis that destroyed the Minoan Civilization on the large island of Crete to the south.

Pulling into the harbor of Santorini is actually pulling into a *caldera,* or volcanic lagoon. This *caldera* is about seven and a half miles long, half as wide, and almost thirteen hundred feet deep in the center. Some claim this may be the site of long lost Atlantis, and seeing the place, I could easily believe it. The island surrounded us on three sides with tall, steep cliffs. Capital city Fira overlooks the lagoon, perched on the cliff almost a thousand feet above.

Alex and I arrived in the late afternoon. A deckhand aimed and threw the heavy rope precisely over the piling, pulling the boat to the dock. As soon as we disembarked we were faced with an immediate challenge. There was no town at sea level. The only way to Fira was a long switchback ascent up a wall of rock all the way to the summit.

A few enterprising locals offered donkey rides to the top for a fee. We looked up, gauging the enormity of the climb, and agreed to skip the ride. *What the hell. We could do this on foot.* With sandals on our feet, knapsacks on our backs, and leaning forward against the ascent, we began, placing one foot in front of the other. Although we were in good shape and took it slow, after a while there was some huffing and puffing.

Stopping to catch our breath along the way, I wondered if we had made the right decision. Right or not, it was too late to change now. Instead of considering how far we had climbed already, I thought about the top, how every step drew us closer and how great would be the view. *Just one step at a time.*

I was light-headed when we finally reached the summit, but the trek had been worth it, shaky legs and all. The panorama was spectacular. Standing on the precipice of this curved inner coast I was struck by the sheer drop. The cliff was composed of solidified layers of lava, reaching to the water. In the distance, I could see two places where the deep blue water of the lagoon merged with the water of the Aegean, and I could see a much smaller island.

The town of Fira stretched out across the cliffs. Almost on top of each other, whitewashed and pastel-colored, cube-shaped stone houses sat nestled into the rock, some with roofs or gates in shades of the sea below. In contrast, bright fuchsia bougainvillea draped some of the walls.

We found lodging and a cafe where a friendly local introduced us to *retsina*, a wine with a pungent odor and a very peculiar turpentine taste. Reluctant to try it, I balked as I had balked as a sick child attempting to avoid the inevitable when my mother was forcing some medicine on me. "Wait a minute. I'm not ready yet. Okay, okay, I'll do it… Just a minute."

Finally resigned, I put the glass to my lips and took a small sip. "Aaagh. I don't think I can drink this," I said to our host apologetically. He said most people initially had the same reaction.

Retsina isn't a type of grape; it is a method of making wine. Originally, wine was preserved and shipped in casks sealed with pine resin out of necessity, but even after the resin was no longer needed, it was added to the wine to give it the familiar flavor. It was possible the residents drank more wine than water because Santorini has no rivers. Water is scarce and much of it is imported from other parts of Greece.

"If you drink *retsina*, soon you will like it," our Greek friend said, "and it is very good for your health."

Maybe he was right about the health benefit, and maybe it would grow on me. That night, I managed to drink a small glassful to be sociable, and after Alex downed his wine we said goodnight.

For the next few days we explored the outer side of the crater island, where the land slopes gradually down to smooth, pebbly beaches. Rock colors varied from red to white to black. The shallow water at the shore was more black than blue because of the black lava rock just beneath the surface. While beautiful in its own way, this beach was not conducive to sport or relaxation.

After a solid night of fresh-aired slumber, we rose early the morning of our last day and headed out. Before descending to the port, we stopped to absorb the magnificent view one last time. The sky was clear and the view unobstructed. At this height, I found it easy to imagine godhead and dominion. Was this where Greek gods and humans met?

Great height allows grand perspective. Everything below seemed inconsequential, including our problems, our worries and our very selves. What did we matter except as an infinitesimal part of the grand theater of the world, with ever-changing elaborate sets, actors with continuous opening nights and curtain calls, and thunderous applause, laughter or boos. The show must go on. Simultaneously Santorini's perspective offered me reassurance that everything mattered. I mattered and what I did mattered because I could appreciate beauty and feel compassion. This place was created for me.

Our next Aegean stop was the charming island of Ios where we rented a tiny cottage for a tiny price. The semi-walled patio was complete with a few chickens and one enthusiastic rooster. The cottage was only minutes from the town square, which was another few minutes from the small harbor. Here we spent more unambitious, down-to-earth days, doing nothing in particular, although we usually rose with the sun and the rooster. We were on Greek time, which, like New Orleans time, is generally slow.

In the mornings, I would greet the sun and write in my journal while Alex would write feverishly on short stories he hoped one day to sell. Because his writing often wore on and on into the day, I tried to make myself scarce during these times. I had learned that when Alex was writing, whatever I did or didn't do was of little consequence to him. He was so totally engrossed in his words that I could have de-materialized and he wouldn't have noticed.

Occasionally Alex and I spent a few hours at the beach, in the astoundingly clear azure sea. Most evenings we would walk to a favorite café for dinner, but much of the time I was alone, emotionally if not physically.

Most mornings I spent at and around the town square, reading, sipping coffee at the café or walking to the harbor. I often shopped for fresh feta cheese and bread at the market, returning with them to the cottage for lunch. The people were friendly, and I learned a few Greek words. "*Cali mera*," I responded to the morning greetings of the residents.

Usually it was pleasant enough, but one day I was overcome with deep feelings of loneliness. Here I was on an idyllic Greek island, young, healthy, full of life and passion, and I had no one to share it me. Alex was living in his own world where I was only occasionally welcome.

I wanted to be out and about with my partner, enjoying the small town, its people, its food, and the luscious ocean air. More than anything, I needed romance. I wanted to make love and be loved and cherished. Alex wanted to write. A writer must write. I understood. But even if Alex couldn't leave his writing, I could have been happy knowing he desired me. Could I seduce him as much as the words he teased from his head to the page? Truthfully, I was beginning to believe I was no match for his mistress, the Word.

If we couldn't feel romance here, when and where would we? Did Alex enjoy the *idea of sex* more than the actual act, or was I being too demanding? He liked conjuring up rich imagery of others in Hemingway-ish romantic situations, and he didn't hesitate to flirt with other women, but I felt he was living vicariously through a novel he was writing in his head. People he knew, including me, were characters in it. Characters conformed to their pre-cast molds or were written out of the manuscript. Often he didn't see me, and I was nowhere on his page.

On this particularly promising, gorgeous, azure-skied morning, I woke up feeling extraordinarily good, strong, and energetic. The windows of our little alabaster cottage were wide open and the air smelled of fresh flowers, sweet earth and sea. I wanted to drag Alex away from his notebook, but thought it best to wait, so I busied myself as several hours passed. In the meantime I started hearing in my head the words of the sultry song Peggy Lee made popular years before. "*You give me fever, when you kiss me, fever when you hold me tight... Fever in the morning, fever all through the night...*"

I felt like Peggy, felt like singing that song to my man, felt like seducing him, or even better, having him seduce me. What better time? It was a great day and there was no place we had to go, nothing we had to do. We could just enjoy each other. I needed terribly for him to take me into his arms and make wild, passionate love to me. I needed him to appreciate my young womanhood.

But Alex sat deep in thought, in some faraway world, in the stranglehold of his words. When I sidled up to him, wearing my best come hither look, he barely raised his eyes from the page.

"Hey, you want to come and play?" I teased.

"No, I'm going to finish this," he said, matter-of-factly.

It was a perfect day and there are only so many perfect days, I reminded Alex. Not wanting to be bothered, he dismissed me, chased me away, intimating I should go find someone else. At first, I was disappointed and hurt, but then I was furious. I thought, "*Okay, if that's the way he wants it...*"

I put on my breezy, short, slim, red cotton dress and stormed out. I escorted myself to the town square, and sat at a table sipping a small glass of wine. I tried to focus on reading a paperback, but my mind wasn't on the story.

Before long I sensed a tall, dark-haired stranger with bedroom eyes using them to undress me. He looked familiar and I realized I had seen him here several times before. We smiled and flirted a little. Soon he approached me and asked if he could sit down. Of course he could. I wondered if my fever was that obvious.

He ordered another glass of wine for each of us. He wanted to know how I liked *retsina*, how I liked Ios, and where in America I was from. He was from Athens and worked for one of the ferry boat companies. He was on the island for just a few days. It was the smallest of small talk, but he had an easy smile and I liked him. His attention exhilarated me. We chatted and laughed together about nothing, as the sea breezes blew a few hours away. His English was faltering, but his eyes were fluent and we both knew what he meant.

As if in a dream, where one moment you're somewhere and in the next you're in a *non-sequitur* elsewhere, this man took me by the hand, and I floated to another realm. I swear I don't remember how it happened. Suddenly, inexplicably, we were in a small hotel room near the square. With my heart aching, my mind abandoned its constraints of sanity, and this perfect stranger and I had indefensibly reckless sex.

Was I insane to throw caution to the wind? Perhaps I was, but I also felt vindicated. Was it so delicious because the fruit was forbidden? Was it that I needed to be needed and pursued? As ethereally and timelessly as it had started, it was over. After a little nervous small talk, this stranger and I went our separate ways.

Back at the café I felt better in the obvious way, but worse in other ways. I had the satisfaction of revenge for Alex's neglect, but this was not supposed to happen. This was not me. I am a faithful and devoted partner, but more importantly, it was dangerous behavior. Or was it?

Was this out-of-the-blue Greek a devil, preying on a young innocent woman, or an angel, temporarily rescuing me from a potentially worse scenario in an erotic world? Did he exist or did I dream him?

After I returned to our cottage, it was quite a while before Alex and I spoke. He was still engrossed in his writing. I wasn't particularly interested in talking to him, but when he eventually stopped writing, he noticed something was different. When we did speak, I told him about my tryst. Whether or not he was covering his true feelings, he didn't display any distress. In fact, he acted quite nonchalant about the whole thing. I sensed a secret relief that I had been taken care of and he didn't have to bother.

They say we teach others how to treat us, so in retrospect, I admit some blame for the way Alex took me for granted and neglected me. I didn't demand otherwise. I probably should have left him before now, but though I knew little about love, I believed I loved Alex, and that he loved me, in spite of his often thoughtless behavior. I held onto the hope that one day we would both be better at this relationship thing and have a family together. My sense of commitment to him was possibly stronger than my commitment to myself, and my ingrained Catholicism prompted me to stick with my man, no matter what. Also, I lacked the confidence to strike out on my own with this odyssey, halfway around the world from my home and family and friends.

The trouble with life, I heard it said, is that it gives us the test first and reveals the lesson only later. It didn't seem fair. Fair or not, I decided that even if I wasn't on the right path, I was going to force it to be the right one. Somehow I would make it work. After all, our experiences, positive or negative, joyous or painful, were simply dross being burned off to reveal strong character, weren't they? On the way to higher ground, we all had lessons to learn, but underneath, everything is truth and beauty. That's all there is.

In the long run, I don't think the Ios incident had much effect on the way Alex and I related to each other, but it did give me cause for new considerations. When would enough be enough?

The very morning we stood on the pier ready to board the boat to the mainland watching passengers file off, we spotted our friends Lenny and Jen among them. It was a happy meeting. We postponed our leaving for a few more days, and arranged to reconnect with them on the island of Skiathos in a week.

Determining to see more of the country, Alex and I thumbed our way northward, stopping above the Gulf of Corinth in Central Greece at Delphi. I had read about this site where the lines between legend and history are delightfully blurred. Delphi, situated on multiple terraces along the slope of Mount Parnassus, was the home of the most important oracle in the classical Greek world. Its prestige continued throughout that culture's Golden Age.

From the eighth century B.C. Delphi was revered throughout the Greek world as the center of the earth and of the universe. It was from Delphi that the god Apollo spoke through the Oracle *Pythia,* offering inspiration and guidance to those who sought it, both the great and the common.

One detail about Delphi intrigued me. The Greeks, Romans, and Christians who are said to have sought guidance there included Alexander the Great, King Croesus, and Oedipus, King of Thebes. They asked for advice about laws or reforms to benefit their states. They asked about declaring war, building temples, or founding cities. They also asked about personal issues.

The Oracle's pronouncements may have been inspirational and authentically prophetic and wise, although doubtlessly some were misinterpreted or lost in translation. I truly believed divinities could communicate with mortals. Now, so it was said, the god at Delphi was silent. As I stood on Mount Parnassus, surrounded by the ruins of temples, a theater and crumbling columns, I couldn't help but feel it's all in how well you listen. Through my distraction, I was trying.

Leaving the mainland once more, we sailed for Skiathos to meet Lenny and Jen. They had been promised a free room by an acquaintance, but we took a different tack. Not knowing when we could earn any money again, we, as always, were trying to economize. A lovely spot on the beach became our camp with no tent.

This beach was pristine and secluded with white sand and crystal clear blue-green water. For the ten days we stayed there we had it all to ourselves. Our place was barely under a slight earthy overhang, about five feet above the sand. Conveniently located, on this little promontory was a full-bodied fig tree, providing both a bit of shade and a lot of fresh fruit within reach for daily breakfasts.

We spread our sleeping bags down on the sand, and *voila*, there was home. We were both outdoor people who didn't require much. In spite of my feminine, conventional American background, I surprised myself at how low-maintenance I was. With very little, I had it all.

Every night we fell asleep under the canopy of stars, and every morning awoke with the sunrise. The days were for swimming in the sea, for reading, writing, talking, playing silly paper games, and lazing in the sun.

Every day I walked into the little town less than a half mile away and bought goat cheese, bread, and wine for our lunch. By now I had learned to like *retsina*. Sometimes Alex came along and we went exploring by ourselves or with Lenny and Jen. At a quiet café we ate dinner on the covered patio with colored lights strung around its canopy roof. We devoured plates of *moussaka, spanikopita,* and *dolmades,* all wonderfully flavored, nutritious dishes rich in Mediterranean vegetables. It was the kind of food that made me feel happy, the taste enhanced by the salty sea air.

In spite of the rich foods we ate, we stayed lean. We soon became tan. I felt as healthy and vigorous as I had ever felt. My long hair was streaked and bleached by the constant fingers of the sun. Everything was quite lovely. Alex and I were a little more intimate than we had been before, and at least we were spending more time doing things together.

I frequently stopped at a public fountain near town to rinse the salt out of my hair. Then one day, I had a less than brilliant idea. Why not shampoo my hair in the sea? It would be efficient. While I was swimming, I could get my hair washed and rinsed at the same time. It turned out, disastrously, I could do neither. When I shampooed my hair, it didn't get clean. The combination of shampoo and salt wouldn't rinse out and turned into a sticky, globby mess. To my chagrin, I couldn't even get a comb through my hair. Finally, I went to the public fountain and shampooed and rinsed there. I felt foolish, but how could I have known that salt and shampoo don't mix?

CHAPTER 12
The Whole Elephant

Take me back to Constantinople; no you can't
go back to Constantinople. If you go back to
Constantinople, you'll be waiting in Istanbul.
—Jimmy Kennedy, Nat Simon, "Istanbul, Not Constantinople"

When I heard this silly song as a child, I was intrigued by the name, intrigued by the geography. I loved map puzzles and world globes. I was fascinated by faraway and exotic-sounding places, but I had never thought about going to Istanbul until the spring of 1968 in Barcelona when some other travelers were discussing this next must-go-to place.

Istanbul had several draws. It was an exotic, truly *foreign* culture. Europe was Europe, but Turkey was the East, straddling the line, literally, between West and East. Venturing into Istanbul was venturing out of the safe familiar womb of western civilization. That city presented more potential excitement because there were more unknowns.

Additionally, we heard reports of cheap and readily available hashish. Not that we were druggies or were inclined to be. We had only "experimented" with marijuana and hadn't even been exposed to hashish, a marijuana plant derivative. Still, the lore of hashish was beguiling.

The biggest danger for Westerners, so we heard, was being caught transporting or dealing hashish, especially across borders. We kept hearing rumors and horror stories, of busted Americans spending eons in frightening, worse-than-primitive jail cells with no hope of release. But surely that couldn't and wouldn't happen to us.

It crossed my mind I had to go to Istanbul to prove I could tempt Fate and still return unscathed. Was this whole, open-ended odyssey my way of teasing Danger or of testing myself?

When I was ten years old, my family moved from an old, too-small, Creole cottage in the lower Ninth Ward of New Orleans to a little larger just-built home in a newly developed subdivision on the outskirts of the City, a fifteen-minute drive from the French Quarter.

A long narrow canal separated our backyard on the mile-long street from an undeveloped large wooded area. Sometimes I enticed my neighborhood friend Karen to cross the canal with me and venture into the woods where we would pretend to be explorers. I pretended I could identify the flora and fauna. I would note and mark our path so we could find our way back. At the same time, I secretly hoped we would get lost so that I could use what I believed were my innate survival skills until we got rescued.

We never got rescued because we never got lost. It could be we didn't try hard enough. Whatever the truth of the matter is, that exploration was my first flirtation with Danger.

It's possible that we all, at times, want to get "lost," some for the challenge, some for the attention, and some to see if there is someone who cares enough to rescue us. Some of us choose to get lost vicariously in the lives of the kinds of people our mothers warned us about. Why were we so drawn to stories about prodigal sons and rehabilitated criminals and druggies, and we ignore stories about the saints, unless those saints were reformed sinners?

Lost or not, the line between make believe and reality is often fuzzy. I had to ask myself if I was pretending now, as I walked along the Galata Bridge, in this very foreign world. Did this floating bridge, which was pulsating with daily necessity, and crowded with more walkers, bicycle riders, and bicycle taxis than cars, really have its feet on two continents? Was I only imagining I might be easily swallowed up in this place and disappear?

The crossing both defined and linked traditional, empirical Istanbul and its religious and secular institutions on the Asian side with its more non-traditional cousin on the European side.

My uneducated eye didn't notice much of a difference between the mélange of housing and business places on the eastern and western sides of the Golden Horn. It was clear, though, which was the traditional side—the one whose skyline was dominated by the *Hagia Sophia* and the Blue Mosque, grand icons of Islam. The western side was largely populated by non-Muslims, foreign merchants, and diplomats in districts like Galata, Beyoglu, and Sisli. The bridge, built in 1912, not only tied two continents together, but two different cultures.

Alex and I crossed into the Beyoglu district to get our pictures taken for the student identification cards required by the youth hostel where we would be staying.

"So, you are students in America?" Mehmet, the young, enthusiastic clerk wanted to know. Not long ago he had been a student himself.

It was only a partial lie when Alex said, "Yeah, we're on a long break." He still had a semester or so of college credits to earn when he left the University of Salamanca, and I could be a graduate student. In fact, we were both continuing students of life.

Mehmet was friendly and helpful and he made sure we got the IDs we needed. He had a better than average command of English and saw a chance to practice it by inviting us to a family picnic that weekend. Of course, we eagerly accepted this opportunity to meet some of the locals and have a non-tourist experience.

In the meantime, we got settled into the hostel. Located on the Asian side of the Golden Horn, the building was a rough, old, somewhat run-down dormitory which housed students during the school year. Although there were several close-quartered, cramped rooms available, they filled quickly and we were lucky to get one, I think. There were no bathrooms in, or attached to the rooms, but shared bathrooms were at the end of a hallway. A great benefit of this hostel was its location in the heart of the Sultan Ahmet district, within walking distance of so many of the places we wanted to explore.

Before much exploring, I had another priority. We had spent a lot of time on the road, literally, and all of it wearing sandals. When a fellow flophouse inmate told us about an inexpensive Turkish bath in the neighborhood, I jumped at the chance to get really clean.

Stepping into the bathhouse was stepping back to a time when bath meant luxury—spacious, high-ceilinged rooms with marble everywhere. Every surface looked scrubbed and whistle-clean. After washing myself, I was instructed to lie on a smooth marble slab where a woman rubbed my skin with a very coarse cloth. I watched, unbelievingly and embarrassedly, as the woman rubbed what appeared to be layers of grime off my arms. It reminded me of what we called "grandma beads", dirt that collected in the creases of little kids' fat necks after they had been playing in the dirt and in the heat of summer. But, my pride was salvaged when I learned it was layers of dead skin, being scoured off my arms and legs and feet.

Never before had I felt as clean and refreshed. I was reluctant to go out into the street and dirty my skin again, just as I had sometimes experienced not wanting to eat again after having my teeth power-cleaned at the dentist, only much more intense.

Walking around town, we discovered street vendors selling *simit*, a type of bread that was a cross between a pretzel and a bagel with a sprinkling of sesame seeds clinging to the dry baked dough. They weren't sweet, but were a little bland. We often saw people eating them at outdoor cafes with a glass of hot, black tea. When we began doing the same, I found it satisfying. Turkish food in general was a robust pleasure that reminded me of home.

It had been almost a year since I left New Orleans. The food and the strangeness of this interesting place occasionally made me melancholy. I had to admit I did miss home, my big family there, and all the Sunday dinners and special occasions when everybody was together. I missed the easy camaraderie, even the arguments.

When Sunday came, I was excited to be with a family, even though it wasn't my own. The picnic was in Beyoglu on a beautiful, clear day. Although Mehmet's sister, Cali also spoke English, none of the rest of the family did, but it didn't matter much.

All dressed in European clothes, they were hospitable, kind, and cheerful. Mehmet's mother was also generous. She had gifts for me—a silver and turquoise bracelet, and a small bronze dish. I thought to decline them, because that is *our* way, but I learned that in many other cultures, it's an insult to the giver to refuse gifts. I also learned if you're visiting someone's home, you should never compliment too much an object you think is beautiful, or the host will insist on giving it to you.

"Thank you so much. These things are lovely," I said, and Mehmet translated for me. I put the bracelet on my arm. We spent a mellow, carefree day on a grassy hillside with these people, ate food they had brought, and communicated mostly in sign language and smiles and hugs. By the end of the day I felt almost as if they were my own relatives. In a sense, they were.

Depending on one's perspective, Istanbul was many things—a bustling, intriguing crossroads and marketplace, and an artful, brilliant gem. To my eyes, she was also an inscrutable, mysterious woman, a true exotic dancer. Certainly Paris and London had their back alleys and intrigue, but the secret life of fabled Istanbul was much deeper and darker to me.

No other city on earth had been raped, burned, and razed with as much wild terror and as often as Istanbul. But still it stood and its people went on eating, drinking, making merry, marrying, bearing children, and dying, though apparently not everybody died. Rumors abounded about a two-thousand-year-old man dwelling in its streets.

What especially lived on in Istanbul was the spirit of tenacity, the stubbornness to survive what is left after all pretenses are blown away. Here, one must go deeper within oneself to find the beauty and niceties of nature. They had gone underground. This was not to say that Istanbul had no trees or grass or parks, but it seemed its soul was much older than a European one. It had seen much more of the beauty and the ugliness, of the passion and the hatred than most of Western civilization. It had seen all the extremes of human nature, and it had solidified its remembrances in grand mosques and monuments, bridges and squares.

Was I ready to face life in this kind of reality? Part of my, and our, ability to function there came from an ability to play act. We were just in a different movie now, with different sets and character names. Alex and I were both ingénues, but at times I felt kinship with the oldest souls on the face of the earth.

This place, called Byzantium when it was founded in the seventh century B.C., became Constantinople in the fourth century A.D. when the Roman emperor Constantine, who introduced Christianity there, renamed it after himself. When the Ottoman Turks captured Constantinople in 1453, it was reborn in its most recent incarnation as Istanbul.

Istanbul thoroughly blankets its geographical area with its sense of self, the blanket punctuated with a wealth of mosques and minarets. The sight of the Blue Mosque with its six tall slender minarets dazzled me. Just as dazzling was the sound of the chant when a single voice breached the otherwise impervious atmosphere, calling the faithful to observe prayer time.

Without trying very hard, Alex and I found evidence of all four of Istanbul's empires. To truly appreciate Istanbul though, we had to allow ourselves to be swallowed up by it. It was almost impossible to be an innocent bystander in this land of the magic carpet ride because the air was thick with history and art, with dreams and nightmares, secrets of ages, and monuments to failed empires, shadows of changing religions, and intrigue, and a mix of dozens of nationalities.

Satiated on the sumptuous servings of history and culture, we digested it all in the serenity of a mosque, not just any mosque, but THE most impressive of all, the Blue Mosque. Located within blocks of our hostel, the Blue Mosque dominated not only the Sultanahmet neighborhood, but also the whole Istanbul skyline.

Just inside the entry I saw an array of several hundred pairs of footless shoes. Shoes weren't allowed in the mosque itself. Born to be barefoot, I happily removed my shoes and Alex did the same. Adding our shoes to the lineup, we trusted we would recognize and be able to retrieve them afterwards.

Inside, I was astounded at the blue beauty. I saw a million blue tiles lining the domed ceiling. Images of flowers and trees and abstract patterns everywhere breathed life into the designs. It was so magnificent that my jaw hung open.

Looking down, I saw beauty of a different kind. Men and women knelt in rows on the floor, heads down, arms outstretched, in obeisance to their God. We reverently joined them in quiet. Had I still been a member of the Catholic Church, this would have been a heretical offense.

I had been led to believe that the Catholic Church cornered the market on Truth. It was, after all, the *true church*, and though other religions, even those within the Christian tradition, had a little of the truth, they still missed the mark.

The problem with most religions though, is they each think they've got the Truth, the Whole Truth. Instead, they're like the six blind men and the elephant, fabled characters in John Godfrey Saxe's poem. Each man laid a hand on only one part of the elephant and took that part to be the whole. Was an elephant like a snake, a wall, a fan, a rope, a spear or a tree? Each, the author noted was partly right, and all were wrong.

When I pulled away from the Catholic Church in my college years, I began to appreciate the liberating nature of spirituality outside of the confines of a church. I became a seeker, looking for the whole elephant.

Here, inside this mosque, a part of the elephant was apparent. The devotees were bowing to that greater authority within and without. The reverence was palpable, something I could respect.

When we walked to the nearby museum, I learned that in 1609 the twenty-six-year-old Sultan Ahmet had commissioned the Blue Mosque to be built with the intention of upstaging the *Hagia Sofia.*

While I couldn't grasp the extraordinary vision and the skillful design and construction of the *Hagia Sophia*, I appreciated the feast for my eyes—the artistry and rich colors of green, white, and purple mosaics, the gold encrusted brick, the marble pillars, and the arcade composed of hundreds of arched windows under the immense central dome. The light streaming in appeared mystical.

Built as the patriarchal basilica, the Church of the Holy Wisdom, this mosque was the largest cathedral in the world for almost a thousand years. All holy relics, bells, altar, and sacrificial vessels were removed and many of the original mosaics were covered with plaster when Constantinople was conquered by the Ottoman Turks. It was converted into a mosque. Finally, in 1935, under the Republic of Turkey, it became a museum.

More than ten thousand people were employed in the construction of the *Hagia Sophia.*

Materials came from all over the Roman Empire. Over the years, it was damaged by earthquakes, and parts collapsed. It was ransacked and desecrated, reconstructed and restored. Today this building still awes and inspires.

The Blue Mosque became an impressive rival of the *Hagia Sophia*. The young sultan, who died just a year after it was completed, and his wife and three sons were buried inside.

Once again, I was struck by the wisdom of our ancestors whose keen grasp of architecture, artistry, and physics allowed them to create massive wonders. I was impressed not only by the workmanship but also by the complete dedication of the workers. In their short lives, what else did they do, what else could they have done in addition to this work? The *Hagia Sophia* was their entire life. Suddenly, I felt small, inadequate, and petty.

Still, these monumental beauties were not as interesting as the people and their traditions. One of our fellow hostel guests, a loud German named Horst, invited us to a circumcision event taking place in a Bohemian camp on the outskirts of town. We found the location described and joined a party already in progress.

Unquestioningly, people welcomed us with smiles. This night a twelve-year-old boy would be initiated into the ranks of manhood after undergoing a ritual circumcision. We sat at long tables outside under a serene starlit sky. Food was passed around, and a few musicians played spirited and seductive melodies. Soon a thin woman with a big belly and long gray hair who appeared to be in her sixties, stood up and belly-danced for the crowd. We were told a big belly was a good thing because it sexily suggested to a man that the dancer wanted to have his baby.

After the food was eaten, the men entered the large tent with the brave youngster. Because no females were allowed in, Alex told me afterwards what happened. The boy sat in the middle, surrounded by all the men who started clapping and chanting. The noise became increasingly louder and more frenetic until it reached a fevered pitch. At this moment of frenzy, the doctor, without administering anesthesia, snipped. Tradition says the frenzy provides the only anesthesia needed.

While it seemed barbaric to me, in the United States it is common practice to circumcise boy babies before they leave the hospital. Because it is done under sterile conditions and with anesthesia, and because the baby can't speak, many people believe the infant doesn't feel it either, physically or emotionally.

We had been in Istanbul for more than three weeks when I began to feel some pain of my own. One of my molars was infected. This was not supposed to happen in a foreign country, especially not in a technologically backward one. Daily the pain worsened; I became increasingly miserable and unfit company for anyone. For several nights, Alex hung out with the gang across the hall, while I tossed and turned, groaning in bed, thinking if I could just pass out I might sleep away the pain. I couldn't.

It was past the point of tolerance. Although I hated the thought of seeing a dentist in Istanbul as much as I hated the pain, I had no other choice. In the morning we searched for a dentist, asking around as best we could in a country where we didn't speak the language and few people spoke ours.

Eventually, we found a woman dentist who spoke a little English. After examining and poking the very inflamed gum, she said, "I will have to take it out."

"What? No!" I resisted. I believed an infection should be treated and cleared up before the tooth was pulled, to avoid the chance of blood poisoning. Apparently, she either hadn't heard or didn't believe that.

"Yes, that's what we will need to do," she repeated, offering no alternative. By now the pain was so horrible I was willing to undergo anything to be rid of it. As she readied her tools, I braced myself.

I believed I had a high tolerance for pain, but I wasn't prepared for this. As I leaned my head back in the worn leather chair, the dentist gave me a shot of what I assumed to be some form of anesthesia. We waited a short time. Although I didn't notice much difference in the feeling of my mouth, she was ready. She approached me with pliers that looked like an instrument of torture, and leaned in. Grabbing hold, she started to pull. I thought I was going to die. I just wanted to escape the pain. Either she wasn't strong enough for the job or my tooth was too firmly anchored, but it didn't budge. She pulled harder. Feeling as if my skull was caving in, I screamed like a child. I screamed like I had never screamed before. Alex couldn't stand it and walked outside. More screaming, more pulling, more crunching noises, until finally the tooth was out, and so was I, almost. The dentist packed the bloody hole and sent me on my way, weak and traumatized.

"Sorry," Alex said when it was all over. "I couldn't handle it."

"Yeah, well, you had the easy part," I mumbled through my tears.

You never know how much you can handle until you do. Although recuperating took several days, I didn't die from blood poisoning or have other complications. I had to go easy on the eating for a while, but what a relief it was to have that tooth gone. I'd returned from a trip to hell.

I suppose you could say as I gathered pieces of the world from now more than two continents, I had begun to *leave* parts of myself in exchange. Not only had I left my heart in San Francisco and my soul in New Orleans, but now a tooth in Istanbul.

CHAPTER 13

Another Perfect Stranger

The rule for overcoming fear is to head right into it.
—ANONYMOUS

"*JUMP!... JUMP!*" THE VOICE INSIDE my head kept insisting. Fritz, bobbing nonchalantly in the tumultuous, muddled Mediterranean water shouted his bait once more. "Come on in, Carroll. It's great!" He made a long-armed appeal. "Look, no problem."

The thoughts and urgings in my mind were as choppy, frantic, and insistent as the water. One side of me nagged the other, "*Stop being gutless!*"

I couldn't jump and I couldn't stay where I was, frozen on this pavilion in this small town in the south of Turkey. I knew why I *couldn't* jump and I also knew why I *would.*

Even in tame backyard swimming pool conditions, I was only a mildly adequate swimmer. I tended to panic when I couldn't touch or see bottom. From where I stood, overlooking the turbulence, there *was* no bottom. I didn't know what I would be jumping into, and except for a few days' acquaintance, I didn't know the tall, lanky Dutchman who was urging me in.

What I did know was, tempting Fate, I had presented myself with yet another challenge for which I was unequipped. Common sense told me not to take the challenge, but something drew me into it. Even as I stood, alone and shivering with fear and mortification, I knew I had to take the plunge, just as I had to board the Spanish freighter in New Orleans a year ago, young, alone, and completely unprepared for my voyage. All I knew then was I was meeting a former boyfriend in Spain, then going *who-knew-where* to do *who-knew-what*.

I didn't imagine I would continue for years to put my life in jeopardy in insane, unpredictable ways, all the while thinking I knew why. At the beginning of this global odyssey, I thought I was rising to the challenge because of romance, love of adventure, and my mother's promptings that I could do whatever I wanted to do.

I would never lose the longing for romance and adventure. I would also never forget my unspoken charge of carrying my mother vicariously with me. But when romance soured and adventure devastated my very soul, I thought I continued for fear of being alone. I thought I wasn't strong enough to command my own life, until I had to.

By the time I was in Turkey I was no stranger to jumping into unknown waters, and this incident would pale in light of what the Universe, with my complicity, would devise.

Conflicting voices resided in my head, urging my obedience in one direction or another. Sometimes they led me to enlightened places, and sometimes they led me astray. I liked to believe I could tell the difference and that I usually complied with the wise forces for good. Yet I cringe to recall those occasions when I couldn't or didn't, typically because my heart was too preoccupied to listen to the voice of right or reason. At least a few of those times happened in Turkey.

Many evenings in Istanbul we spent hanging out with a mixed bag of European and American students, nomads and expatriates, smoking pot, swapping stories, talking, and laughing about nothing. On most of those nights, Horst, a self-appointed dean of dissipation, uncannily spotted the low point of our dissolve and our collective need to munch. He would stand and announce loudly, "Okay, pudding shop time."

Somehow we would all obediently revive from our foggy-brained inertia. We would sort ourselves out enough to march, not quite in step with each other or anyone else, to the shop that sold sugary sustenance. There we indulged in the creamy sweet rice dish, known to us as pudding. Delicious. I would never forget its taste. It was lucky someone in our motley group not only could recognize that our brains needed glucose, but also could rally the troops to get it.

After almost four weeks, the routine was getting old. I didn't want to squander any more days and nights getting wasted. I was anxious for our next move and next adventure. Alex wasn't ready to go yet. I felt the arrival of a couple of new attractive females had some bearing on his sentiment, and tension was building between us.

Two of the group, Fritz from Amsterdam and Adrian from London, were leaving in a couple of days for the south of Turkey, which is where Alex and I planned to go soon. "Why don't you just head down with them? I'll catch up with you in a few days," Alex suggested.

"What do you mean?" I didn't believe what I heard.

We had never traveled separately. Taken aback, annoyed that he would suggest such a thing, I also realized he wanted to be rid of me for a while. Alex didn't display, and possibly didn't feel jealousy. Probably he knew I had no intention of leaving him for someone else. I supposed I had become too clingy and dependent, like an extra appendage to him. But no more, I thought.

"So, this is what you want to do, is it?"

"Yeah, it'll just be for a few days," he said, shrugging off the concern in my voice.

That was it then. Fine. There were a few more things I did in Istanbul before leaving. One was to visit the *Topkapi* Museum, a former palace with a blinding and incomparable array of jewels and queenly artifacts. I couldn't own them or even touch them, but my eyes drank in their unapproachable beauty.

I also returned to the bazaar to buy a puzzle ring. Although I didn't often buy anything, this was special. It was the first gold jewelry I ever bought, and it was inexpensive for gold. The slippery smooth old gold ring had four misshapen, interlocking parts that fit together only in one particular way. It felt luxurious and sexy on my finger. Once I learned the trick of putting it back together, I took it off frequently. Rearranging the puzzle pieces had a calming, self-satisfying, therapeutic effect on me. My hands memorized the feel of each piece, separately and united. It was a small but true treasure.

When it was time, Fritz, Adrian, and I sailed down the west coast of Turkey and south to Antalya on the northern shore of the Mediterranean Sea. It felt good to get away, even though a part of me wondered if I would ever see Alex again.

While it was true I didn't flirt with other men, I also had no chemistry with either of my new traveling buddies, perhaps because we had so little in common. The trip was quiet and uneventful. I found my center again. Looking at open water helped dissipate my cares.

When we arrived in Antalya, I found the broad, clear sky and small town atmosphere more than a little welcoming. It was a nice change from the venerable, claustrophobic air of Istanbul.

Disparaging dense city living in his book *Emile,* Jean Jacques Rousseau said man's breath was fatal to his fellow man. I agreed. Beautiful and exciting cities fascinated me for short bursts of time, but I found they eventually imprisoned my spirit.

As soon as we stepped off the ship, Fritz, Adrian and I scouted for a restaurant for a good meal. In Turkey, a good meal was easy. I couldn't argue with the claim that Turkish food was one of the three major cuisines of the world. All of the food that had touched my tongue was hearty and zestful, full of flavor and color.

After a heavenly meal, we found an unremarkable hotel. In the morning, I awoke curiously refreshed and energized. Fritz suggested a swim in the sea. Adrian wasn't interested, so Fritz and I walked to a nearby restaurant on a wooden pavilion that stretched out over the water's edge. No sign prohibited swimming there, so six-foot-three Fritz dove into the choppy sea. I held back, standing on the pavilion while he bobbed in the restless Mediterranean about forty feet away.

Fritz called to me and waved. "What are you waiting for?" The weather was warm, with blue skies and buckets of sunshine, but the water was muddled and dark, offering no clue to its depth.

My hesitation was strong. At the same time, a nagging voice in my head kept berating me. *Quit being a coward and do it*! Back and forth the dueling voices argued.

As a child I had taken swimming lessons several summers, but I had a fear of letting loose in the water. There was something I didn't trust, and in my freshman year of college I found out what. The something was me. I learned this when my date took me to a pool party at the home of a friend whose parents were out of town. After having a few mixed drinks with his parents' stash, I became fearless, if not foolish, and dove into the pool. I was ecstatic as I swam its length back and forth, laughing crazily. My date had to practically drag me out.

From then on I knew I *could* swim, however gracelessly and weakly. *Okay, then*, I asked myself, *what's the problem?* I could feel my mouth drying. As I moved closer to the choice I knew I had to make, my knees became shaky. My internal coach reminded me I should either bow out, or take the plunge. *Just go for it,* the bold voice urged. The timid one argued that I really couldn't handle it. I started to feel embarrassed for being frozen there, sure everyone on the pavilion was staring at me.

Fritz, still effortlessly treading water, looked sideways at me, motioning and calling to me one more time. I could tell he was about to quit.

Then suddenly, without any more internal argument, I took the plunge. I swam a little and wound up a few feet away from Fritz. He grinned.

The water temperature was perfect. "See, it's great," he coaxed, still at ease. I attempted a very brief nonchalant smile. My nervous feet felt for the bottom, and terror struck when there was nothing solid beneath them. I drew my legs back up underneath me, as if withdrawing from the unknown offered some protection against it.

All right, don't panic. I tried to be, or at least to appear to be, calm. *Just see if you can swim back to the ladder, and you'll feel better.* I started to swim towards the pavilion, but the waves held me in place in their back-and-forth sway. I tried again, but failed.

I remembered a lesson I learned many years ago. Never grab onto someone else in the water for help, because that could cause both people to drown. I heeded the warning, instead saying almost matter-of-factly, "Fritz, I don't think I can make it." I paddled faster. My breaths were shorter, my heart raced, and my head pounded with fear. I knew I wasn't strong enough to keep treading water for long. I was too panicked and too poor a swimmer to return to safety.

He looked at me genuinely puzzled. "What do you mean?"

"I mean I can't make it. I need help!" My voice cracked. Poor Fritz didn't understand my predicament, because it was so easy for him. I had to convince him. "Fritz, I *can't* do it!" My voice was more strident. Either he was unbelieving, or he didn't know what to do. But I did.

I screamed, as loud as I could, summoning everything in me. "HELP! HELP!" *Tread water! Tread water! Just keep your head above the water*, I told myself. *Hang on!* I had no idea if anyone would come to my rescue.

But someone did.

Although it seemed like a lifetime, within seconds a muscular young Turk in tight swim trunks dove in, swam to me and motioned for me to climb onto his back. I didn't hesitate to put my arms around the neck of this perfect stranger. He swam easily to the pavilion and delivered me to the ladder. I was embarrassed that as the choppy waters worked against me, I didn't have the strength to pull myself up onto the ladder. My rescuer hoisted me while someone pulled from above.

As I recovered, all the attention was focused on me on the wooden pavilion and I didn't notice that my hero had slipped away without a word. I didn't get to thank him. I didn't know his name.

The next day or two found me in a state of semi-shock. I tried to figure out what had happened, and what lesson the Universe was trying to teach me.

CHAPTER 14

Smugglers, Too

Life is either a daring adventure or nothing.
—HELEN KELLER

IN A FEW DAYS, WHAT do you know, Alex did arrive. We made, or at least went through the motions of making, peace. We talked about the next leg of our trip and how to accomplish it.

I'm not sure when or if we decided our journey would trace a complete circle around the Mediterranean. I'm not sure we thought about what might be involved in such a trip. Hand and hand with the Fates, we kept re-shuffling the cards and playing whatever hands we were dealt, brazenly or timidly, sometimes bluffing, but always choosing to stay in the game, together.

Our next move was to the eastern shore of the Mediterranean, and then to North Africa. From North Africa we would cross at the Strait of Gibraltar to return "home" again to Spain.

In our own way, we were fearless. Sometimes I held onto Alex's brazen coattails, and sometimes he held onto my trusting ones. Perhaps we were just bumbling and foolish enough to know no fear, trusting that we would be taken care of. Whatever the case, somehow we would find a way to do whatever we set out to do. Alex wasn't afraid of talking to people and finagling for their assistance.

Originally we thought we would go to Israel first, but learned that if we did, the Israeli visa stamped on our passports would prohibit our entrance into any of the Arab countries, which meant of course, all of North Africa.

Syria was closed to Americans, so a workable alternative was to hopscotch to Lebanon, and from there to sail to Egypt—much easier said than done.

Alex's easy familiarity with ports enabled him to chat up local skippers even if he didn't know their language. Fortunately, a small steamer soon leaving for Lebanon, had a first mate who spoke English. Steve was half American and half Lebanese. Somehow Alex convinced Steve who convinced his Captain, to give us passage to Beirut the next day.

What luck! The Captain surrendered his cabin to let me sleep there while Alex took a bunk down below with the crew. Impressed by the Captain's magnanimous gesture, we didn't know what he would claim in exchange for our passage and accommodations.

I was sleeping comfortably on the bunk's firm mattress when first a noise and then a light startled me. The Captain came barging in. Although my first thought was he had come to retrieve something he needed for the night, it didn't explain his rudeness. He wasn't apologetic and wasn't smiling when he stepped abruptly to where I lay watching him. His dark, heavy eyebrows combined with the narrowed slits between his eyelids almost obscured his eyes, but not his intent. He spoke some words in Arabic in a tone meant to be seductive, as I lay shivering under a thin blanket. The Captain quickly pulled the blanket down, and, to his dismay, found me fully clothed. Still, he reached for me and I knocked away his groping hand.

By now, my adrenaline had kicked in. I sat bolt upright, yelling at him, extending my arms in front of me, pushing against his chest. He laughed at my efforts to fend him off, as if I could not be serious. I took the split-second opportunity to jump up from the bunk, intending to head for the door, but there was a hundred pound difference between our sizes and he stopped me. He held my wrists and pulled me closer. I kicked, screamed, and screamed again. No one responded to my screams. The Captain squeezed my wrists tighter and sneered. Then suddenly, surprisingly, he dropped my wrists and shoved me away, angrily yelling something I didn't understand. He opened the cabin door and left as abruptly as he had entered.

I couldn't go get Alex because I didn't know where he was, only that he was bunking on the deck below. The rest of the night I spent awake, thinking about what had happened and what could have happened. When I rejected his advances I didn't think about the possible consequences. He could have killed us and thrown our bodies overboard. No one would ever know what happened to us. At the least, he might have demanded his "pay" and forced himself on me. What could I have done about it? Apparently screaming was of no use. How crazy was I, how crazy were we, to believe this captain gave us free passage on his ship out of the goodness of his heart. Thankfully, we were spared and made it to Beirut intact.

Disembarking the next morning, we encountered Steve. Briefly I told him what happened during the night and he was sympathetic. In what I read to be an attempt at reparation for the Captain's behavior, he invited us to have dinner at his home. He also offered us a place to stay for the night. Since Steve spoke English, it might be an interesting cultural learning experience. It would also save us a few lira, so why not take him up on his offer?

My first inclination has always been to trust people. It's in my family genes to trust first. It's in my nation's genes. Under our laws, a person is innocent until proven guilty. Perhaps naiveté has led both me and my countrymen into trouble, but I hate being disillusioned about people. I hate disbelieving in their basic core of decency. When I first heard about JFK's womanizing, I was distressed. He was brilliant, charming, witty, and, I believed, a good leader. How could he disappoint me? How could he disappoint the rest of the country? I was young and impressionable.

Since Kennedy, many other people have self-tarnished their images. I should have developed more discernment, but I was still wearing the tag of an innocent abroad. For good or bad, what happened that evening with Steve, pushed me along the road to distrust.

Steve was easy to talk to because he had a wealth of knowledge on a variety of topics, including his country's history and government. He said in fact, he had friends in high places. He lived alone and knew his way around the kitchen, cooking lamb that smelled delicious. Dinner would be ready soon, but there was enough time for Alex to buy some supplies from a nearby store.

I was helping Steve set the table and enjoying our conversation when Alex left. But no sooner had Alex walked out the door than Steve sidled over, drew me to him, and aimed puckered lips at my neck. "What are you doing?" I yelled, quickly sidestepping his moves. "Get away from me!"

This couldn't be happening again. It was unbelievable. Steve had seemed like a "nice guy." He had even apologized for the behavior of the boat captain. What was he thinking? What were *we* thinking? It was distressing. Apparently, neither Alex nor I was very good at reading people and their intentions. I wondered if this behavior towards women, at least towards Western women, reflected a deeply embedded cultural bias of men in the Arab world. Maybe they believed Western women were undeserving of their respect. Was this behavior a result of something I was projecting? Could it be the freedom I represented was anathema to the men of this culture, or was I making a dangerous generalization? Were Steve and the Captain exceptions to the rule? Did most men in this part of the world treat women respectfully?

Whatever the case, Steve took off his friendly face as I loudly rejected him. As soon as Alex returned and I reported what happened, he had a few angry words with Steve. Alex then grabbed my hand, we picked up our belongings, said a hasty good-bye, and found a hotel room.

Setting our sights on North Africa, we spent hours the next day hanging around the docks, and discovered a way to get there. We bought two tickets for an overnight passage on a large, run-down passenger-only ferry boat leaving in a couple of days for Alexandria, Egypt.

In the interim, we had the opportunity to see a little of what Lebanon had to offer. In Beirut, the old and new, the Middle Eastern and Western influences were in contest to define the city's character and personality, but at the American University of Beirut, I sensed a genuine blending of the best of the opposing cultures. The red clay-tile roofed buildings sat peaceably, half-hidden among the trees, as views of the Mediterranean peeked through.

The university was founded by an American, at the end of our Civil War. Except for Arab studies, its classes were all taught in English. One of the most prestigious universities in the world, the A.U.B. had produced many leaders.

The land of Lebanon offered much in the way of natural beauty and important historical sites. Ruins of some of the most significant and best-preserved temples of the Roman Empire were in Baalbek in Lebanon's Bekaa

Valley. A foray to the Bekaa Valley though, was both time consuming and dangerous.

The Valley was noted for its cannabis cultivation and trade. From Roman times, cannabis was a large revenue source for the tribal drug lords. Lebanese ships stocked with hashish found customers in Egypt, Israel and Europe. The trade had gone on for centuries and would continue long after we passed through this country.

Seductively interesting as it was, we had a different focus. We were both eager to travel, to sail to another continent. It was the same urgency I had felt time and again—an urgency to move to new places, a hunger to taste different flavors.

With knapsacks on our backs, we arrived at the Beirut harbor very early on our sailing date. Already swarms of people, eager to board and lugging bags and bundles, clustered near the gangplank. As we rushed to join the crowd we were intercepted by two Arab men in their thirties. The taller one said in halting English that they were from Egypt and would be on board this ferry too.

He had a proposition for us. "This boat will be very crowded, and you will not have a place to sleep, or rest, but we can help you."

Comparing the burgeoning swarm of people to the size of the boat, I knew at least part of what our potential benefactor said was true, but how could they help and what did they want in trade? Admittedly, I had grown wary of offers from strangers.

The ship had no cabins, sleeping spaces, anything resembling beds or cots. There were only scant wooden benches with first-come-first-served squatters' rights, our Egyptian friend explained. Those rights were easily lost with a trip to use the toilet. The tall Egyptian said they could assure us a place on a bench where we might stretch out for the night, if we would agree to carry some clothes for them in our knapsacks. It was just some Western slacks and sport shirts which would cost them money in import taxes, if they brought them into Egypt in their own bags.

"Customs officials will not check your bags because you are American," our friend said. "I am sure of it."

Weighing the request against my newly acquired skepticism, I wondered for a moment. What might these clothes have hidden in their seams? Should we or shouldn't we? Ultimately, the decision wasn't too difficult because the prospect of having no place to sleep or sit comfortably for so many hours was daunting. Our prospective partners in crime showed us the clothes. What's the worst that could happen? We didn't have the time or inclination to consider the possibilities. *We were Americans, by God. We were among the chosen, young and invincible. It would all work out.*

Shrugging our shoulders, Alex and I agreed to the deal. "Okay, we'll do it."

Stuffing the contraband into our overstuffed knapsacks, we followed the Egyptians onto the ship. True to their word, they secured a spot for us on a bench. Whether it was by their power of persuasion, by bribe, or by threat, I didn't know, nor did I care.

In a semi-reclining position with my head resting on my knapsack, I eventually fell asleep, awoke, and fell asleep again, over and over. Eventually, I opened my eyes to see the sun well above the horizon and masses of people bunching towards the port side of the ship approaching the dock in Alexandria. Alex and I jumped up. There were no lines, but only knots of people forming a large, potentially unruly herd. In their rush to disembark, some people pushed, squeezing and re-shaping the amoebic mass. Alex and I did our best to stay on the perimeter, though there wasn't any space on deck to separate from it.

Eventually, our portion of the herd exited the cattle ship and we were channeled through immigration and customs lines. As predicted, the customs officials did not open our overstuffed knapsacks. Our Egyptian partners, with smiles on their faces and families in tow, caught up with us to claim their contraband. Everybody was happy.

CHAPTER 15

Walk Like an Egyptian

We should be careful to get out of an experience only the wisdom that is in it—and stop there; lest we be like the cat that sits down on a hot stove-lid. She will never sit down on a hot stove-lid again—and that is well, but she will never sit down on a cold one anymore.

—Mark Twain "Pudd'nhead Wilson's Calendar"

If you're young and don't allow any preconceived notions of limitation to intrude on an experience, your body and mind respond with a remarkable ability to adapt and endure.

When Alex and I emerged from the customs and immigration building into the streets of Alexandria, we emerged into a true third-world, materially-impoverished culture, many years behind our own. We found more bicycles and bicycle-pulled wagons than cars snarling traffic in the streets, a scarcity of food items in the markets, and extremely limited menus in the cafes. In one shabby place, the offerings were simply beans and bread.

An obvious dearth of electricity meant inscrutable darkness in many streets. The shortage also left many homes and small business establishments without adequate refrigeration. In America, where electricity was practically a birthright, refrigerators and freezers kept our food safe, but an experience in Alexandria gave me a new appreciation for that taken-for-granted blessing.

Always opting for the adventure of new experience, Alex and I joined a few Egyptian travelers as guests in the home of a driver we hired to take us westward. For dinner we sat on the floor and dipped pieces of bread into a common bowl of beans. Then we slept on the floor in our sleeping bags.

When sunlight broke the darkness and streamed into the room, everyone roused themselves and packed. We would leave shortly, but not before we had breakfast—the same bowl of beans we shared the night before. The driver pulled the half-empty bowl from under the bed where it had spent the night. As hungry as I was, the look of the day-old, probably bug-visited, and possibly dangerous beans, made me lose my appetite. I skipped this meal.

The day after arriving in Alexandria, we took a bus to Cairo. At some point, the bus followed a road near the mighty Nile River. As we rolled along, I watched women washing their clothes in the river, while children played beside them, and I considered Egypt's history, from the royal pomp and pageantry to the industry, and the use and abuse of slaves.

In downtown Cairo, it was disturbing to see tall blocks of concrete standing in front of the doorways of many buildings. A measure taken in recent years, the concrete prevented bombs from being thrown into the doorways.

Our visit to the National Museum allowed an escape to a very different and magnificent ancient Egypt. We walked through grand halls housing truly astonishing art, statues that seemed to breathe, to hold emotions and secrets of the universe within their stone bodies and behind their impenetrable eyes. My eyes were riveted on intricate carvings telling detailed stories of life that was, and would be, in the hereafter, and brilliant, natural colors that have remained true for thousands of years. My mind struggled to grasp the actuality of bodies of royalty before me, artfully wrapped and scientifically preserved, and sheets of papyrus bearing the writing of some individual's hand.

The jewelry and the funeral mask of Tutankhamen, made from almost twenty-five pounds of gold, were the most fascinating works of art I had ever seen. I was never overly impressed by or covetous of expensive jewelry, but these pieces inhabited a realm far different from what I knew as jewelry. The broad collar necklaces of gold sheet were so brilliant and fluid they seemed ephemeral, making it plausible that the gold and the design must have come from the gods themselves. I felt as if I were looking at a magnificent natural landscape that had been melted down and compressed into its godly essence.

In stark contrast to this display of dazzling antiquities was the rattletrap bus we boarded when we left the museum for the ride to Giza. The bus was full of local passengers, most of them dressed in ankle-length, long-sleeved cotton or wool hooded robes, many carrying babies and cloth-wrapped bundles.

Though all of the windows were open, the air was stiflingly hot. Flies buzzed around us, but Alex and I were the only ones who swatted at them. A young woman sat across the aisle from me holding a semi-swaddled sleeping baby in her arms. The faraway look on her face and the slump of her shoulders told me that she had resigned herself to a life of deprivation. I cringed to see evidence of that resignation. When a fly buzzed around her child's face and flew into his mouth, the woman made no move to shoo it away.

The bus continued, trundling along on rugged, ill-maintained roads, past rows of shoddy dwellings. It was odd when, in the near distance, one of the seven wonders of the ancient world incongruously and abruptly came into view.

Thankfully, a great deal of space and sky surrounded the pyramids at the actual site. Next to the great one called Cheops, I felt especially dwarfed and insignificant.

Its surface was pocked and much rougher than I had imagined it would be. Much of its smoothness was lost many years ago when a massive earthquake loosened many of the white limestone casing stones. Centuries of erosion caused more damage, yet, the Great Pyramid was no less spectacular. It's not surprising that over the centuries so many people still wonder how it was constructed. How were more than two million immense stone blocks, each weighing a couple of thousand pounds, lifted into place, and fitted so exactly? How is it they were leveled and oriented to the four directional points? However the construction might be explained by architects and engineers, I was satisfied to appreciate the mystery of it all, allowing that mystery and wonder are necessary elements of a happy life.

During our visit we were the only sightseers. There were only two other people in the area—two very unofficial-looking "guides" who asked for tips in exchange for letting us wander around. I rubbed my hand over a part of the pyramid's rough surface, and Alex persuaded one of the guides to let him climb up one of its sides.

For an additional fee, the men said we could ride their camels, one of which was named Lucky, of course. We had to do it. When Mustafa ordered the camels to lower themselves to the ground, they slowly obliged, folding their legs partly underneath their bristle-haired bodies and yawning profusely as they did. We mounted, wearing pith helmets we bought in Beirut. Both beasts registered their annoyance, grunting and groaning like ornery old men, when they were forced to stand with passengers on their backs. The guides held onto ropes attached to the camels' halters and walked along as we rode about the length of a city block. Alex handed one of the guides his camera to take our picture before we carefully dismounted when the camels knelt down.

Returning to Alexandria, we made plans to head west through Libya, Tunisia, Algeria, and Morocco, traveling on a road that both crossed and skirted the Sahara Desert. Most of the cities hugged the shore of the Mediterranean, but the long stretches between them were barren. Because there wasn't public transportation available, we arranged for a ride in a private station wagon. Squeezing in with the driver and three other male passengers, we failed to consider what danger our travel arrangements might pose, particularly to me. We didn't have the opportunity to find out if the men were dangerous because we were forced to part ways with them at the Libyan border.

"Where are your visas?" the bushy-browed, gray-uniformed, severe looking border official wanted to know as he checked our passports. We had not applied in advance because we assumed, mistakenly, we could get them at the border, as we had done in many other countries.

"Sorry, you will have to stay here," the official announced. Though we protested, he let us know he would have to send to Tripoli to get permission for us to enter his country, and that it would probably take until the next day.

Our driver pulled away. We were detained at this outpost in the desert with no town or other buildings around, but the official was agreeable, speaking kindly and assuring us he would provide for us while we waited. We had no choice but to accept his kindness. Our hospitable host immediately opened his larder to us, offering us food and drink and asking if there was anything else we might need. He wanted to make sure we were comfortable.

Only one other person was at this outpost, a male assistant, and only an occasional car or truck passed through the border crossing for the rest of the day. It must have been a very lonely and boring job. Before I could feel too sorry for our host though, I discovered an ulterior motive for his generosity.

Yet again it happened. Alex left the room briefly and the Libyan border official came on to me. When I rejected his advances, he acted surprised, even when Alex came back into the room. What must he have thought of our relationship? In the process, the man had the gall to push his luck by whining that he hadn't had a woman in a month. Although I tried to hide my fear and the weakness of our position, I knew we were treading on dangerous ground. He could hold us hostage and deny our visas. Although he didn't push further or threaten us, his hospitality disappeared. My sleep was fitful that night.

The next afternoon I was somewhat surprised when the official announced we had our visas and were free to go. Facing about two thousand miles of mostly desert road, we still needed a ride to go anywhere.

Eventually, one came. We were in our hitchhiking mode again. Now though most of the drivers asked a fee for the ride, and we were happy to pay. After having a variety of drivers and vehicles, my faith in humankind was alternately shaken and restored.

On a ride to Tobruk, a smiling peasant farmer took us to his home on the outskirts of the town. After introducing us to his wife, he insisted we spend the night with them, and proceeded to step outside and slaughter a lamb for our dinner. We didn't have a language in common, but we had beautiful communication, and I was extremely grateful for their kindness. If only all our encounters across the top of the African continent would be so fortunate.

They weren't. Once we were picked up by a suave looking Libyan who spoke fluent French and said he was going all the way to Tripoli, just what we wanted. The driver was genial. Although he drove a bit erratically, we didn't mind because, except on occasion, there weren't any other cars or obstructions on this straight road. He stopped occasionally to let us stretch and look around. It was a pleasant ride.

But circumstances, as I had seen, could change in an instant. During one long sweep of road in the late warm afternoon, Alex and I were both dozing, he in the front seat and I in the back. Suddenly something awakened me. It was the hand of the driver groping my leg! My scream woke Alex. All of a sudden, we were at odds with this French-tongued Libyan. Alex berated him in English and I used all the relevant French I could muster to convince him not to try anything again.

He was red-faced angry, but then shrugged his shoulders, appearing to brush things off. As he drove, the red-orange sun just above the horizon was calling the day quits. After a few hours the driver announced he was tired and was going to stop for the night so we could all sleep. It had been a long day and sleep sounded like a good idea, but we were nowhere near a town. We were in the middle of the desert with nothing around but endless sand, stars, and a crescent moon.

The driver pulled off the road and cut the engine, leaving us in an immense resounding quiet, like the sound of eternity. Breaking the beautiful silence, he told us he would sleep in the car. Alex and I laid our faithful sleeping bags on the sand, and crawled into them. I stared at the ceiling of stars for a long while.

I am not a desert person, but I could appreciate the desert now. It made me feel less fearful than I did in close spaces, because I believed I could see danger long before it could reach me. I didn't know anything at all about the dangers, but I couldn't be concerned about them now. After sensing the driver was asleep, I let myself drift off.

Sand makes a lovely bed. You can move it around with your hips, your shoulders, and your hands to make it conform exactly to your body. I slept soundly.

The morning sun was barely above the horizon when I opened my eyes, stretched, and looked around. My eyes weren't fully focused, but focused enough to see something was missing.

"Oh my God, Alex, wake up," I said. "He's gone!"

"What?!" Alex sat bolt upright and rubbed his eyes as if dismissing a nightmare. True, the car and its driver had vanished.

We both jumped to our feet and stared. For 360 degrees, nothing interrupted the flat landscape except for an occasional clump of dry grass. *What do we do now?* This was certainly a new kind of experience. We couldn't walk or run away from the danger. There was nowhere to go and no way to get there. You can figure your way out of some situations, but clearly there were no options here.

We had no compass and only a little water left in the two canteens we habitually carried with us. Although the air still held a bit of the night's coolness, I knew that it would quickly evaporate as the sun climbed higher in the sky. And there was no shade.

Hours crawled by. We sat on our sleeping bags and talked, trying to entertain ourselves and encourage each other, ignoring a growing hunger, and trying not to think the worst. Alternately, we stood up, paced, rolled up our sleeping bags, then laid them out again, tried to nap, read distractedly, wrote in journals, and watched the horizon for any sign of life.

What if no one came? What would our end be? I learned the meaning of the word *stranded*. I started bargaining with God, listing all the ways I would be a better person. Was it too much to ask for a single ride to somewhere? Anywhere. Any kind of ride. I have always hated waiting. It seemed like such a waste of time. Now I learned *waiting*. Hours seemed like days.

Then what I first saw as a vague moving spot on the horizon approached and became a sand-colored car carrying a kindly older man. He nodded his head, smiled kindly, and picked us up. We traveled with him, thankfully, uneventfully to Tripoli.

On another of our waits between rides in the desert, we had a small diversion when we witnessed a spectacle straight from a page of St. Exupery's wistful fable, *The Little Prince*. In the story, the little prince, a pilot who has crashed and is wandering in the Libyan Desert, encounters scenes which illustrate the absurdity of much of civilized pretense. In one scene, there is a king who rules, but has no subjects.

Alex and I had been sitting on the sand just off the road when a strange sight brought us to our feet. An incongruous eerily silent pageant played before us. Armored personnel carriers led a line of long black limousines, racing away from where we were going. Through one limousine window we could see a hand moving in a royal wave to us. It was none other than the hand of Libya's King Idris II. To me the absurdity was that the procession had no other audience. In my mind, the purpose of limousines is to impress those who aren't in them. Neither Alex nor I was particularly impressed.

As fate would have it, the King wouldn't wave from a limousine much longer. Soon after our sighting, the monarchy ended in a coup led by Muammar al-Gaddafi while King Idris was getting medical treatment in Turkey.

Alex and I walked through living history as we passed, and sometimes muddled through, various cultures. We encountered an odd assortment of cultural and historical relics and remnants all across North Africa, from roaming Bedouin tribes to World War II artifacts at El Alamein.

At El Alamein we took turns sitting on the rusted out hulk of an abandoned Italian tank. I contemplated what went on there, and how many men had spilled their blood on the ground around our feet. One of the signs crudely painted on a crumbling stone wall caught my eye: "*You will not laugh if Jerry straffs. Safety first. Keep dispersed*," the forced rhyme warned the troops.

We walked around the town of Oran in Algiers, the place Albert Camus made famous in his existential novel, *The Plague*. Everywhere we traveled on this Dark Continent, we encountered stories, some in landmarks, and some written on peoples' faces. In some stories we were characters ourselves, and in others we were only observers, passing through. Without making a commitment to one culture or community, we had the luxury of choosing how much or how little we would be involved. An unspoken, but understood immunity, natural to footloose travelers, afforded us an emotional, if not moral detachment from scenes we encountered. Unless we chose otherwise, we bore no responsibility for anyone's plight but our own. The most I could do to help was to pull a smile out of a child or to meet a stranger's eyes with compassion, and show respect for him and his situation.

Traveling more westerly, we gradually moved into more modern territory. Tunis, Tunisia was a welcome stop with a good, clean pension and showers, and some heartening news. A French-American movie shooting in town needed extras for a masquerade ball scene. It was *Justine,* a screenplay adapted from Lawrence Durrell's novel. We trotted down to the location. "Can you do the samba?" a director's assistant asked.

"Sure," was the only possible answer we could give, although neither of us knew the samba. I could dance to anything, and Alex was just uninhibited enough to pretend. We were immediately signed up for the parts.

A number of other Americans, Europeans, and Tunisians shared the dance floor with us every night for the two weeks of shooting our scenes. Between takes, we relaxed and feasted on couscous with lamb and other fine fare provided by the company.

Dirk Bogarde, the dashing male lead, and his co-star Anouk Aimee made a handsome couple, but she apparently could not do the samba. While she was learning, she insisted everyone leave the set.

It was all great fun, and even better, we were paid handsomely, relatively speaking. The only drawback was that the Tunisian dinars could not be exchanged or taken out of the country. We would have to spend the money there, but we made the best of the inconvenience. After our scenes were wrapped, we stayed a while and indulged ourselves with a little shopping and eating at a few excellent Tunisian and French restaurants. It was a nice change to spend money without worry.

Exploring the maze of shops in the Sousse Medina we came upon a talented artisan making beautiful silver-inlaid brass trays. "It will be good price for you," the man said. I barely had to negotiate the price with him for this perfect wedding gift for my sister.

Once we had spent all of our dinars we moved on down the road to Morocco, stopping in Fes, Meknes, Tetouan, and finally Tangier. With the exception of Tangier, Morocco had a more oriental feel than the more easterly Tunisia.

Taking our time in Tangier, we contemplated the end of our African adventure and our move back to Europe. We basked awhile in sunny outside cafes, sipping cup after cup of highly sweetened spearmint tea. Occasionally we were approached by young entrepreneurs wanting to show us around the town for a fee.

One particularly eager young boy who already had learned some sales skills, approached our table. "What you want see?" he asked. "I take you. Small guide, small price."

Sure, why not? It was our last shot at exploring the African continent. The small guide gave us our money's worth, leading us up and down alleyways, through the *souks,* past zealous vendors, and finally to someone's home; I didn't know whose. We were invited into a windowless room. Its floors were covered in hand-woven rugs in various shades of red and gold and its walls were draped in multi-colored tapestries.

A tall mustachioed man in his thirties promptly appeared, wearing a light-colored *djellaba,* and a slight smile on his face.

"Please," he said, pointing to a covered, thickly cushioned wide seat. We sat, not knowing, but guessing, what to expect.

"You like *kif*?" our small guide asked, though he didn't wait for an answer.

At this point, the boy stuck out his hand for a few more *dirham* as the man pulled out his *hookah* and loaded it with hashish.

Although I felt apprehensive, I put my lips on the mouthpiece of the long hose leading to the bubbling water pipe. The room was comfortable, the hashish smooth, and the apprehension soon melted away. Our host sat quietly while we relaxed. When it felt right, we simply took our leave.

Somehow unscathed, we found our way back through the maze of streets and alleyways, to the town's open and ordered space. The next day we said good-bye to that world and boarded a ferry bound for Algeciras, Spain.

CHAPTER 16

Play It Again, Sam

Do not marry a man to reform him. That is what reform schools are for.
—Mae West

Gibraltar looked different during the day. No cover of darkness lent it mystery, as it had more than a year ago when the freighter first carried me past it. The huge rock in the Strait now seemed much more pedestrian. Real people, going about their mundane tasks, lived and worked at its base.

Gibraltar was still the same rock. The change was in me. My perspective was no longer that of the ingénue abroad. Although I was still wide-eyed, some of my "heavenly ignorance" was replaced by what I had read in the eyes of so many strangers. After seven months of circling the Mediterranean, covering the cradle of civilization by thumbing rides, by train, by boat, and by beat up old buses, we closed the circle when we crossed the Strait and arrived in Spain.

Once again on the mainland, we had an uneventful trip back to Barcelona. This time around, instead of the kind of dark, dank living quarters on narrow streets we had inhabited before, we found a spacious, airy room on *Calle Pelayo.* The sunny, wide avenue allowed light to reach our window in the afternoons. Breathing and smiling seemed easier there.

Splurging at Christmas time, we bought ourselves a small *tocadiscos,* a record player, at the modern department store *el Corte Ingles,* and two records.

One, an album called "A Man and a Woman," sung in both French and English, was music from a movie of the same name, one of my favorites. In fact, its star, Anouk Aimee, was the same actress we had met and worked with in "Justine."

The other record was Otis Redding's *Dock of the Bay*. On its flip side was *Try a Little Tenderness,* which we occasionally danced to in our room. We started in time with the music, slow and romantic, my style, as close, touching partners, but by mid-song, Otis had worked himself into a frenzy. This suited Alex more, so we split apart and moved to our own personal rhythms. The lyrics were especially poignant for me. "Oh, she may be weary. Young girls they do get weary, wearing that same old shabby dress, but when she gets weary, try a little tenderness..."

Our pension was within a few blocks of the Berlitz School where we had worked before. We were hired again. A few of the same teachers were still there.

I felt twinges of melancholy being back in Spain, now a second home to me, particularly in Barcelona, which reminded me so much of New Orleans. Both cities are important ports and both have older quarters within them. Barcelona has its Gothic Quarter as New Orleans its French Quarter, but in the French Quarter the architecture is Spanish, not French.

The City's Catholicism, including its many churches and cathedrals, its strong family units, its readable language, its familiar art, and its love of good food, wine, and music, all made me homesick for my hometown.

We spent most of our days teaching English and many of our nights drinking dark red wine and eating *tapas,* alone or with our friends in neighborhood bodegas and in a place called the American Bar, which it wasn't really. What distinguished the American Bar was its modern, updated interior, and that some of the music played there was by American artists.

We lived very frugally. We drank the most inexpensive wine, and reverted to our habits of the year before, including eating suppers where the locals ate. I still shopped for our midday meals at the enormous farmers' market. Again, cooking wasn't allowed in our room, and again, we did it on the sly.

Occasionally we had lunch at a neighborhood eatery, although I did enjoy the regular trek to the market. The wonderful mix of aromas from the fresh fruits, vegetables, meat, and fish was the smell of life at its heartiest.

We spent money for little other than food. I almost never shopped for clothes, and I never bought jewelry, perfumes, or special toiletries. Unlike many of the women I knew, I never treated myself to any of the little luxuries. Although we lived very basically, that's what I had signed up for. This is not to say that I didn't occasionally long for some particular thing I couldn't have, like the stunning pair of knee-high, soft, brown, leather boots that a tall, attractive French woman co-worker wore almost every day. They were the most beautiful boots I had ever seen and I truly coveted them. I told myself one day I would have a pair like that.

Although I had no idea how, magically, one day we would have money. I could have the things so many other women took for granted. Eventually, I was so used to this doing-without lifestyle I even stopped missing what I didn't have. It helped that my family never had much materially anyway.

On rare special occasions Alex and I went to a "nice" restaurant with white tablecloths and great Spanish food. Our favorite was *Los Caracoles* (the Spanish equivalent of *escargots*). In an ancient stone building in the *Barrio Gotico*, the restaurant oozed authentic, rustic, old world charm and hospitality that made me feel like royalty. The walls were lined with immense wooden wine barrels, and salt-cured hams and braided garlic hung from the ceiling.

The owner and chef, Senor Bofarul, was a rotund, happy, aim-to-please kind of man. All of the food—the *sopa*, the *paella,* the *pescado*, the *postre*—was superb, as was the wine. This special treat was truly a rarity for us. Usually we were satisfied with the knowledge that we were squirreling away enough of our paltry incomes to be able to travel again whenever that right time revealed itself to us.

Once in a while, when I had an afternoon free without Alex, I would pinch enough pesetas from our stash for the less-than-a-dollar matinee at a small movie theater on the *Ramblas* where they often showed old American movies. Always the audience was a smattering of people and always, the smell of cheap lemon cleaner pervaded the theater air.

It was fun to watch Donald O'Conner skipping around in some schmaltzy flick or the ever suave Gene Kelly doing his foot magic while he was "Singing in the Rain." Spanish was dubbed over the English dialogue, and I didn't understand everything, but the story lines weren't important to me. The songs were in English, and the dancing made me feel light on my feet, and lighter in my heart. And why not? I put myself in the movie along with the cool, elegantly smooth Kelly. I knew how to sing in the rain.

Occasionally we were invited to a party. One Saturday night party, at the apartment of a co-worker, was especially memorable in an unfortunate way. Not long after we arrived, Alex made haste to lose himself in the crowd, abandoning me. I didn't know more than a couple of people there, most of whom were Spaniards. I did my best to introduce myself to people and make small talk. A couple of glasses of wine helped to loosen my tongue. I was beginning to feel a little comfortable until I caught sight of Alex who was obviously coming on to a raven-haired young woman with intense dark eyes. He was drinking deep from the cup of liquid courage and shaking his tail feathers. I would have been fascinated by the seduction process if I hadn't been so angry and so jealous. I couldn't pay attention anymore to the people I had been talking to. All of my mental and emotional energy was focused on the man who was supposed to be *my* man.

Alex didn't notice me watching him make his moves. As far as he was concerned, I wasn't even there. I waited as long as I could. Finally, when I couldn't stand it any longer, I called out to him. Visibly annoyed, Alex relented and walked over to where I was standing.

"What is it?" he shot at me.

"What do you mean, what is it?" I shot back.

He argued he was just having a good time and that I should do the same, but I was livid. I let him know I felt certain if I hadn't interfered and if he could have arranged it, he would have had the woman in bed.

When Alex shrugged off my concern with a "so-what" cock of his head and started to step away to return to his prey, I lost it. I really lost it, and did something I had never done before. I hauled off and slapped him hard across the face. "That's what!" I screamed. I didn't care who heard or saw what had just happened.

Alex was momentarily stunned, but then he was angrier than I would have thought, if I had even thought about it first. I surprised myself too, but it stunned him so much he was speechless, which was a rarity.

When he did speak, he let me know he had every right to "hang out with" other women. My choices were I could keep my distance, fuming in silence, or find someone else to entertain me. The trouble was my mind and heart didn't work that way. My mother had always reminded me of the old folk adage: "You go home with who brung you." Alex had "brung" me to this party, to this odyssey, and I was determined I would go home with him.

Otherwise, there wasn't much justification for staying with him. I felt pathetic. My life now was this odyssey which I believed I couldn't do alone. I didn't know how long it would last or where it would take me, but I had to continue. Obviously, I had conflicting emotions and thoughts because I believed, we were somehow meant to be together.

Why wasn't there a course in school that taught kids about relationships, about how you are supposed to act? Why couldn't we all have emotional intelligence especially when we are young and need it so badly? Why was this so complicated and difficult?

I continued to hold onto the hope that one day I would have children. Alex would grow up and grow out of his selfish and sometimes mean-spirited ways. Maybe I would learn how to keep my cool and respond to him in an emotionally mature way. Maybe I could make it all better. I would forgive him. I would give him the family he never really had, and he would see, dammit, what I saw—that he needed me to complete his life.

After teaching several more months and saving enough money to move on, Alex and I were ready to launch ourselves eastward again, this time to the Far East. We had to go because traveling was what kept us alive, the desire to see more, do more, and learn more, to break out. Travel was the glue that kept us together. Besides, staying in one place too long called for commitment, to the place and to each other. Neither of us was ready to commit to one place, and at least one of us was not ready to commit to the other one.

Mid-morning on a Saturday, our Berlitz friends met us at the dock where the Turkish ship, the *Iskenderun*, was waiting to be boarded. Tall, handsome British Bob and his ebullient girlfriend with the lovely name, Gladwyn, were there. So was genteel, black-haired Jane who promised to write, Michael, the Australian to whom we had donated the Taunus, and Gabrielle, the statuesque French woman with the coveted brown leather boots. Gabrielle didn't offer me her boots as a going-away gift, but they all wished us well and waved good-bye as the ship pulled away.

I stood on deck happy and excited for yet another trip with little definition. This was what we were all about, ready for an adventure.

On our last journey, we had put only our toes into the shallow waters of Asia. Now, we were ready for the big time. This time we would swim.

CHAPTER 17
The Orient Expressed

The first condition of understanding a foreign country is to smell it.
—Rudyard Kipling

Winds blowing rootless souls were blowing in the direction of India. That country was apparently The Destination for growing numbers of the new breed of experimentally brave seekers and confused travelers.

We were just foolish enough to know little fear, and India, the mysterious ancient culture worlds away from our own, would be the test of our commitment as Serious Travelers. There was no question we must continue this odyssey to discover where it would take us. I suspected India was the place where whatever else you were looking for, you accidentally might find yourself.

I wished we could have traveled the fabled Orient Express to Istanbul, our jumping off point for India, but seafaring on the small Turkish line was more affordable. We had interesting port stops on the way, and the *Iskenderun,* we agreed, had been a good choice. A smallish, no-frills ship, it was clean and well-kept and the food was excellent.

On a bright morning, we steamed into the port of Marseille, the oldest town and second largest city in France. The open arms of its white limestone hills welcomed us. My first glance at the dockworkers and people milling around confirmed that this city was more international than French. Founded by Greek sailors twenty-six hundred years ago, Marseille's trade ran the gamut from oil to ceramics and everything in between, all from ports just as varied.

This city's history was tumultuous, ranging from independence and prosperity to Roman rule, to battles for its control, and crises like the Great Plague of the Eighteenth century. The plague, which was brought in by a ship, killed half the city's population. Marseille had opposed the rule of Louis XIV during the Revolution, and its battle cry, *La Marseillaise*, eventually became the French national anthem. Unquestionably it takes a certain amount of conflict to make a place, or a person, intriguing. Could this have any bearing on my relationship with Alex?

In Marseille, I immediately sensed an air of in-your-face independence that many port cities develop, as if the populace, who live next to open water, know they can leave whenever they are unhappy with their circumstances or want to seek new fortunes. I could relate.

"Independent as a hog on ice" my mother labeled me when she was at a certain level of exasperation. I had taken it as a compliment. Then one day, trying to trace the origin of that metaphor, I learned that when farmers "in days gone by" took their hogs to market, they hauled them standing on blocks of ice in their truck beds. The hog might be independent, the source said, but helpless.

Making the most of the few hours our ship would be in port, Alex and I explored side streets and shops, found a bountiful farmer's stand, bought some fresh fruit, and ate it while sitting on a grassy public area. As we people-watched, Alex mentioned offhandedly he was glad I was with him. Nice. Feeling good, we both stretched out under the sunny sky until re-boarding time.

The *Iskenderun* followed the graceful curve of the southern edge of Europe, hugging the coast of Italy. It stopped in Napoli and gave us glimpses of the city's staired streets and people working in them. Sailing back into the Mediterranean, we rounded the long-tailed peninsula and entered the Aegean Sea. We docked at Ismir, Turkey, a beauty, sitting like a princess on the bay, commanding a view of her Aegean domain.

Since the *Iskenderun* would be in port for several hours, Alex and I took a bus to nearby Ephesus, the remains of a two-thousand-year-old city, reputed to be home of Mary the Mother of Jesus. As we walked around the broken columns, we encountered facades and marble arches belonging to an ancient marketplace. We stepped over a wealth of Biblical history, even walking on the Marble Way which once led to the sea. I was fascinated to learn the city once had terra cotta pipes carrying hot and cold water to the homes of the wealthy. What would they think of next? Some people would have responded "so what?" to this information, but for me knowledge was among the treasures I collected. I carried bits of knowledge with me in my pocket, like pet rocks. I liked to touch them and share them when I could.

In this slow, studied, relaxed way, continuing our voyage, we arrived once again in Istanbul, but this time for a much shorter stay. Hand in hand, for a day, we roamed the Buyukada, an island in the Sea of Marmara that was at once a destination both for wealthy royalty and political exiles. Mansions and wooden houses built in the early 1900s still stood. No cars or other motorized vehicles were allowed. Locomotion was by bicycle, by horse-drawn carriages, or on foot, which meant a refreshing lack of noise and fumes.

On the ferryboat ride back to Istanbul, Alex felt a ceremony was necessary. He decided we should both cast our pith helmets, which we had bought in Egypt, into the water. I liked and had grown accustomed to mine, and saw no good reason to throw it away, but eventually I agreed. Who was I to deny ceremony? Here was another lesson in non-attachment, not to just material things and places, but also to opinions and long-held beliefs. I decided it was an important lesson to learn and as often as necessary. Now we were ready to head to the East.

The bus ride through Turkey was unremarkable, except when we were almost to the Iranian border, and someone pointed out a particular mountain in the distance. Tall, massively wide, and snow-capped, the mountain stood alone except for one smaller peak nearby. This was Mt. Ararat, the tallest mountain in Turkey. Many people believed it to be the site where the Biblical Noah's Ark came to rest. Ararat's summit, at almost 17,000 feet stays frozen, preserving the Ark from decomposition—that is, if it were actually there, and if, in fact, it had ever existed.

Mt. Ararat, a dormant volcano, last erupted in 1840. Because of the broken lava rock covering its sides and the ice that caps it, it is extremely difficult to climb. Still, there have been many expeditions, studies, and accounts of alleged sightings of the Ark, although scientific evidence and photos are lacking. The search continues.

Moving past Mt. Ararat, our bus took us to Iran, to Tabriz, then to Tehran. In Tehran we boarded a rescued, rickety, American school bus, to continue east. All the seats were full.

Women were dressed in brown or black burqas, their faces completely covered except for a small, eye-width piece of lace, allowing them to see out. With temperatures hovering near eighty degrees, I wondered how they could stand the heat. I was wearing long, somewhat loose pants and a modest, long-sleeved blouse and I was too warm.

The farther east we rode, the more remote areas we traveled through, the more primitive were the conditions. Traveling for long stretches through the desert I saw no buildings of any sort, and thus no bathroom facilities. At irregular but very welcome intervals, the driver stopped on the side of the road. We all got out, stretched our legs, and found places to relieve ourselves, men on one side of the bus and women on the other. At least the women's long, cumbersome clothes allowed them to be discreet.

One stop wasn't a pit stop, but a necessary one. A sand storm arose suddenly, initially turning the sunlit day into a dark, forbidding landscape until the dark brown swirling cloud enveloped us and the landscape was completely obscured. Quickly, Alex and I pulled large handkerchiefs from our backpacks and wrapped them around our faces.

Even though the windows were closed, the maddened sand forced its way in at every window frame, every metal seam, or possible crack. Our face covers at least made it possible to breathe. When the storm was over and the sand had settled, I felt dust in my hair, and like a thin blanket, it covered my clothes. I understood then why a burqa might be a good choice in the desert, the greater part of the land of Iran.

The bus driver started the engine, which thankfully turned over, and we were on our way again to Afghanistan. The driver, apparently not a graduate of a driving school, drove insanely fast and recklessly around narrow, curved, sub-standard roads. The Muslim passengers didn't share his nerve, and neither did we. As we raced and bumped along through one or another extremely perilous spot, when we could have easily flipped over and careened down a hill, a sudden cry would go up from all the passengers except us. "*Allah, Allah, Allah!*" they screamed, almost in unison, begging for protection. My heart was racing so fast I thought it might explode. I prayed silently and tried fruitlessly to find something to grab onto, as if it would make a difference in my safety if we did go off the road. And then, once more we were spared.

We changed buses in Herat, not far past the Afghani border, but not before briefly exploring this town. We found no modern section. All of the houses or buildings looked as if they had been constructed during the time of Jesus. Modern civilization had passed Herat by without a second glance, leaving the town with narrow dirt streets bordered by primitive, colorless, dirt-floored, stone or wood structures.

Kabul, Afghanistan's capital, situated in a valley of the Kabul River in the Hindu Kush Mountains, was a giant improvement from Herat, but in 1969 it still bore no resemblance to a modern city. Alex and I stayed in a two-story inn right off the main square in the center of town, and shopped at its marketplace for various goods. Here, in the square, vendors sat on blankets on the ground with their merchandise laid out before them.

From Turkey eastward, the accepted practice was to negotiate the purchase price of everything. No one simply gave the vendor his initial asking price. Although we didn't know the language, we knew our numbers and could and did bargain for everything.

One purchase we made was a unique knife. It was handmade of brass and rough steel, with its blade completely hidden within the handle. Only when the handle was manually separated and folded back against itself was the blade revealed by sliding out.

The knife was one of the few items we bought during these traveling years. Not only our frugality but also our lifestyle, made carrying or storing things almost impossible. We lived with little—a few clothes, essential toiletries, notebooks and pens, and not much else. For a while I did keep a small bag containing a few pieces of jewelry, including a pearl ring which was a gift from my mother, my high school senior ring, a watch, and a few pairs of earrings. One day in some hostel, my jewelry was stolen. Initially I cried, but then learned to live without them, ever lighter.

From Kabul another bus took us to Pakistan by way of the Khyber Pass. This gorge winds its way through shale and limestone cliffs, and is infamous for being both a gateway and a battle-way for a multitude of invaders, defenders, conquerors and would-be conquerors, from Alexander the Great through Genghis Kahn to the British.

Locals warned it could still be a perilous passage, but the Fates and my mother's prayers led us uneventfully to and through Peshawar and Islamabad, stopping finally at our destination, New Delhi, India. It was June.

So this was it. Climbing out of the hot, dirty bus, Alex and I stepped into the hot, dirty, clogged streets of this burgeoning city. Everything and everyone moved sluggishly. Wafts of spicy, curry scents rode on the heavy air waves. Steamy cow dung percolated in the streets. Lounging, undisturbable cows dictated the flow, halt, and direction of traffic, in the midst of the insanity of driving in streets without defined lanes.

One meandering cow lay in the middle of the road we were on, while drivers of cars and buses found a way around her or stopped and waited, lest the sacred creature be bothered. The cow's sacredness in this setting was difficult for me to comprehend. In the United States, for better or worse, it couldn't happen. In recent years, there was a distinct shortage of sacred cows.

Thin holy men sitting by the side of the road held empty begging bowls, waiting patiently for alms. Their spiritual tradition directed that they not eat anything unless it was given to them.

On sensory overload, dizzy from the heat, and terribly thirsty, I licked my lips to give them some bit of moisture while my eyes searched for relief. Spotting a man at the end of the crowded block selling some liquid from a wheeled cart, Alex and I swam through the sea of people to reach him. The vendor was unconvincingly swatting at the slow-moving flies flitting about his cart and the liquid. A couple of rupees bought for each of us a *lassi,* a surprisingly refreshing unsweetened, thin, yogurt drink.

For the time being, we dismissed the warnings we had heard about food contamination in India. So many Westerners who suffered through it and lived to report the cramping and awful diarrhea, said they felt as if they could die. But we were different, we told ourselves. We were invulnerable. We hadn't been sick yet and we had eaten and drunk all manner of things. We were desperately thirsty.

Once the thirst was quenched, my brain fog cleared and I asked myself what we could have been thinking. June, the hottest time of the year, was absolutely the wrong time to come to India. We had to do something, but first things first.

Finding a hotel was made easier because English was the second language of India. In my mind, the language and the train system were happy outcomes of the former British rule. Following careful directions from a couple of locals, we found lodging for a few nights while we considered our options.

Daily threading our way through the impossibly congested streets of New Delhi in June became overpowering. No particle of physical space was unoccupied by some jostling living creature, two-footed, four-footed, man or molecule-sized being, in perpetual scuffle for survival.

Layers of noise, interconnected and overlapping, blurred the boundaries between one sound and another. The incessant din, shouting, handout-begging, rickshaw-pedaling, bell-ringing, clanging, bus engine belching, honking, screeching, and amorphous rumbling made me feel as if all the centuries had funneled their entire clamor into this time and place.

Most staggering was the oppressive heat that sucked whatever usable oxygen was left over from the necessarily shallow breaths of the throng. Air was at a premium and it couldn't be bought. I felt as if I were truly suffocating.

Alex and I had come to this vast mysterious sub-continent of India to explore it and discover its secrets, but the heat was unbearable. Exploration would have to wait. For now, we must escape to a cooler, higher place.

Thanks to the grapevine, we chose for our refuge Kathmandu, Nepal, a truly exotic, mysterious place, eons old and forbiddingly remote. High in the land of the Himalayas, it would provide a cool respite.

Without a railroad or any highways to Kathmandu, traveling there could be complicated, arduous and dangerous. *Think. Think. Think.* We didn't as yet have a plan B. We never had a plan B. Most of the time we were lucky to have even a plan A, but something was developing.

CHAPTER 18

A Trek in the Himalayas

One's destination is never a place, but a new way of seeing things.
—Henry Miller

A day's search didn't turn up any public transportation options for the crude mountainous road to Kathmandu, but our ferreting found us another mode, not even meant for passengers. All the truck had to recommend itself were six wheels and an engine. Less than basic, it was excruciatingly uncomfortable, and although we didn't know it beforehand, downright dangerous. But it was cheap and all we found.

We left New Delhi in the evening, just before sunset. After Alex and I and a half dozen Indian and Nepalese men paid our rupees, we climbed into the back of a dilapidated, wooden-sided truck, also carrying a load of iron rebar to Kathmandu. The entire truck bed was covered with a deep layer of the long, rusty metal rods that shifted and scraped as we bounced along. Try as we might to settle in, we couldn't find any place or position offering even a modicum of comfort. Sitting and then lying on top of the rebar with only our backpacks and sleeping bags beneath us was barely on the other side of tolerable. Still, I told myself this ride surely couldn't last very long and I could bear anything with a foreseeable end.

The moonless overnight trip was up and down narrow, steep, sometimes treacherously curving mountainous roads, and the loose sides of the truck bed shook all the way. I could hear the gears of the transmission grinding at times, and the strain of the low gear as we climbed. I prayed the brakes wouldn't give out.

The noise and bumps and swerving, and the iron rods beneath us made sleep impossible. After hours of trying, I finally gave up and instead immersed myself in thought about where I was, where I was going, and why I was going there. I started to wonder if I had lost my mind.

There was no logical explanation, nor any reason for us to entrust our lives to some random driver, a broken down truck, and so many unknowns.

At the time, as we calculated means of getting to where we wanted to go, the concept of distrust was not part of the equation. We were at point A and wanted to get to point B, and this was the way to do it; period. So, yes, on numerous occasions we put our lives into the hands of people who could have been at best, inept drivers and at worst, raving lunatics or killers, going down treacherous roads, or in vehicles without integrity, but held together with rubber bands and hope. We had the daring, blind faith of youth.

Day had already broken when wonder of wonders, we made it. I was sore, exhausted, and disoriented when we climbed from the truck into the dirt and cobblestone streets of Nepal's capital city.

Landlocked and isolated by the Himalayan Mountains, except for a minor airport, Nepal is difficult to access. It is sandwiched between the Indian and Tibetan borders with India on the west, south, and east, and Tibet on the north. Kathmandu lies in a valley, nestled in the muscular arms of the tall Himalayan foothills.

That old chameleon time wore very different colors in this medieval city. The pace was extremely slow and, although I couldn't identify the century we parachuted into, the religious foundation of the culture was unmistakable. As I looked around to find my bearings, I saw stone and wooden pagoda-style Hindu temples, Buddhist *stupas*, mound-type reliquaries, and many small shrines. A parade of men and women, some towing children, on the way to their daily obligations, stopped to ring a bell, turn a prayer wheel, or touch the stone images.

I didn't see anything like a grocery store or a gas station, or any other evidence of the twentieth century. I didn't see much commerce at all, except in a few bedroom-sized shops selling the most basic necessities, and a limited selection of foods. Because we had become accustomed to eating whatever the locals ate wherever we traveled, the limited food choice was inconsequential. It wasn't so much the food we depended on to nourish us as it was the customs, the people, both residents and itinerants, and the ways we found to relate to them.

Century aside, there was something I found a bit odd. As we walked past one small shop—a government shop, in fact—a man called out to us, hawking their brand of hashish as the best. "Come, you buy, good hashish," he had mastered. We didn't stop for a taste test.

Before long we bumped into a fellow traveler who told us where we might find lodging. Following his directions, we came to a small, unpainted, rough wood and stone abode. It bore little resemblance to any building you would imagine to be a hotel, other than its having four walls and a roof. Winter there, I was sure, would have been quite inhospitable because daylight shone between some of the wall boards. There was no electricity. Our bed was a mat on the "upstairs" floor. It was not exactly the Ritz, but was infinitely better than the rebar in the bed of the truck. The measure of comfort, as the measure of most things in life, I learned, is relative. I was grateful to have a place to call home for the duration.

There were a few minor incursions of our late twentieth-century culture into this place. One of them was just across the narrow dirt street from our inn. It was a Nepalese tea shop, a tiny cafe of sorts, also serving rice and water buffalo burgers. It did have electricity and a very basic record player, brought in by some American counter-culture folks who had recently discovered this exotic place.

Throughout most of the day two types of music streamed out of the café's open door. Strains of Eastern raga, both cheering and soothing, alternated with the earthy, heady music of Jim Morrison and the Doors. In this primitive place, the incongruity of hearing cryptic lyrics like "riders on the storm" or "break on through to the other side" lent the scene an air of unreality. Alice hadn't walked in any stranger places in her Wonderland.

The cafe became the epicenter of activity for members of our traveling community. Within a matter of days, we met several of them from the States and various countries of Europe. Not unlike ourselves, most were shaggy-haired people in their twenties, dressed in unpretentious, loose-flowing, Indian-made clothing, or in quiet, natural fibers. No one was trying to make a fashion statement, or any other statement, for that matter. We were posing questions instead. A few were rebellious expatriate types, but no one lent them much of an ear. We acted as if politics, at least in this situation, was irrelevant. We existed in a world outside of, perhaps above, the mundane.

Days had no routine. People drifted from one activity or non-activity to another, in and out of one or another's "hotel" room. We didn't have and didn't need, telephones. No invitations were issued and no one was excluded. Movement just happened, like a breeze gently blowing fallen leaves on an autumn day. Somebody always had some stash to share. As a pipe was passed around the room, in the background I could sometimes hear, "*Come on baby, light my fire...*"

Sharing a pipe made easier the most important business of the day—attempting to relate to and fathom this magical part of the planet in the neck hollow of the earth. The air resonated with ancient wisdom as profoundly as the vibrations of the immense brass gongs being struck on temple grounds.

Many evenings, and parts of days, we spent gathered with others—most of whose faces and names will forever remain a blur—and smoking, sometimes drumming on Indian *tablas.* We made our own music on whatever was available. Conversation topics sometimes turned philosophical or spiritual. My introduction to mysticism caused me vague discomfort, as I found it so foreign, even threatening, to my formerly espoused Catholic beliefs. Did I really have to examine what I believed so microscopically? I had my reservations. When the student is ready, they say, the teacher will appear. Maybe I wasn't quite ready, or maybe everyone on my journey was my teacher and I was learning only as much as I could from each one, even if only a spoonful at a time. Sometimes the messages came too fast and heavily, and I couldn't put the pieces together to make clear sense. *What did it mean?* I felt at times like Wonderland Alice, remembering the silly king:

"If there's no meaning in it, that saves a world of trouble, you know, as we needn't try to find any. And yet I don't know,..."

My most profound realizations usually came to me in wordless awe in nature's theater. And here I was in the grandest theater of all, in the neighborhood of the Himalayas, the most revered, majestic, and unearthly mountains on the planet.

I never had any aspirations to climb mountains. Why subject myself to the arduous danger of the climb? I could be content for the rest of my life without ever trying to climb Mt. Everest or any other mountain peak, content to see their majesty from a distance. I could feel the primordial essence in the cloud-kissing air around me on this land where the elevation was more than forty-five hundred feet closer to the heavens than my below-sea-level home.

I learned though, it was possible to reach taller heights without doing rugged hand over hand climbing. Many travelers who went before us had already blazed the trails so that we could go trekking in the mountains. Why not go?

We easily obtained the government permit for trekking, and planned to set out the following morning. Much of what we did was done simply on the strength of what we heard from others who had already done it, or from those who had heard from others. So it was with the trekking venture.

Our plan was to trek for just a few days. Wanting to avoid carrying excess weight, we packed only sleeping bags, a change of clothes, toothbrushes, a couple of knives and a few small bags of nuts and dried fruit. We had been assured we could find food and lodging in the mountains with families who lived along the way.

Just after daybreak, Alex and I, without any guide, started by walking out of town across the valley. Then suddenly, without fanfare, we were face to face with the foothills. Locating a narrow path, we started the trek upward. At first it was easy. Sometimes the path was shaded. For a time it meandered next to a vibrant mountain stream. I knelt beside the stream, cupped my hands into it and drank the most delicious water I had ever tasted, so clear and vibrant it sparkled. The water more than quenched my thirst; it tasted like food, full of minerals and life-giving substance.

As we climbed, we were sometimes winded. Occasionally, we were overtaken by Sherpa tribesmen who lived in these mountains. Their legs looked as solid as tree trunks as they by-passed us speedily without breathing hard, carrying large loads on their backs. I would soon learn they survived on very little food. Could it be this water and mountain air gives them their strength? How easily nature provides. How little we need to survive.

Even as the well-worn path became steeper, hand over hand climbing wasn't necessary. We passed through wooded areas and reached many plateaus. On each plateau I thought we must be at the top of the mountain where we would have a clear view, but each time I was wrong. Finally, by late afternoon, I was right.

What I saw my eyes could hardly absorb, much less my mind. The absolutely stunning Himalayan Mountains must be where the gods resided, with the heavens as their backyard. This panorama was an entirely new perspective. Seeing the earth from the surface of the ball that it is, I felt its roundness in space. Sucking in the rarified air like a newborn at her mother's breast was a new experience for my lungs and a natural high. *Aha!* I thought. *Maybe I have an inkling of what makes mountain climbers climb.*

Following the widening path, we climbed higher and higher. Seeing the peaks in the distance was astonishing. As high clouds drifted past, other peaks in the background revealed themselves. Far away, one peak was so high it appeared to curve forward, bending to avoid hitting its head on the sky.

Now we were on a plateau. The path continued for a while on more level ground, before gradually ascending again. While we walked on, the day didn't wait for us. The sun announced his intention downward.

By this time, I was tired and realized we hadn't eaten anything of substance all day. I hoped we would find a place to spend the night soon. Not much farther along the trail, we came upon a couple of rough huts. A few of their inhabitants stood outside.

Once again, body language and gestures were essential for communication. Pointing first to me and then himself, Alex then put his hands together and leaned his head sideways onto them to indicate sleep. Next he pointed to the family's abode with a questioning look. The man and woman of the house only stared at these foolish intruders, either not understanding or not trusting.

I couldn't blame them for their mistrust or even for their lack of hospitality. We came from a different world from theirs, and perhaps it was rude of us to be there. Still, we were quite vulnerable, the sun was sinking fast, and "those who had gone before us" said we would be welcome.

Gesturing again to no avail, we were waved away. What could we do? Walking on, we found another small hut around a bend and tried again, but found no door open. What could I think about this refusal? Maybe some previous foreign trekkers were terrible guests. Whatever the reason, we found ourselves without shelter as the sky began to drop its curtains. Although we were several feet from the cliff, I walked gingerly.

Knowing that we couldn't continue walking or even find a place to lay our heads once we lost daylight, we searched for a spot for our sleeping bags. When we stopped, I gaped in awe at the sun taking its final bow. On the side of the path away from the cliff was the only flat area. There was a slight rise above it. This, we decided, would be where we would spend the night, and we snuggled our bags up next to the rise, ready to bed down.

A few minutes after we resigned ourselves to our situation, a young man appeared on the rise above us. He motioned excitedly to us in a way we read as a caution against staying there. He must have come from the home of the last family that had refused us. Although we did not understand what kinds of dangers he might have been warning us against, we did understand he wanted us to go with him. Rolling up our sleeping bags, we then obediently followed him back to his home.

Much less than what westerners would call a house, it was a primitive, insubstantial, raised wooden hut with a semi-enclosed barn-like space below that housed a donkey. A ladder led to the only entrance to the one-room family living quarters above. The room held no furniture, but a place for sleeping mats and a small fire pit hearth in the center.

We sat with the young man, a younger girl, and father, cross-legged on the floor around the pit while the mother threw lumps of unseasoned dough—nothing more—into a big pot of water. When the "dumplings" were done, she ladled some liquid into each bowl and handed us each one. As lacking in flavor and substance as it was, I determined to eat mine, not wanting to offend them. In Europe and North Africa it is insulting to the host to refuse their food. I supposed Alex read the situation differently, and he chose not to eat much of the tasteless gruel. When he set down his mostly full bowl, the young man picked it up, ate some, and proceeded to pass it to the others to finish. I didn't know whether to feel badly or not about having eaten mine.

Mealtime was a quiet communion, the repast taken for both physical and spiritual sustenance. Afterwards, the young man showed us where to lay our sleeping bags. Almost immediately after crawling into my bag, I left the planet. Alex and I both slept so soundly we didn't hear anyone stir in the morning. When we finally awoke everyone was gone. We left the family most of our food supplies and went on our way.

Inebriating and invigorating is the only way to describe waking up near the top of the world. The sky was much bigger and the sun much closer. I drank in the nutritious air as we followed the path farther upward, seeing my giant mountain friends against the sky. The more magnificent the view, the more insignificant I felt. When the path wound perilously close to the mountain edge, my heart stayed in my mouth. I felt light-headed, as if I were floating. Simultaneously, I was imagining the ease with which I could fall, not just from the mountain but from the earth itself. With one misstep I could be cast out into space to float around forever. It was too high to fall to a bottom. There *was* no bottom. I felt extremely vulnerable, and life tenuous at best, but at that moment it didn't matter. What mattered was only the breathtaking experience of being there, witnessing the naked universe. At this point in my life, when I owned nothing, I felt I owned the world.

We stopped to catch our breath and simply to gaze into the magic. I didn't know how much farther or higher we would go. Under the circumstances, with no more food supply, and with the knowledge we couldn't count on finding other food and lodging, Alex and I discussed whether or not to shorten our sights.

The Universe stepped in with an answer. Clouds had been gathering as we walked, and there is was. Rain started to fall. Now we were even less prepared, as we had brought nothing waterproof. Making a quick about-face, we found minor shelter in the lee of a rock ledge. We stood there for half an hour as the rain slowed. As the sky became clear again, so did the message: Retreat. Even so, I didn't count this as a defeat, but as a victory. We hadn't reached the roof of the world, but we had climbed at least to its double digit floors, and we had found space and air to breathe.

CHAPTER 19

Wild Monkeys of Kathmandu

When you've come to the edge of all of the light
you know, and are about to step off
into the darkness of the unknown, Faith is
knowing one of two things will happen –
There will be something solid to stand on,
or you will learn how to fly.
—UNKNOWN

NATURAL INSTINCTS OF ANIMALS ALERT them to danger, allow them to read the winds, and connect them to the world. The human species has largely traded or submerged those instincts in favor of electronic telecommunication. Too often true communication is silenced behind the electronic buzz, but living as we did, Alex and I fell somewhere between the two worlds. In these years before cell phones and Internet, mail was slow, long distance phone calls were prohibitively expensive, and neither we nor most of our itinerant friends had permanent addresses. Consequently, we depended on the grapevine not only for our news, but also for broadcasting our situations, questions, and needs.

We put the word out we wanted to find some LSD to try because we felt we needed to experience the drug as part of our education. Seeking to experience, know, and understand, we determined this called for expanding our consciousness in a way we believed only LSD could do. It was almost like scientific research. Almost.

The grapevine did its job. We learned that a young California man who was currently living in a small house outside of Kathmandu, had a couple of hits of pure acid for us.

How did we know it was for us? As fate would have it, Jonathan had been given this LSD with specific instructions, that he not sell it, but that he give it away, and only to individuals who had never taken LSD before. Perfect. Not only did the grapevine do its job, but it provided what we needed at a price we could afford.

Shouldn't I have been frightened? Shouldn't I have distrusted this stranger and his gift?

Probably to any rational mind the answer would have been "yes," but these were not questions I asked myself. We were operating outside of the realm of reason. I could not trace the reason for many of our decisions any more than the poet Shelley could find the cause of his sonnets.

I was wide open like a child, driven by honest motivation. I tried not to harm anyone, and I assumed the favor would be returned. The Universe had protected us so far, so why wouldn't it now? Besides, we told each other, the use and culture of LSD had not become so common that hacks and big drug dealers would have gotten into its manufacturing and marketing, so the product was most likely pure and unadulterated.

Of course I felt a little trepidation on the day we were to have the experience, but I attributed it simply to a normal fear of the unknown. Admittedly, this was a big unknown. Although we had already ventured into many wild, strange, and unknown geographical areas, this was different. This was exploring the unknowns within.

Blind faith. We defined it. We had decided when we returned from our trekking in the mountains, we would visit this bearer of gifts. His house was on flat land at the edge of a field, not far from where we descended. We couldn't phone ahead, but I had the feeling he knew we would be knocking.

Jonathan came to the door, saw us and smiled through his full beard and mustache. Like a priest, he was dressed all in white, with cotton drawstring pants, and a loose-fitting, long-sleeved, Afghani-style, soft cotton shirt. His manner was gentle and serene. "Come on in," he said, as if expecting and recognizing us. He invited us to sit with him on cushions on the floor. We were clearly Americans, apparently on a mission, and obviously green by California counter-culture standards.

"So, you're the ones," he said, almost matter-of-factly. Someone must have told him we were coming. But still, he asked why we had come and what we were looking for.

Alex started to explain. This was a very important moment. Jonathan must understand we were not looking for a recreational drug. We made it clear we were essentially looking for a teacher, and that LSD could be one.

Concerning drugs, Alex and I were less than neophytes. Except for the brief Istanbul stay, we had only occasionally smoked pot—experiences I felt were sometimes eye-opening and usually mellowing, but benign.

"Listen, I don't know what you've heard about acid, but it's not like anything else," Jonathan said. "It really does open up your mind. It can show you things you've never seen before, but you have to be careful and treat it like a sacrament. You should be in a safe place and have some food with you because your brain will need it. And you should have somebody with you who's still on this planet."

We would find out this was very good advice. Jonathan gave us the two tiny tabs as if he were delivering communion. In a sense he was. We asked if he had a third tab for Rudolph, an Austrian we met on a train who had become a traveling buddy.

"Unfortunately, no," he said. As it turned out, it was probably *fortunately,* no. Rudolph would be our spotter, protector, and guide as our feet walked through the potential worldly perils, while our spirits explored other realms.

Our rosy-cheeked, teddy-bearish friend was perfect for the job. He was unshaven and a little scruffy, but he had strong arms. One look at him and you knew he could take care of himself and anyone else. He had a good enough grasp of the English language to understand what he needed to know and to make himself understood, in a charming, roguish way. Rudolph had a quick incisive wit, a unique, broad perspective, and an easy, though sometimes unusual sense of humor. A fearless no-nonsense guy, he knew how to get things done, and had a soft side. I knew we could trust him to take care of us. We planned our "trip" for the following day.

In the morning we bought flatbread, dried fruit, and nuts, stashing it all into a backpack. The three of us walked to Monkey Hill, a tall, grassy, partially wooded hill, away from the foot traffic and bustle of the center of town. The hill came by its name honestly. It was populated with dozens of wild monkeys who subsisted on whatever they could.

In my limited experience, monkeys were those harmless, silly little animals whose antics we watched and made fun of at the zoo. My illusions were about to be shattered—about monkeys and about everything else.

It was a mild, sunny day. When we arrived we climbed a short distance up the hill, high enough to give us a good vantage point of the surrounding area, as well as to keep us out of view of curious eyes. We sat on the grass with our bags nearby. Alex and I, first looking around, then at each other, took some deep breaths. In preparation we took our food out of the backpack.

"Okay, Carroll," pronouncing my name with his heavy Austrian accent like '*cattle*,' "you ready to do this *ting*?" Rudolph asked me.

"I think so," I said. "Yeah, I'm ready."

"And *vat* about you, Alex?" Rudolph asked.

"Let's go for it," he said.

"Okay. I'm here," Rudolph assured. "I stay *vit* you. Don't worry."

Meanwhile, we didn't notice that several of the hill's permanent inhabitants had descended and were eyeing us, but even more so, our food. Quick as a bee sting, a couple of the monkeys ran down, making awful screeching noises, swiped most of our bread, and ran defiantly back up the hill. Chasing them to attempt retrieval of our food was out of the question. We were foolhardy, but not stupid. Instead, we decided to eat what they hadn't swiped to avoid the possibility of losing that too.

Ceremoniously, we unwrapped our small treasures. Alex and I put the tabs into our mouths and lay back on the soft grass.

I wasn't aware of how long it took for the LSD to take effect because the borders of time and space began to blur. Everything seemed to happen simultaneously. Time, a human-contrived concept, ceased to exist. This trip into inner-outer, space-no space, time-no time, matter-no-matter realms was already reaching way beyond anything man-made or man-conceived. I turned onto my stomach on the grass, and began to sink into it.

I could feel the blades of grass as if they were hairs of my skin. I let go of all doubts and trepidation, all limiting and inhibiting thoughts, all reason and no reason, all excuses not to release my body and soul into the care of the Universe. I abandoned myself completely and became only a vehicle of exploration. As my body relaxed into the ground's embrace, I felt the firm earth beneath the grass as the living, breathing flesh of a loving mother. Ultimately, I felt no distinction between my body and the hill, no physical line separating my flesh and bones from the earth, and certainly no ego. I had melted, but I had become something greater, like a grain of sand on the beach. I *was* the beach. My real education had begun.

Monkey Hill became my residence for an eon or two as I was totally engulfed in and awestruck by this new land I was inhabiting and that was inhabiting me. I was able to notice all manner of insects and creepy crawly things which ordinarily escaped my vision. They weren't frightening or repulsive to me, only curious. I didn't see any ogres, any ugliness, or horror. There was no judgment or appraisal of anything.

I didn't feel any violence or other danger, only wonder, and a stronger sense of being at home and at ease in this home than I had ever experienced. I saw the universe essentially laid bare, as if a great magician's tricks were all suddenly revealed to me. I was on the inside of all of life's workings with only the finest of lines of separation between the cells of my body and the cells of everything else.

I had a million "*Aha*!" moments. All my sensory gates were wide open. All my physical, mental, and spiritual gates were accepting the whole world, overflowing my vessel. Simultaneously, whatever *I was*, was spilling out unreservedly back into the universal pool. There was no loss of function in any of my body parts, and my mind, if anything, was sharper and able to grasp whatever I focused on. I had no fear or thought of fear. I needed nothing.

I understood physics as simple science. I understood what Einstein had uncovered, that matter and energy were one and the same, but only in different forms, so that whatever I was doing I became—matter undergoing a change into energy.

I understood the meaning of mind-blowing, because my mind truly had been blown. It could be called an out of body experience, because I wasn't aware of my body as apart from its surroundings. If anything apart, my body was perhaps like a suit of clothes that housed and distinguished "my" group of cells from the other groupings of cells, dressed as flowers or grass or windows. In fact, at some point I wanted to be rid of my clothes, as I didn't see any need for them. Fortunately, Rudolph intervened, because by that time we were walking through town headed back to our primitive hotel.

After Rudolph deposited us in our small room, he disappeared. Lying there on the mat on the floor, still wrapped in the expanded world, I became absorbed in observing tiny creatures on the wall, including a spider on its fine, hair-thin legs, weaving an intricate web. I saw the fibrous makeup of the boards on the wall. I saw colors everywhere. The blues, greens and aquas were splendid, but I experienced every color and understood how all together they made white.

Because words cannot adequately describe what I saw and felt and what happened, in the attempted recounting, I risk being considered a drug-crazed fool, but what I experienced was real. I glimpsed a world ordinarily too large to be contained in my small individual mind. I was left with the "logical" explanation that this lysergic acid chemical breaks down the walls that contain and restrain the individual mind, allowing it to merge with the over-mind, the Universe.

However it could be understood, I knew I would never be the same again. I had had a spiritual, mental, and maybe even a kind of physical dying and rebirth. No longer could I claim innocence or ignorance of any thoughtless actions. I understood how whatever I did affected every other person or being in the world, and how I was in turn affected by every other person or being. I learned I could stand back whenever I needed or wanted to and observe my life objectively. I realized I had the power of choice, not only in how I acted, but also in what I thought and consequently what I felt, since thought clearly precedes feeling. I learned that I alone choose the "meaning" of my life, as others, consciously or subconsciously, do the same. I learned only by letting go can you control your life.

Would I ever do this again? Who knew? Would it prove to be a costly, unhealthy, or dangerous experience? What had I traded for my insights? Would those insights remain with me and direct me to living a more satisfying or evolved life? What had I sacrificed on the altar of knowledge or curiosity? And what had I really gained? Only time would tell, if indeed time did. Would I dare to recommend to others using LSD as a means to spiritual growth? No, I would not. Even in a "safe" environment, there are too many variables and too much potential for dangerous outcomes.

In Kathmandu though, I hardly thought about any possible consequences. At some point that night, the parts of the universe that had previously configured themselves into the individual I call me, collected themselves, and we slept soundly.

First passport

Barcelona, Fall, 1967

Hitchhiking in Southern Turkey

Kabul, Afghanistan

Volunteering at an Israeli kibbutz Farm

Regrouping in Formentera, Spain

Osaka, Japan

CHAPTER 20

Wuddy'ya Want in Bangkok

You grow up the day you have the first real laugh at yourself.
—Ethel Barrymore

Before arriving in Kathmandu, I hadn't known what the cosmic plan was for me there. Possibly I still didn't, but it seemed we had accomplished what we were meant to accomplish, and we left Nepal.

We wouldn't be going back to India just yet, except to pass through and fly out of Calcutta to Bangkok, Thailand. We were enticed by Don and Mary, an American couple we had met and become friends with earlier, who were now working in Bangkok as English teachers.

The war in next door Vietnam was still going on, though massive troop withdrawals had begun. It was still a place for R and R for troops in that part of the world, for military wives teaching English, for troops who legitimately or illegitimately had stayed behind, for increasing numbers of tourists, and for explorers like us. Bangkok was waking up to Western influence and Western influx.

Because of the war, the Thais were learning the value of the American dollar and learning that signposts on the road to wealth were written in English. They all wanted to learn it. Children were taught English grammar in their elementary schools, but they found out as adults they couldn't understand or be understood by the American G.I. on the street. What they needed was practical instruction in conversational English.

We happened to get aboard that ship at the right time to ride that wave. Two of Don and Mary's American teacher friends in Bangkok would be exiting the country soon, creating openings for two more teachers. We stepped into a couple of part-time positions at Madame Chalao's Language School, a small private school, and also at the much larger American University Alumni School of Languages.

AUA began a few decades ago predominantly as a social organization for Thai students returning from their studies in the United States, and for their American friends in Thailand. During the Vietnam War years AUA grew. The wives of American servicemen stationed in Vietnam needed a place to stay and something to do. Eventually, an enterprising American PhD educator devised a series of English courses which served purely as verbal communication aids for the Thais.

The classes were fun to teach. Initially, it was hard for me to keep from laughing as I presented the lesson of the day. Standing in front of a classroom of twenty attentive and bright-eyed young adults, I would have them repeat after me phrases like "*Wuddy'ya, wuddy'ya, wuddy'ya want?*" and *"where ya', where ya', where ya' goin?*"

In their elementary and secondary schools, the Thais might have learned the meaning of "What do you want?" They might even have learned the correct pronunciation of those words, but the words sounded nothing like what they heard from the Americans on the street.

Madame Chalao's school was an entirely different experience. Housed in a more traditional building wrapped around a picturesque courtyard on quiet grounds, the atmosphere was much friendlier and more personal. The students there, all adults, were extremely appreciative and generous, insisting I take the thoughtful little gifts they brought me. A few invited me to go with them to watch a program of intricately beautiful Siamese dancing. My students tried to interpret for me the stylized movements and gestures of the dance depicting ancient stories and legends. Although I didn't understand all of what they described, I was totally taken in by them and by the elaborate costumes and headdresses the dancers wore.

Madame Chalao's School was where I met Jim, a fellow teacher and fellow American who had been living in Bangkok for a few years now. Jim was soft-spoken and a true gentle man. I don't know whether his mild manner was in his nature or whether he had acquired it while living among the gentle Thais, but he had learned their language and had a Thai girlfriend.

Jim lived in a rented house, one that, in my mind was an ideal habitat for a human. In this country where there was no cold weather, the house, like many others, had few walls, but plenty of gauzy mosquito netting, and ample light. The lines were simple and uncluttered. The floors were smooth and waxed. The house, surrounded by banana trees, bamboo and vines, had a wonderful clean fresh scent.

Jim's circle of friends included Klaus, a pre-maturely gray, flamboyant German who lived like a prince in a low-slung secluded house surrounded by lush tropical gardens and greenery. Klaus was wont to have elaborate, multi-cultural parties, and we were wont to be a part of them.

We also became friends with Jeff and Katy, an American couple who were living comfortably in Bangkok after Jeff's Army stint in Vietnam was finished. Jeff was a rock music aficionado, and he became our connection to the States for the latest popular sounds. It was in their living room in the more modern section of the city we first heard some of the terrific songs of the highly energetic Credence Clearwater Revival, like *I Heard it Through the Grapevine.* Happy reconnections to my own culture. They were good times.

For the months Alex and I lived in Thailand, we had good, regular jobs and a very active social life. Thailand for me wasn't fully western or fully eastern. It wasn't either industrialized or third world; it was pleasantly "other world", and a feast for my senses. I enjoyed many aspects of life there.

I loved that on my way home from work I would pass in the streets local vendors squatting at their low makeshift tables deftly cutting fresh juicy pineapples lengthwise into long chunks and selling them for five *baht* apiece, the equivalent of about five cents. More often than not, I stopped, bought one and ate it on the spot, and my energy level jumped up.

Alex and I lived in a very traditional, very low income section of Bangkok in a one-room wooden dwelling on stilts across a small courtyard from the one-story, three-room home of our landlords.

In the center of the little secluded courtyard was a bathing pond where men and women both bathed, standing next to it wearing cotton wraps, pouring water over their bodies. Of course we did the same.

It was an interesting and organic place to live, sharing our room with a couple of geckos. We watched them hanging out on the ceiling or the walls, and felt their bulbous eyes watching us too.

From the landing outside our door I could see the balcony of the next door home of a group of Buddhist monks where some of them often stood in their saffron robes. When I encountered them in the streets of the small community, I noticed they did indeed live according to the Buddhist code of not doing harm to any living creature. I watched them carefully stepping around, not on, insects that were in their path as they walked. Considering this was a climate where bugs abounded, I wondered how they might possibly avoid stepping on at least some.

All things considered, with the possible exception of the Greek islands, living in Bangkok was more akin to an extended vacation for me than any other place we had been. The climate and open-air activities greatly contributed to that feeling. So did the vibrant colors everywhere—the bursts of color in nature, native clothing, temples, and the many small ornate neighborhood spirit house shrines which were built to appease the spirits. Whether or not they accomplished this purpose, they certainly appeased mine.

The food too was colorful, not only in appearance but also in taste. While it was undoubtedly the hottest spiced food I had ever tasted, it was probably the most flavorful. Unlike so many dishes from other countries, in Thai cuisine, the ginger, the lemon grass, and each different seasoning distinguishes itself to the palate. When I ate dinner, even in the most unpretentious hole-in-the-wall restaurants, dinner felt like a celebration happening in my mouth.

Bangkok is crisscrossed by waterways—rivers, and canals, known as *khlongs*. Some waterways were quiet and lazy, meandering through neighborhoods passing crooked, ramshackle, hobbled-together, wooden houses on stilts. Others, like the wide *Chao Phrya* River, were alive daily with commuters in speedboat buses, vendors in small overloaded *sampans*, and floating wooden shop houses noisily selling fresh produce and fish.

One of my favorite things was to do errands via the *Chao Phrya*, including making the weekly trip to the post office downriver. I rode on the commuter "boat bus", a long, wide speedboat holding two dozen passengers. It wasn't for the frail or slow, as it made regular, or irregular, stops at various points, and passengers needed to be ready to jump on or off quickly before the boat sped away again.

I hardly missed a Sunday flea market at the *Pramane* grounds when the large open field became an enormous beehive of buying and selling and social activity. The market had outstanding buys on colorful batik fabrics, sarongs, and handmade jewelry, all price-negotiated, of course, making it more fun. Happily for me, so much of what we did in Thailand took place outdoors.

In spite of Thailand's geographical and cultural distance from America, I was reminded occasionally of some of the curious ties that bound both countries.

Thonburi, the neighborhood where we lived, was near *Wat Phra Kao*, a large compound consisting of a number of gilded, architecturally stunning buildings, including the Grand Palace and its most revered temple. The imposing ornate gate of the compound was a block away from where Alex and I stood watching the parade carrying visiting President Richard Nixon through the streets in a long yellow open-topped convertible.

A banner draped on the car broadcast the familiar American message, most likely incomprehensible to the Thais: "Sock it to 'em, Nix." Several hundred school children lined the parade route near us, each quietly holding a tiny American flag. Most stood stone-still, looking as if they had not an inkling of who this was or why they were there.

Alex and I were a few feet from Nixon's car as it passed. Though he wore a guarded smile on his face, the President looked directly at me and waved. A shudder of electricity ran through my body as I became aware of a distinct aura of raw power emanating from this man and his position. This power could exist only through common agreement to bestow it on the office of the

Presidency. It was maintained by so many others who were all focusing their energy on him.

Another procession along this same route calling for Thai schoolchildren to swell the crowds was the one carrying the Apollo 11 astronauts, Neil Armstrong, Buzz Aldrin, and Michael Collins, after their moon landing. This too left the children with wondering looks on their faces. Did anyone really comprehend what had happened? Some people were skeptical that the moon landing had even happened. One elderly Thai gentleman made known to one and all his sentiments: It was all Hollywood make-believe.

I was of course convinced of the moon landing, but I could understand how some might not be. I was also convinced of the need we all have for some make-believe in our lives.

Alex and I had our second make-believe honeymoon in *Hua Hin*, traveling a hundred miles or so south of Bangkok by train. Situated on the Malaysian Peninsula bordering the Gulf of Thailand, the town was edged by white sands and clear blue water.

Hua Hin was home to King Rama VII's summer palace, built in 1928, and named *Klai Kangwon*—Far From Worries. And so were we for a time, far from worries, even if this wasn't a *real* honeymoon after a *real* wedding. We succumbed to the magic of it and grew close again.

During our tenure in Thailand, we were faced with having to renew our visas. There were two options for doing this: One involved money, and the other, exiting the country. We chose the latter. It was more interesting in any case, and we could do it without flying anywhere.

Our choice meant taking a train from Bangkok north to next-door-neighbor Laos. We packed a lunch and relaxed in the train as it rolled past rice paddies and benign water buffaloes that stopped their munching long enough to lift their heads and stare apathetically at the iron monster crossing their paths.

Once we crossed the Mekong River we were officially out of the country. After getting off the train in Vientiane, we had our passports stamped, and then re-boarded for the return trip to Bangkok. And that was that.

I lived more lightly in Bangkok than I had anywhere else. Not everything here was easy, but in Thailand, problems didn't seem to weigh as much. The city even had an annual Water Festival which one of my students described to me as a just for fun time during which residents threw water on each other.

Perhaps a better example of the nonchalant attitude happened when I was a passenger on a bus in Bangkok. Because the weather doesn't get cold, the buses have no doors. Instead there are open doorways at the front and back of the buses where passengers can, if they choose, stand and ride while holding onto a vertical metal pole.

On this particular day, my bus was almost empty. I was seated and there was a man standing in the rear doorway. Bangkok bus drivers were mavericks who drove fast and one-handedly. Our bus driver was typical. His left elbow was hanging out over the window, his body leaning towards it, as we sped through the streets and he maneuvered the long bus around cars and corners. At one corner, the driver made an especially sharp turn to the left, causing the man standing in the rear doorway to fly off into the street, away from and behind the bus.

As soon as the driver looked in his rear view mirror and saw what had happened, he stopped the bus, but made no attempt to get off the bus to help the man in the street or even to find out if he was okay. Before possibly twenty seconds had elapsed, all of us aboard the bus watched the man get up from the street, dust himself off, and walk away. The driver, satisfied his former passenger was alive, took off again, resuming his fast pace.

At first I was appalled, but then I was amused. In my country, this would call for a lawsuit. Even though no one was obviously hurt, except perhaps the flying passenger's pride, in the U.S. we might have had a battle about whose fault it was, but not in Bangkok. Sure, the bus driver was carelessly freewheeling, but the passenger didn't have to stand at the exit. He could have sat in a seat. I wasn't thrown off.

It was just a thing that happened, as things tend to do. Some may be avoided and some not, but they can't be undone, and some should just be left alone. I made up my mind then and there I wanted to be more like that passenger. When I found myself flying off a bus in the future, I would get up, dust myself off and go on about my business. There wasn't much dust to brush off from Bangkok, but soon, there would be ample opportunities to do that.

Friends told us about a Yoga course they had taken at an ashram in a town south of Madras in India. I knew next to nothing about Yoga, but Alex and I were both intrigued. This had to be the next learning adventure and chapter in my life.

CHAPTER 21

Between the Rails

What if the hokey pokey really is what it's all about?
—Anonymous

Dawn sent a pale yellow stream of light through the curtainless window of our cheap second floor hotel room on that first morning back in India. Looking out of the window, I was startled to see bodies strewn across the sidewalks in every direction. Not dead bodies, but live ones, homeless ones, sleeping as they did every night, on thin, raggedy blankets or cotton cloths on the ground. This was Calcutta.

We flew to Calcutta from Bangkok with plans to study Yoga at an ashram in a town far south, on the Bay of Bengal. Because we were several weeks early for the next course to start, we used the time to explore some other parts of the country. In India, hitchhiking wasn't an option. We would travel by railroad, a much-used British legacy.

Many of the trains were still coal-driven, and since there was no air conditioning, we kept the windows open for the journey across interminable stretches of hot plains. By the end of the line, more often than not, our faces were smudged with black soot.

The third class cars in which we rode were always packed with people, people who didn't expect to ride in comfort, crammed into hard seats and everywhere else. A sign posted at the front of each car made me laugh: "Ticketless travel is a social evil." The reason for the sign quickly became apparent. When the train pulled into a station, almost invariably, a number of people were hoisted from the station platform to climb in through a window, find a space to sit, and after nightfall, a place to sleep. That place was often on the floor or even in the overhead luggage rack. I assumed these trespassers were some of the social evil-doers. But where was everybody going?

Finding a place to sleep was apparently an all-too-common daily challenge in this overcrowded nation, attested to by the plain and simple prohibition posted on some Calcutta train station platforms: "NO SLEEPING BETWEEN THE RAILS." Bewildered when I spotted this sign, I wondered what kind of people would sleep between the rails of busy train tracks. Were they complete fools without any idea of the danger? Were they sensible but without the survival instinct? Were they holy men who simply trusted their gods to protect them, or were they so haughty as to dare the fates?

While grappling with the question, I had an unsettling realization: Whoever these people might be, I was one of them. At least figuratively, I had already slept between rails a number of times, and frankly, I girded myself to sleep between more of them.

While our train was stopped at any given station, at any time of day, we saw vendors walking up and down the platform, hawking steaming hot tea with milk and sugar. In spite of the hot climate, cold drinks didn't exist. There was no ice to be had, and the rationalization for drinking hot liquids was founded in science. The heat would cause the body to sweat and the evaporating moisture would cool it. In my mind, an added benefit was that presumably, the water had been boiled. We became converts, and when a vendor walked by yelling, "*Chai, chai*!" we usually each had a cup, making the two-rupee transaction through the window.

The tea was served in what was a primitive, ecologically agreeable clay cup, not ceramic or even kiln-dried. I didn't know, and didn't want to know, how unsanitary or unhealthy it was. This small, thin, crude brown vessel appeared to have been formed from the clay dirt along the road and dried in the sun. In the truest sense, it was completely disposable and instantly recyclable. When we finished our drinks, we threw the cups out the window, watching them crash into bits of hardened dirt to disappear into the ground. Perfect. Cycle. Re-cycle.

I had never been in a place, perhaps other than Nepal, where the cycles of life were as apparent, where so many people lived so close to the earth. In philosophy as well as lifestyle, there appeared to be a seamless transition even between life and death.

Memories of my childhood's Ash Wednesdays filled my head. "*Remember man that thou art dust, and unto dust thou shalt return,*" the priest said, as he smeared a thumbful of ashes in the form of a cross in the middle of my forehead the day after Mardi Gras every year. Like the cup, I came from dust and would one day be dust again.

Although I was too young to imagine my own body going through that transition, in India the concept was easier to grasp, especially in Varanasi, on the holy Ganges River. Varanasi, also called Banares, is one of Hinduism's seven holy cities and the spiritual capital of India. Many people in their declining years come here in the hope it will be where they take their last breath. Hindus who die in Varanasi, tradition says, go straight to the un-place that releases them from the cycle of life and death. Wanting to know more about this holy tradition, we stopped at Varanasi on our circuitous route to the beach village of Goa on the Arabian Sea.

As we walked through the streets on our way to the holy Ganges River, a local resident approached us, offering to be our guide, but not for any recompense. I think he sensed our genuine curiosity, and his inclination was to share what he knew.

He called our attention to several emaciated, elderly men, sitting on their haunches or cross-legged on the ground, in the crooks of buildings, or leaning against walls, eyes mostly closed to the world around them. "Some of them have come from far away," our guide said, "and now they are waiting here to die."

A wooden wagon went by in the street, being pulled by a barefoot man wearing only a *dhoti,* a rectangular piece of cloth, folded and tucked around the bottom half of a man's body and secured at the waist. In the wagon was a body wrapped in a plain white cotton cloth. The wagon was headed for the river bank where the body would be cremated.

As we neared the river, the disconcerting odor of burning flesh was pervasive. Our guide friend took us to an open pavilion on the high riverbank. Several funeral pyres were visible below. The smoke rose and filled my nostrils.

"You see," he said, "after the body is burned, the ashes are thrown into the river. Sometimes the families cannot afford to pay for enough wood so the body does not burn completely."

"What happens then?" I wanted to know.

"Then they will toss the remaining bones into the Ganges," he said matter-of-factly. I struggled with the image, so foreign and outside of my frame of reference. The Catholic Church discouraged, and at one time outlawed, the practice of cremation. But even when practiced in my country, cremation was never out in the open like this. Because of my cultural bias, it felt wrong to me, disrespectful of the dead.

In America, death was hidden and hushed. Dead bodies, if seen before burial, were dressed in nice clothes, with carefully made up faces and neatly styled hair. The bodies lay on satiny beds in dignified caskets. At wakes in New Orleans, always minor family reunions, we waited in quiet lines to pay our last respects to the departed souls and sat in funeral home parlors talking in hushed tones.

The funeral the following day would be a somber affair, unless it was a jazz funeral which celebrated the life of the deceased with music, and in a procession.

In Varanasi, India, death wore a different face. Could both cultures be right? And by what ruler can we measure *cultural correctness*?

As we stood next to the Ganges, I glanced a little farther upstream. Dozens of people occupied the *ghats*, the sacred, wide slab stairways forming the river's embankments. Some were performing ritual ablutions, purifying themselves by bathing, some washing clothes in the river, and some occasionally drinking the murky water. I felt sure some were bound to become ill from it. On the other hand, I felt just as certain that some *wouldn't* become ill because of the strength of their firmly held faith in the powers of this holy river.

Since the Monkey Hill experience in Nepal, my mind was much more adaptable to other realities, and accepting of more possibilities. I now saw faith worlds away from my past viewpoint. My faith was no longer something apart from me, something I kept in a box and took out when I needed it. I felt faith more as a part of my flesh and blood, like one of my senses through which I could interpret the world and grow. And there was certainly no lack of new settings and situations on this subcontinent in which to interpret the good, the bad, the ugly, and the astoundingly beautiful.

One of the sweetest and most beautiful nights I spent in India was in Agra, sleeping on the ground on the lawn of the Taj Mahal, watching it sparkle in the moonlight.

During the day Alex and I examined this awesome white marble structure, originally inlaid with precious and semi-precious stones, including diamonds, sapphires, jade, crystal, jasper, turquoise, cornelian, and lapis lazuli. In later years, many of the stones were stolen, particularly during the Indian Rebellion of 1857 when British soldiers and government officials chiseled some out.

But the Taj remains a jewel in its own right. A blending of Persian, Indian, and Islamic architectural styles, it is a masterpiece. If the Taj were made up of words they would speak incomparable eloquence. The great pyramids astounded me and the Blue Mosque was magnificent, but this fairy tale structure, erected by the Mughal emperor Shah Jahan as a mausoleum for his wife, was a monument to love. To me, it exuded love. Glowing in the sun or moonlight, it is an architectural marvel, and yet it is so much more. It is passion wrapped in stones. I felt the passion as I rubbed my hand over the smooth marble walls of the exterior, and saw the captivating black marble inscriptions and colorful gemstone flowers and swirls inlaid in the creamy white interior walls.

Material for the building was brought from all over India and Central Asia with the help of one thousand elephants. Twenty-thousand workmen took over seventeen years to complete the building on the bank of the river Yamuna. Construction began a year after the death of Mumtaz Mahal, a Persian princess who was the third, and reputedly favorite, wife of Shah Jahan. Even while she was alive, poets wrote about her beauty, gracefulness and compassion. Mumtaz was the trusted companion of the Shah and had a great influence on him. Although she bore fourteen children in their nineteen years together, she managed to travel with her husband throughout the Mughal Empire. In fact, it was while she was with him on one of his military campaigns that she died just after giving birth to their fourteenth child. He was crushed by grief.

As I lay on the ground on this starry, moonlit night gazing at the glorious Taj Mahal, I wondered about the great love this man had had for his wife that caused him to create such a tribute to her. I couldn't know how he treated her while she was alive, but I could easily believe that it was also with great love and passion. I let myself imagine how it might have been to be treated like a queen.

I had always been a sap for romantic tales where the heroine is whisked away by a brave knight on a white horse. Since my childhood, I believed that one day, after all my hard work and devotion, my Prince Charming would come and rescue me. Instead, was I just an observer to the great love stories of others? Was it that Prince Charming really didn't exist, that he didn't exist for me, or that I had been whisked away by a prince of my own fashioning—one who wouldn't put me on a pedestal and would let me be an independent dreamer? If I had truly been "rescued" by a brave knight, would he have let me sleep on the ground? Would I have been able to ride a camel in the desert or climb the foothills of the Himalayas? No, more likely I would be gazing out of a castle window yearning for escape.

We drifted off to sleep with our knapsacks for pillows. They were handy like that. In other places, sleeping in the open, like railroad station platforms where we waited for late night trains, we kept our knapsacks under our heads not only for comfort but also to prevent our belongings from being stolen. This had worked for us so far as a deterrent, although a few other travelers we knew had their knapsack contents stolen from right under their heads.

To fight the tedium of some of the long train rides, we invented games to entertain ourselves and made sport of confounding fellow passengers. Indians have an insatiable curiosity, and weren't shy about asking us whatever questions crossed their minds. They never tired of asking, though we sometimes got tired of answering, so we would make up foolishness to give ourselves a chuckle at their expense.

"Where are you from?" was usually the first question. We had answered this so many times that we occasionally gave the inquirers the name of a fictitious country. Our favorite, Alex's invention, was "Atlas." We pronounced it with the British open "a" sound rather than the flat nasality of the American. Inevitably our fellow passenger would screw up his face and try desperately to place this country of which he had never heard. In the meantime, we would quietly suppress laughs. Maybe that was cruel, but we thought it harmless enough. It broke the monotony and making fun of the world gave us some comic relief.

One day a smiling, dark-eyed Indian man sitting across from us wanted to know, "What is your purpose in traveling?" A fair enough question. His eyes probed our faces, waiting for a response. Because we were a novelty, we had heard this question before. Initially we gave, or tried to give, a straight answer to that question, though this was doubly difficult. First, our answers were insanely involved and mostly incomprehensible to the inquirers, even though English was their second language. Second, we weren't sure of the answer ourselves. When we tired of giving straight answers, again we fabricated them. We could be anybody, because we were traveling incognito. At times, even we didn't know who we were.

Standing in train stations waiting for our next ride, we were often surrounded by a number of men and boys, staring and watching our every move as if we were animals in a zoo. Unabashed, lengthy staring wasn't taboo in India as it is in much of the western world. They stared because we looked very different from them. These staring Indian eyes were ink pools, looking past the surface and peering into our purposes. They weren't undressing us in a sexual manner, as I had experienced on occasion with men in some other places, but they were undressing us in another way. They wanted to see what we were made of. The attention was frequently unnerving though, especially when we were fatigued from a day's travel.

Finally we made it to Bombay and then traveled to Goa to the south, a town in the province of the same name. It was worth the wait. Goa had all the components of a tropical island with long stretches of sandy beaches, tall coconut palm trees, pineapple and mango trees, and glorious open sea air. I had had enough of inland places. This was my element.

Some of our fellow travelers had spread the word about Goa. It was a paradise, they said. It wasn't surprising then to run into a number of Europeans and Americans when we were looking for a beach cottage to rent for a few weeks. The colonial-looking, small building we found backed up to a stand of trees and was just far enough away from the shore to be safe from rising tides. It had two sparsely furnished rooms, a kitchen, and a front porch. Pigs roamed freely outside. Several feet to the rear of the cottage stood an outhouse which was a clear step above the Indian squatter toilets. The place was just what we needed. It was clean and open to the sea.

We arrived during the short "winter" season when daytime temperatures were in the mid-eighties during the day and dropped to cool upper sixties at night. The weather was ideal for us and for the growing itinerant community who became our friends. A short walk took us to the farmer's market in town where we shopped for our meals and snacks of fresh pineapple. The daily routine involved lazy days romping on the beach, and collecting ourselves around a fire at night, telling stories and making music together.

Some of the itinerants opted out of wearing clothes on the beach, much to the dismay of the locals who saw them. A funny circumstance was that in the deep interior of India, some of the populace were quite casual about seminudity. I frequently saw women breast-feeding their babies in full public view, and some older women didn't seem to care if they were covered, but here in Goa it was different.

Ironically, when the Portuguese had barged into Goa in 1510 and defeated the ruling Bijapur kings, establishing a permanent settlement, they found natives often *au natural*. The Portuguese, bringing their Christian mores, eventually converted many of the Goans, and shamed them into modesty. Now, it was absolutely the other way around.

Alex and I didn't go native, but we did join the nightly pow-wows. One day as I was looking through a cabinet in our cottage, I found a six-inch slab of hashish that someone had apparently left behind. It only made sense then to put a chunk of it into cookies I baked and pass them around at the fire circle that night. It proved to be an interesting new experience, with a few revelatory moments and even some funny ones, but it was much too heavy for my liking. The word "stoned" comes to mind, for more reasons than one. It stole my legs and made me feel useless. I didn't see myself making a habit of hash.

While we were in Goa, Alex became distant again. A gregarious type who enjoyed being the center of attention, he found a willing audience with some of the itinerants. Otherwise, he seemed more focused on the fictitious life he had created for himself in the pages of his notebook, hanging out with characters he met in Hemingway novels.

Still, I enjoyed Goa, especially the late afternoon beach ritual of the fishermen not many yards away from where we stayed. Just before sunset every day, they hauled in their catch in the huge nets they had thrown out earlier. Four or five fishermen lined up on either side of the net, each holding a different part of the rope. It was a ballet. Thin, sinewy, leather-skinned men slowly inched backward, keeping pace with the rolling in of the tide. Pull, step back, release, and reach. Pull, step back, release, and reach. Hands moved farther up the rope after each step back and the net came closer to the beach. Finally, a net full of squirming mackerel was laid out on the sand, and people rushed in to buy the fresh catch. On a few occasions I was among them, and we cooked them over an open fire. The fish were delectable.

Every day after sunset, when the air had cooled and residents and itinerants strolled up and down the beach, one mysterious character appeared among them. With his brown leathery skin, he looked Goan and may have been a Goan, but he could just as easily have been from another world, a surreal character dropped from nowhere into the scene of a Hollywood movie, who was there to mentor, or bedevil the protagonist.

Although I never saw him engaged in a conversation with anyone, as he sauntered past me, he looked over, with eyes twinkling and a bemused smile on his face. He sang slowly and deliberately... "*Boo-gal-oo*," only "*Boo-gal-oo...*"

every evening. That was it. The word meant nothing to me, but it flew straight to my heart and perched there like a bird. This stranger knew something I didn't know, or that I didn't know I knew yet. What in the world was it?

CHAPTER 22

No Place Like OM

When I let go of what I am, I become what I might be.
—Lao Tzu

Dr. Swami Gitananda was a lion of a man with a broad, gray-bearded face, framed by long, gray-brown locks and flashing blue eyes. Unlike the thin, frail-looking yogis and gurus I had seen, he was stocky, with a massive barrel chest. Born in northern India of an Indian father and Irish mother, he was a reachable, likeable blend. Because he had spent many years as a physician in Canada, he understood the Western mind. He also understood and respected Hinduism as well as the spirituality at the base of all religions.

Swami founded Ananda Ashram in 1968 when he returned from the West. He was someone who was still in a world I recognized and from whom I could learn. Not that I didn't appreciate and admire the holy men who had forsaken the material world to be better able to dwell in the spiritual one, but I couldn't see myself following that path. I wanted to experience a fuller spiritual life, but from within the framework of the life I was living. Not someone who would drop everything to bow at the feet of a guru, which some teachers might expect, I was happy to discover Swami wasn't looking for that kind of student. Generous with his knowledge, he wanted his students to question and become teachers themselves. Every day, all day, he would guide us through the dining halls of discovery and we would feast as we went.

Alex and I met Swami soon after we arrived in Pondicherry in the province of Tamil Nadu. He smiled as his eyes searched our faces for honest intention. Passing inspection, we were taken across the street to a rudimentary two-story, white-washed, thick-walled building—our home for the next several months. The plaster of Paris walls of the small rooms were unadorned. The floors were bare and there were no beds or other furniture. Our sleeping bags on mats on the floor were our beds, providing all the comfort we needed. We had rested our heads in far worse conditions.

Despite the tropical climate, the rooms had no air conditioning or even fans, but the building's accessible flat roof would provide an escape from the still, hot air in our room, and a lovely bed under the stars.

We began every day at dawn with the practice of hatha yoga, the physical form of yoga that has become most familiar to the western world.

Swami instructed us in all the traditional yoga positions, called *asanas*. In the process I learned the only thing keeping me from accomplishing some of them was holding on too tight, not letting go, and not trusting my body. Despite the fact I was young, healthy, slim, and relatively limber, it took me a few weeks to accomplish the plow pose. Day after day, from the shoulder stand, I lowered my legs over my head toward the floor. And day by day, little by little, I released the muscles in my hips and legs, allowing my toes to finally touch the floor. I was thrilled I could do it because I had never been very athletic. Once I accomplished the plow, my body didn't forget how to do it, how to trust, and how to release those muscles.

As I made similar discoveries with other *asanas,* it became clear the accomplishment of the various postures had everything to do with learning awareness of the body-mind and with releasing control. Yoga's physicality helps to remove bodily obstructions and distractions, facilitating focus and meditation. Although it isn't a religion, yoga enhances the spiritual, and while its aim is mastery over the emotions, it fully engages the heart. This was perfect for me.

"The focus is on awareness," Swami said one day, as he was teaching the more comprehensive, higher level *Raja* Yoga. "It's a four-fold awareness—of the body and how it works, of the emotions and how they use the body, of the mind and how it can control the emotions and the body to transcend itself into higher mind, and of awareness of awareness itself."

At first, it was difficult to decipher and I wondered what Swami was saying. Because I've always been a good student, though, I determined that while I would guard against the possibility of being taken in by a charlatan, I would apply myself and do the best I could to get a new education.

Our fellow students were an odd assortment from a variety of countries and backgrounds. Some were simply curious, while others were serious seekers for whom this ashram was the next logical step. Whatever the original motivation, we were captivated not only by what Swami had to offer, but also by what he was able to draw out of each of us, the mark of an excellent teacher. I wanted a guide and mentor, but not someone to whom I would relinquish the sovereignty of my life. This worked out well for me at Ananda Ashram, where Swami didn't pretend godhood. While he had a strong personality that commanded respect, he exalted wisdom, not himself. I felt directed to adhere to the truth I recognized in his words.

Among the students were some remarkable people, like Eliezar, a paraplegic from Israel. He sat on the floor on a mat like the rest of us and did many of the *asanas.* He had a finely developed power of insight and great personal warmth, and didn't let his crippled legs cripple his mind or make him any less whole.

And there was Clara, a sixty-three-year-old woman who met Swami in Canada. Vibrant and youthful looking, except for her long gray hair, she was the one who led the pack when the class climbed a tall hill to get a better view at a Hindu festival field trip. She was a role model for me.

One day she spoke to the group about childbirth. She had delivered her babies at home naturally, without drugs and without fear. "There's nothing to be afraid of," she said. "Our bodies were built to do this, and women have been delivering their babies naturally since the beginning of time."

Clara showed us a book she carried with her called *Childbirth Without Fear,* written by a British doctor named Grantly Dick-Read. In it, the good doctor explained the psychology of fear about childbirth and how to combat it. Based on sound research, the theory, greatly simplified here, is that fear, fed by generations of old wives' tales and poor health practices, is responsible for the biggest part of the pain involved in childbirth and delivery. There is little reason, Dick-Read said, except for ill health or mechanical abnormality, a woman shouldn't be able to deliver a child naturally and happily.

While it's true some women cannot safely deliver at home, the author impressed me with two realities. First, the infant mortality rate in the United States, where most babies are born in the hospital, is higher than in England where many are born at home. Second, in England, it is common practice for the midwife to have a mobile emergency unit outside of the home of a woman giving birth, just in case medical intervention is needed.

I was happy to hear this information. While living in San Francisco, I had met a bright, strong, independent woman who delivered her two babies in her apartment, assisted only by her husband and a friend. I admired her and decided then if I ever had a baby, I would do it that way. Clara's introduction to this book reaffirmed my belief and doubled my determination. I began to comprehend what it meant to gain control by letting go.

Each day at the ashram was a new learning experience, exciting to me as I started to see how all the parts fit together. Life began to make sense when I learned yoga is a science, an artful science, and is much more than something you *do,* but is a way of living a balanced, conscious, integrated life.

Swami's teachings were based on the *Yoga Sutras*, the writings of Patanjali, an Indian physician of more than two thousand years ago, who codified the philosophy and practice of yoga. The sutras offered a blueprint for living a right life and achieving harmony and freedom.

Swami didn't allow us any props or shortcuts in the performance of some challenging *asanas*. His approach was structured and methodical as he guided us through them, and through a process of sense withdrawal, in preparation for concentration and meditation.

A wealth of knowledge and wisdom flowed through him, effortlessly and unpretentiously, as he spoke without contradictions or lapses, and without notes, as if he had a direct connection to cosmic consciousness. And yet as I absorbed and practiced what was being imparted, it was less like learning than it was of recognizing the truth.

Once a week just before dawn we walked to the beach for sunrise yoga on the sand, including an expansive and nourishing *Surya Namascara*, a salute to the sun, done as a flowing series of poses. Throughout the day we followed a regimen of sessions on various aspects of the whole.

We learned how to truly relax. We learned how to "walk" on someone's back to adjust it, and practiced other forms of body manipulation, all very gentle and enormously gratifying. We learned about philosophy of the ancients and about *ayurveda*, a holistic form of medicine whose emphasis is on the natural prevention of disease. We practiced mantras and various mind cleansers. We learned about nutrition and the effects of different foods on the body. We did fasts and internal body cleansing.

I learned to enjoy the meatless, eggless, and all-but dairy-less meals, prepared by the Indians who worked at the ashram. Meals included a tortilla-like flatbread called a *chappati*, and rice and vegetables, mostly *dhal*—a yellow split pea dish cooked almost to a mush. When we had fruit, it was usually a banana. Although this was a fairly ascetic diet, I usually ate my fill. I was also being nourished in other ways. "Meat will make a scientist, but never a philosopher," Swami reminded us.

Various teachers of yoga emphasize different approaches, any of which might work, depending on the teacher and the student's commitment. I believed the approach at Ananda Ashram was the best for me.

Down the road from our ashram, at the western end of town, was Aurobindo Ashram where the prevailing approach was Bhakti Yoga, or the yoga of devotion. That ashram had its beginning in the early 1900s when Sri Aurobindo developed a method of spiritual practice he called Integral Yoga. There, devotion to the Supreme was channeled through the personage of "The Mother," a Frenchwoman who helped Aurobindo start his ashram.

Unlike Ananda, Aurobindo Ashram wasn't a quiet retreat. There were no obligatory practices, rituals, or systematic instruction. Members were provided all the necessities of daily life, including food, clothing, shelter, and medical care. In exchange, they did a certain amount of the productive work of the ashram, accompanied by surrender to the Divine Force so it might work in their transformation.

At Ananda Ashram, life was also full, but simple. It was an ascetic, frugal, slow-paced, ponderous, eye-opening, soul-searching, profoundly instructive, wonder-filled, and happy experience.

Until now, I had been a stranger to my body, almost a stranger to my soul. I had depended on a third party to be an intermediary between me and the Divine, but in Pondicherry I became able to recognize and communicate with the Divine dwelling within me. I began to keep my own counsel.

At the ashram I learned how to be quiet, to listen, and to be the observing self, a non-judgmental self that could, when I allowed it to, be free of self-pity, self-loathing, or self-importance. In the next few years that skill would be sorely needed and sorely tried.

CHAPTER 23

The Gods Invited

A journey is like a marriage. The certain way to be wrong is to think you control it.
—John Steinbeck

When you walk through the streets of India you must be prepared to confront yourself in myriad forms, like beggars who really and truly beg. "*Bakshish, bakshish,*" they implore with unfathomably deep dark eyes, often set in nearly skeletal bodies.

You soften and put a few rupees into an outstretched hand, only to find minutes later, word of your gift has spread to other beggars who now trail you. By nature you are generous, or so you thought. By nature, you are compassionate and your heart breaks a thousand times, imagining that you or someone you love were the beggar. You can't possibly give to them all, or you could give away everything you own and become a beggar with them. Where do you stop? When do you close your eyes, refusing to see any more? Our friend Rudolph sometimes dealt with the question by turning around and, with a flick of his hand towards the beggars, yelling, "*Ya lah.*" Go away.

The number of beggars in India was staggering. I was told one of the contributing factors to so much beggary was even if these people could find jobs, their pay would be less than they could make begging.

Hardest to confront were the child beggars. It was rumored some were maimed by their own mothers in order for them to elicit more sympathy and be more effective at their daily task. I wondered how a mother could do that to her child. Could it be she had no alternative for the survival of her family? Based in fact or not, these questions were beyond the usual thought-scope of most people I knew. They certainly were beyond mine.

At times I felt like Dorothy in the Wizard of Oz. Before discovering the truth that would take her home, she had to first confront her fears and certain aspects of her character, as seen in her friends Scarecrow, Tin Man, and Cowardly Lion.

"Don't pay any attention to the man behind the curtain," said the counterfeit wizard, trying to derail her intentions, but it was too late. The curtain was pulled back for me, and I couldn't look away. True, I didn't know all the answers, but I had a growing cache of questions.

In a quest to explore, Alex and I one day rented bicycles and rode them far out into the countryside. We had a small picnic there, as well as our second encounter with lysergic acid. Our first 'trip' in Kathmandu had opened a new door into the universe for me, not a different universe, but an expanded and exploded one, seeing life as a movie in four dimensions. It was at once an exploration of the macrocosm and the microcosm, an interpretation of the whole of life by scrutinizing its minutest parts.

A friend had sent us from the States a couple of doses of LSD on tiny strips of paper. We decided to put on our lab coats once more. This time wasn't as dramatic as the last. The landscape was more familiar. I recognized the earth as my home, my beautiful and magical home. I wasn't disoriented, but rather super-oriented. I was able to function quite well in it. In fact, never in my life had I felt as clear-headed, strong, magnificently healthy, and capable as I felt that afternoon.

After our picnic, while we were riding back to town, we soon found ourselves in the midst of throngs of people walking in the same direction. I got off my bike and pushed it as I walked. I had total focus and felt as if I could walk forever. I was a walking machine with no interference, no sore feet, and no tiredness, only walking. As in Kathmandu, I *became* the walking. I felt limitless energy and recognized my purpose at the time to be only to walk, just as the throngs were doing, just as we all do, through life.

"What is your purpose in traveling?" the Indian man on the train had wanted to know, and I still had no satisfactory answer. Perhaps no one answer was more satisfactory than another, and I agreed with the French writer Anais Nin who suggested there is no universal meaning of life, but only the meaning we give to it.

As we all seek, discover, and invent meaning, we travel, walking down myriad paths. We are all transients, even those of us who stay in one place all our lives, thinking we are stable and secure. We walk, choose places, partners, and to a great extent, experiences. We certainly choose our attitudes towards them.

For better or worse, Alex and I had chosen each other. Nearing the end of our Yoga Teacher Training course in Pondicherry, we decided to make a formal commitment to a path together for our future. We talked about children and wanted them to be a part of that future. Why not begin the future here? Our Indian visas were almost expired, but we wanted to get married at the ashram, and we would try for another visa extension.

After first clearing our intentions with Swami, who was delighted with the ashram wedding idea, we started preparations.

I shopped for my wedding dress at a little open-air, street-side seamstress shop. Indian brides don't wear white, but colorful saris instead. I bought a deep satiny green, sari. I would wear sandals on my feet. Alex needed only a simple shirt and a *lungi,* a cloth wrapped sarong-style at the waist.

The person we chose to perform our ceremony was our fellow yogi and friend, Richard. A tall, slender, dark-haired, dimpled, and mustachioed American, he was always smiling, or grinning, as if he knew a secret nobody else did. He had a barbershop quartet look about him. Richard was a Universal Life Church Minister, a calling that has significance depending on the genuineness and reverence given it by the particular minister. Reverend Richard was genuine and his signature would be enough to satisfy legal obligations.

The wedding would happen as a special part of the evening *satsang,* the nightly meditative assembly designed to collect the day's blessings and wisdom into one celebratory whole. This was perfect because that night Alex and

I would not only be joining forces with each other, but also with the entire ashram.

On the morning of our wedding, Swami, Alex and I walked to the Shiva Temple to have a ritualistic, symbolic bath in the *Ganga Peeth,* a shallow pool in the temple, to invite the gods to be present for our ceremony that evening. For that, I wore a white, gauzy sari which I held up as we stepped up to our ankles into the pool.

Clara was the surrogate mother of the bride, an honor which I was sure pained by mother to miss. That night, before the ceremony began, three local Indian ladies, friends of the ashram congregation, helped me to dress, pulled my hair into a kind of bun, and made up my eyes with dark eye liner.

The woman with the steadiest and nimblest fingers skillfully applied a pinch of vermillion powder in a perfect circle on my forehead, just between my eyebrows. This *bindi,* the sign of a married woman, is said to usher in prosperity. It holds added significance for students of yoga. Placed at the point of the sixth *chakra* or energy center, this spot is said to retain energy and control concentration. I hoped it would. Looking in a mirror, I didn't recognize myself.

We entered the room and sat together in the place of honor, on cushions on the floor, in the midst of all of our ashram friends, and Swami. With the sweet fragrance of sandalwood incense wafting in the air, two Indian temple drummers played their *tablas* and chanted. It was a lovely tableau, and not one I would have ever dreamed of as my wedding.

Swami presided over the Hindu portion of the ceremony, speaking words of wisdom and unity. Alex and I fed each other cubes of sugar to make a sweeter life, and then the unconventionally western part of the ceremony began.

Reverend Richard, our minister and fellow student, read the ceremony and marriage 'vows' Alex had written, without my input. When Alex requested the task I had left it to him because I was confident his words would be beautiful, and they were—beautifully crafted.

Apart from the general call for the congregation to join with us in celebration and a reminder to them that this marriage should not serve to set us apart from them, I wasn't prepared for the stipulations and admonitions Alex had included.

The minister read Alex's words: "...I would like to remind them both, that a marriage is a vehicle of joint evolution. This evolution may be slow or rapid, but if either Alex or Carroll uses this legal sanction as a chain of entrapment or as a club of subservience, one to the other, instead of for the elevated nature for which this sanction is intended, then I declare the Cosmic Union terminated and the legal contract invalid pending certification by the civil authorities."

As the ceremony continued, at least some of the words were heartening and inspirational, like the appeal for us to promise "... to seek daily for renewed union with the Higher Self in each other," and "to seek nourishment from the stream of life as it passes through your partner, and replenish that stream as it passes through yourself, thus finding sight through each other's eyes that you may see as one..."

But then, what was apparently of utmost concern to Alex, was this: "Will you weigh always against the banality that, in time, robs the best companionship of flavor?"

I thought marriage was supposed to be for better or worse, in sickness and in health, till *death*, not *banality,* do us part. What was I getting myself into? What kind of bond was I agreeing to? It was as if Alex's main intent were to leave himself escape clauses, rather than to declare an undying love.

Even the conventional ceremony words of culmination, "I now declare you husband and wife," had been changed to "I now declare you whole in the Universe."

The most promising words of the whole ceremony to me were that our marriage might "forever be Divine reunion," and that Eternal celebration might reign. That's what I held onto. Although Alex's words didn't sound like ones of devotion to a woman with whom he was head over heels in love, I settled for what I did hear.

I was hoping as time went on, so would his devotion increase. His eyes would open to the wonder of his bride. He would be willing and ready to do anything to keep her, protect her, and love her. Wasn't that what every woman wanted of her man?

I could wait.

In the meantime, we were forced to leave India because our visas had expired. Although we pestered immigration officials to extend them, they refused. There wasn't enough time for the Indian bureaucracy to process our marriage certificate before we left, so we left married in the eyes of the Divine, but not in the eyes of man.

I had been hoping by the time we left India I might have a third member of our family growing inside me. We both wanted children, and when I missed my period, which almost never happened, I had a pregnancy test done. But when a few of the other women at the ashram had missed periods too and all of our tests came back negative, I had to attribute the missed period to the drastic change in diet and lifestyle. Though I was a little disappointed, I felt fine.

It wasn't long after the wedding when Alex and I collected our things, said good-bye to Swami and our ashram friends, and climbed aboard a third-class car on an outbound train.

CHAPTER 24

Sidetracked

Let us become the change we seek in the world.
—Mohandas Gandhi

On our slow moving train, heading north from Madras, I stared out of a wide-open window. As I watched now familiar scenes appearing and reappearing, dirt-poor people in a dirt-poor countryside stared back, piercing my heart.

In my five plus months in India, I had crossed the country on her rails, eaten her curries, yielded to her sacred cows, peered into the ebony eyes of her beggars, abided the unabashed stares of her ever-curious, worn her saris, lived in her ashram, and married my traveling partner.

If personal change could be measured in inches, I would have needed several yardsticks to account for my time here. Some changes I might not realize for years to come, but I knew living in this vast, close-to-the-bone nation, and absorbing the tenets of yoga had profoundly affected me. I had had a total lifeblood transfusion. No matter where I went or what I did, even if I ignored the yoga I learned, I knew that it would always be with me.

The wisdom living within each of us, I discovered, often lay buried beneath layers of conditioning, prejudice, egotism, fear, disregard, inattention, and what Hinduism called *chitta vritti*—non-stop chatter and clutter in the mind. I wanted to be clear. I could see a right path ahead, yet I knew I would need help to stay on it.

Still, I realized an important element of wisdom is keeping a sense of humor about everything. Life could be unbearable without it. As metal screeched against metal when we braked into one town after another, I had to laugh at some of the signs I saw. "Govindh Razor blades—sold everywhere—and here too," one said. I chuckled, took notes, and added it to my funny bank for use in an emergency. Who knew when I might need to make an emergency withdrawal in the near or distant future when I needed a grin?

I should have made a quick withdrawal when we left India, passed through Pakistan, and arrived once more in Afghanistan. In no other place had I encountered such a paucity of humor than in this rugged nation. Even the mountains looked forbidding.

Almost all of the women were under the veil, and I wondered sometimes what their faces looked like. What expressions did they wear? What did they think of me whose face was not covered? Was there contempt, disgust, or envy at my freedom? Did they live in fear and sadness? Their worlds were so small compared to mine. Or were they? Perhaps strict adherence to their social and religious code had won them more expansive freedom within. I would never know, because without a common language or opportunity, we couldn't talk.

By contrast, the men I saw were striking in their rigid bearing, long, colorless clothes, and turban-wrapped heads. Many had rifles slung over their shoulders. They seemed taller than they really were. I felt uncomfortable, even intimidated by them, and I couldn't imagine tangling with one. Some stared stonily out of eyes that have seen only harsh lives. No laugh lines scored their faces. In the bazaar, I didn't hear laughter or banter from anyone; it was all such serious business. Shopping was never a sport here, but was carried on only out of necessity.

Westerners, especially Americans, had the luxury of laughter. Even in the aftermath of disasters or when we were totally down and out, we frequently uncovered something to make us laugh. Often it was ourselves and our plights. Could it be that our plights, day in and day out, year in and year out, century in and century out, had never been as trying as those of some populations like Afghanistan's? Or was it that we westerners had a "funny bone" in our skeletons, in our very elbows, which they lacked?

Change was slowly creeping into Kabul, some good and some not, depending on the perspective. There were noticeably more Westerners on the streets now, and many more who had passed through. This caused a mutation in the old method of marketplace negotiating for prices—at least it did for foreigners.

The last time we were in Kabul, I understood bargaining was the custom and rule of the marketplace. No one was ever expected to pay the initial asking price of a thing. On the second day of this visit though, I was confronted by a change when I saw a cloth bag I admired and asked the price.

"Fifty *afghanis*," the vendor threw out.

After a thoughtful pause to figure how much that translated into American dollars, I countered with "Twenty-five."

But my merchant didn't counter. He only shook his head and repeated, "Fifty *afghanis*". I tried again. He was immovable, and unflinching in his stare. Finally, he shrugged one of his shoulders, stuck out his bottom lip and said, "You like, you buy; you no like, you no buy."

By now, too many Westerners had plunked down exactly what the vendors initially asked. They had ruined the game, I thought at first. On the other hand, the merchants had begun to learn how the larger marketplace and capitalism worked, and maybe it would be good for them. I caved in and handed him my *afghanis*. It was still a good price for the bag.

The water system in Kabul left a lot to be desired. Truthfully, it left *everything* to be desired. Small open ditches carried wastewater from the small cafes and shops in the downtown area. When I saw one tea shop worker rinsing glasses in a ditch, I could only imagine what immunities these people had acquired over the years, even boiling the water before drinking. I supposed Alex and I had built up certain immunities too, but we decided to confine our eating to the dining area of our little hotel on the square. Because I didn't know and didn't want to know what happened in the kitchen, I could enjoy the meals we ate there. The *pilaf* made with carrots and raisins, minus the lamb, was my favorite.

On our third day in Afghanistan, we took a side trip northward to explore another area. Riding in a reconditioned, barely-running American school bus we traveled fourteen miles west of *Mazar-e Sharif* and we exited at Balkh, one of the oldest cities of the world. The Indo-Iranian tribes had moved here between 2000 and 1500 B.C. For several centuries the city played an important role in the spread of the Aryan civilization and in the development of Persian language and literature. Many early Persian works were written by poets from Balkh. At one time, Balkh was also the center of Zoroastrianism. Zoroaster first preached his religion here, and this is where he died.

Balkh held extensive ruins, including several miles of ancient wall, some Buddhist reliquary mounds, and Islamic shrines and mosques. All that remained of Afghanistan's oldest mosque, the *Masjid-e No Gombad*, were a few arches, yet the lingering history clothed the area in intrigue.

Rummaging around the grounds as I was wont to do, I found small bits of broken pottery in the dirt and picked up a few blue and brown shards to keep for souvenirs. Although their actual age was a mystery, I told myself I had just pocketed tiny pieces of the town once captured by Alexander the Great and destroyed by Genghis Kahn. I had a pocketful of history. With these small treasures, we headed back to Kabul to regroup.

The next day I awoke feeling rundown and sickly with the beginning of a sore throat. I took myself down to a shop a few doors away from our hotel. Its function was a pharmacy, although it was indistinguishable as one.

Unlike American pharmacies, this one didn't carry items other than medicinal concoctions. The unadorned walls of the small shop had no shelves displaying accessible products in neatly labeled packages. Instead, customers had to ask the clerk at the counter for something specific.

Here again, hand gestures were invaluable. Greeting the man behind the counter, I then used my best actress skills, pointing to my throat and pantomiming pain. Seeming to understand, he pulled out some small package and handed it to me. I paid what he asked and left.

When I got back to the hotel room, I looked more carefully at the package. Something told me it wasn't what I needed. Whether it was or not, I was afraid to try it, and decided not to open it. Common sense said to throw it away and count it as a small loss. Instead, I determined to take it back to the pharmacy for a refund.

What was I thinking? This was not the United States where in many stores you could return or exchange almost anything, a practice Americans took for granted. I knew better, but I foolishly made up my mind to go back to the pharmacy. When I walked up to the counter and tried to communicate to the clerk what I wanted to do, he didn't understand, or in my mind, he didn't *want* to understand. I gave him back the box of whatever it was.

I tried a few times to get him to refund my money, and then, I don't know what came over me, but I lost my mind. Suddenly I became someone for whom I had no tolerance and always avoided associating with abroad—a true ugly American.

In my defense, if there could be any defense, I was sick, I was having a bad day, and I was feeling frustrated at not understanding the language or of being understood. I was missing my home and my culture, missing certain creature comforts, and missing little things like the relative ease with which many normal activities such as shopping were accomplished.

The more I insisted the more adamant and fiery-eyed the clerk became. He wouldn't budge, and I wouldn't quit. By now ridiculously unreasonable and enraged, I was resolved that one way or another, this was a battle I needed to win. After one final try and his last refusal, something in me snapped.

Scanning the counter in front of me, I noticed a cheap paperweight type object. I quickly snatched the thing, glared at my adversary in defiance, and bolted out the door. I had never done anything like this before, always strenuously avoiding confrontation. Clearly I was out of my mind, yet I immediately recognized the stupidity and peril of what I had done.

Once outside, glancing to my right and seeing Alex standing in front of a building a few doors down, I ran to him. "Alex, I'm in trouble!" I yelled, hysterically.

Seconds later, an Afghan policeman showed up behind me and ushered us both back to the store. The clerk stood there taller and angrier, arms folded in front of his chest, feet in a wall-like, wide stance. Standing beside me, Alex urged me forward with my ill-gotten object.

Carefully placing the paperweight on the counter, and now more scared than anything else, I gestured my apology to the scowling clerk. With eyes narrowed at me, he nodded. The policeman tilted his head in the direction of the door, and we happily took the hint *out*.

We took the hint *all the way out* of the country. The next morning, we boarded a westward bus and rode it to the end of its line.

We bought tickets for a train through Tehran, Iran to Turkey, and introduced ourselves to a few other Westerners on the boarding platform. Max and Danielle, a young couple from Amsterdam, spoke English fluently. They, and thin blond California surfer Tom, quickly agreed to share a sitting room with us. With the compartment to ourselves, we were shielded from curious eyes and relieved of the weight of struggling to communicate. We talked easily for hours.

In Tehran where we had a layover of several hours before changing trains, the five of us naturally spent the time together and went walking in the middle of the downtown area. We shared the wide sidewalks with swarms of other people.

Although Danielle's and my arms and legs were properly covered, we still stood out from the crowd. Apparently many men here held a dim view of Western women, as they weren't at all subtle in demonstrating their lack of respect. My blond hair made me a special target.

As we walked and talked, an Iranian man approaching from the opposite direction made a point of passing very close to me, and exactly at the time of passing, jutting his elbow out at the level of my left breast. After his cheap thrill, he quickly moved away. This angered me, but I didn't say anything. What could I do? Alex was behind me talking to Max, unaware of what had just happened.

We walked on. Within a few blocks, astoundingly, it happened again. This time, though, I was infuriated. I pushed back the man's elbow and shouted. He ran. Seeing what had happened, Alex ran after and caught the man, who was dressed nicely in European slacks and collared shirt. Although he was a few inches taller than Alex and far outweighed him, Alex grabbed him by the front of his shirt and yelled in his face. At this point, the perpetrator drew back and slapped Alex across the face. No one expected that reaction, least of all Alex, and it prompted a rapid chain reaction.

A number of men stopped in their tracks, curious about what was going on, and the crowd quickly swelled. The five of us were surrounded and swallowed up where we stood in this busy intersection. Driven by mob instinct, a few of the now incensed men took the opportunity to grab and hit at Max and Tom. Others yelled and thrust their fists into the air. It was as if someone had struck a match and dropped it onto a pile of dry leaves. Overcome with fear, Danielle and I stood frozen, as close to each other as possible, shivering. What was going to happen to us and to our men? Was this going to be the way my odyssey ended? Was this going to be the way our lives ended? Completely vulnerable, we knew there was nothing we could do. The fray grew, taking on a life of its own.

Fortunately, a policeman on foot patrol came to the rescue, squelched the chaos, and broke up the crowd. Everyone was still standing and thankfully no one suffered any serious injuries. The officer took our party and the original perpetrator to the police station. Eventually, we saw a magistrate who spoke some English, and we explained what had transpired. He acted as if this were a common occurrence, telling us nonchalantly if we wanted to press charges, we would have to stay until the next day to do it. Because no one had been seriously hurt in the scuffle and no one wanted to spend the night in Tehran or become embroiled in some local civil battle, we declined.

Instead, we asked if the offender could be made to pay for the men's shirts he and others had torn. It was agreed, and we left the station. We used the money to buy ourselves lunch.

We were thankful the rest of the trip was calm and we all breathed sighs of relief when we stepped off the train in Turkey, which now felt like the west again. We exchanged addresses before going our separate ways, the Dutch couple back to Amsterdam, Tom back to the States, and Alex and I to Israel where we hoped to work as volunteers on a kibbutz.

CHAPTER 25
A Sense of Place

Destiny is not a matter of chance; it is a
matter of choice; it is not a thing
to be waited for; it is a thing to be achieved.
—William Jennings Bryan

"*Boker tov*! ...*Boker tov*!" THE guard barked as he banged the butt of his AK-47 rifle against the door frame of the raised wooden cabin where we slept. It was 4 a.m., and the wake-up call was jolting. I hadn't finished my sleep and was disoriented when I opened my eyes on that first morning at Kibbutz Yehi'am.

Except for the Sabbath and Sunday, this was the daily wake up call for the volunteers, sharing barracks-type cabins on the woodsy grounds of this communal farm. Once roused, we made a forty or fifty-yard sprint in the pre-dawn darkness down a footpath to the bathroom and shower facilities. We started work in the orchards at dawn, finishing early in order to avoid the unbearably hot afternoon sun.

Barely three years had passed since the cease-fire after the Six-Day War. Hostilities between Israel and her Arab neighbors were still in the air. They never ceased. The normalcy of everyday life co-existed with the threat of explosions on buses or other violent eruptions, and with soldiers ever visible in the streets, always ready to respond. This was the atmosphere we found in the clean, wide, busy streets of Haifa. We had arrived by ship from southern Turkey in June.

Right away I liked Haifa, perhaps because of my affinity for port cities—the breathable air, the open-ended invitation of the sea, the special brand of commerce, and the exciting mix and industry of the people. But in this place, I could also sense the resolute spirit of the Israelis, determined to work, build, and embrace a positive future for themselves in spite of the threats to it.

Since its establishment as a nation in 1948, Israel had fought for its survival, but the country didn't look like a war zone. It had much to offer and explore, and Alex and I intended to explore as much as we could before offering ourselves as live-in volunteer workers.

First we contacted Per and Ruthie, a couple whose names had been given to us by Max and Danielle, and who would, at least temporarily, be our touchstones in Israel. They welcomed us into their home in Kiryat Tivon, in the hills outside of Nazareth. Here we had our introduction to rural Israel, beautifully wooded and green, and not the desert landscape I expected.

"You see all these trees," Ruthie remarked, as they chauffeured us around various sites. "This used to be mostly desert after the woods were destroyed." She was referring to a time before Israel became a nation and the land had been ravaged. The Jewish nation reforested the area.

Per, a biologist who worked as a bird watcher for the Israeli government, had an extremely powerful pair of government-issue binoculars. Because our stay coincided one night with the appearance of a full moon, Per drove Alex and me up a hill where we could have a clear view of it. Looking through those binoculars, I was surprised to see not only the shadows of the craters on its surface, but also the outlines of the craters on its otherwise round edges. It looked as near as a ceiling light.

I remembered the Apollo moon landing and the skepticism among the elderly in Thailand about its validity. Looking at the moon this night erased any doubt in my mind that such a feat was possible. If I could just stretch my arm out I could probably touch the moon. And why not? If I had reached moons so distant within me, why couldn't I reach one outside of me?

Visiting the Sea of Galilee with our new friends also called for an illusory adjustment. In my mind, a sea was a sea, a very large body of water, but this Galilean water before me was not a sea at all. It was a freshwater lake, much smaller than my Louisiana's Lake Pontchartrain, which is about forty miles in length and twenty-four miles in width. The 'lake' at Galilee measures only thirteen miles by eight miles. I could almost see the other side of it from where we stood. Yet Galilee was described in the Bible as the place where Jesus called the fishermen to be his disciples, where he calmed the sea, and where he walked on water—events much grander than a lake might host, or so I believed.

Remarkably, we human beings sometimes hold images in our minds that are far removed from reality, especially current reality. As an adult, visiting the home of my childhood, I found it much smaller than I had remembered. Although the size discrepancy could be attributed to the disparity between the child and adult versions of me, I wondered if it weren't also true that places, like troubles, shrank as the time and distance between them and us grew. Did places themselves change? What once allegedly happened at Galilee made it what it was then, but now it was no longer that place.

Though I tried to go back in time, my mind balked at the task. For me, the Sea of Galilee didn't exist anymore, except as fable. On its quiet lakeshore, we sat and ate lunch, skipped rocks across the water, and then moved on.

Of course we visited Old City Jerusalem, a place suffused with the piety and presence of all three major religions that claim it. Roaming the narrow cobblestone streets was not only roaming through ancient history, but was also walking through pages of the Bible, replete with its conflicting interpretations.

As a child and teenager, I had dutifully walked the symbolic Way of the Cross in church dozens of times during the seasons of Lent. I was told this path was the one Jesus had walked on the way to his crucifixion. Now as I stepped along the real *Via Dolorosa* to the Church of the Sepulcher, the holiest of Christian sites, I let their heaviness envelop me. Countless pilgrims intentionally made their way here. Even though we were among the throngs, we were *accidental pilgrims*, if there could be such a thing.

At the *Wailing Wall*, I was moved by the constant flow of petitioners for God's ear. Coming face to face with the tangle of stories and legends from various traditions in this region, I wondered where Truth ended and Myth began. Did they overlap? Were they interchangeable from one culture to another?

I thought about these things and about my place in the whole scheme of things as we overlooked Jerusalem from the slope of the Mount of Olives, unrolled our sleeping bags onto the ground, and took our night's rest under the stars.

Every new view of every place I traveled offered me the opportunity to discover something about myself—information I may have resisted seeing or accepting before, whether my nobility or dishonor, selfishness, or even treachery. Consequently, the same information was often presented to me in different ways in different locations until I understood it. Although some people don't need to travel geographically to learn about the world as reflected in their eyes, apparently I did. Perhaps I simply found it more interesting to *find* myself in exotic, beautiful, or even dangerous places.

The truth, as I understood it, was whatever we are seeing, we are only recognizing it as part of our own makeup, whether the good, the bad, or the ugly. And if believing is seeing, we decide, whether consciously or subconsciously, what we want to see before we actually do. Thus, I continued my search for the song inside, and continued to find it, sometimes in unlikely places.

From an office in Tel Aviv, we were directed to an agency that was a clearinghouse for kibbutzim workers.

"Yes, we certainly do need more help," a friendly administrator told us. "There is a kibbutz in the north that has just requested a few people. I think you will like it."

Armed with an address, contact information, and a hand-drawn map, we left her office and boarded a bus for the hinterlands. It was early June when we arrived at *Kibbutz Yehi'am* in the upper Galilee region of Israel, east of the coastal town of Nahariya, and just a few miles from the Lebanese border.

Ester, a stocky, middle-aged, fiery redhead, met us. She was bright, articulate, and passionate. She had a sixteen-year-old, equally luminescent son, by the name of *Yakov,* Jacob to us. Ester was fluent in English, as was *Yakov*, and it was among her responsibilities to welcome, orient, and situate kibbutz volunteers. She obviously enjoyed and was good at her job.

Sitting in Ester's office, we heard a lively explanation of kibbutz life. It was a true working farm with pear and banana orchards, tobacco fields, and drying sheds. There were immense chicken houses and a processing plant for manufacturing chicken hot dogs.

All the members took part in the farming, domestic, or administrative work of the place. *Yehi'am* was a collective community providing economic and familial support for its members. Members were employed according to the need and their suitability for the job, whether driving a tractor, cooking in the communal dining hall, teaching children, running the processing plant, or managing an office. Jobs could also change from time to time.

Ester told us the kibbutzim originated from necessity. Groups banded together in order to have a livelihood, and protection for its members. Economically and socially, independent farming made less sense in these times.

What she described sounded to me like socialism, minus the power structure. I knew that socialism as a form of government had never been successful, for a number of reasons, including its inherent de-motivation of the people. It did seem to be working here though, on this small scale. Perhaps it was because the way of life on the kibbutz was inspired by the Zionist ideology which embraced equality, mutual help, farming, building the land, and the re-establishment of Jewish settlements. These people had a common motivation and zeal I had not seen anywhere else.

The farm was owned and managed by its worker-members. What made it especially interesting to me, and undoubtedly more workable, was that it was governed by direct democracy. Everyone had a part in the discussion and decision-making, even concerning which jobs individuals would have. All the members shared in the profits of the farm, received a monthly allowance, and were provided with basic needs from housing and healthcare to meals and transportation.

Ester took us to the dining hall, a large, clean, efficient place where everyone went for daily meals, if they chose. No one paid to eat. In addition, the adults all had apartments with little kitchens where they could cook instead. To me this sounded ideal. After a hard day's work, if I wanted a good meal, I could have one waiting for me, and I wouldn't have to clean up the kitchen afterwards.

One of the greatest benefits of life on the kibbutz was the safety of the children. Because of the never-ending conflict, Ester explained, many of the children might lose their parents. On the kibbutz all adults were parent figures, so the loss of a parent was not as devastating for the children as it might otherwise be. They really were one big family, she said, and the children learned to be independent, because they had to grow up fast. So that we might see firsthand what she meant, Ester took us to a modest house.

"This is where our three and four-year-olds live," she said proudly as we walked into the dining area of the house. Pint-sized people were setting the low, elfin dining tables. One of the housemothers showed us around the sleeping quarters, play rooms, and bathrooms, where even the sinks and toilets were at child level. Everything was designed for the children to be able to do as much as they could for themselves.

They learn self-sufficiency early, Ester explained, "and they do well."

Each of the other age groups had their houses as well, including the infants. Special accommodations were made for nursing mothers. I tried to imagine what this would be like, and I suggested to Ester it must be hard for the parents not to have their children live with them.

"Every evening after dinner, the children spend a few hours at their parents' apartments," she said. "It's for the good of everybody."

To prove her point, Ester knocked on the door of one couple's apartment. They were all smiles when we went in. Ester repeated my concern to these parents, but they shrugged it off.

"Look," the mother said, "we do what we have to do, but we like this. It works out fine, all things considered. You see, when our children come to visit in the evening, we don't have to bother with making them do their homework or do chores or anything else. They just visit and we enjoy each other's company." She laughed. "Maybe it's the ideal situation."

I doubted I could handle this kind of situation if one day I had children, even if it did make them stronger. Yet, in the days, weeks, and months that followed, I became impressed by the strength, independence, maturity, and spirit of the children brought up in these conditions. They were surrounded by love, their self-esteem was healthy, and they were self-disciplined and self-directed.

Some of the fifteen and sixteen-year old *kibbutzniks* in charge of the various volunteer work crews handled their jobs as well as any thirty-year old. It was easy to have intelligent conversations with them about life, war, their country, and their futures. By comparison, I thought about the frivolous lives our American teenagers lived, my own adolescence included. Even though I came from the lower end of the economic ladder, my parents were hard workers. Like everyone I knew, we didn't have much, yet we did have the luxury of a safe and stable environment, making the lighter side of life our prevailing approach.

On the kibbutz, it was refreshing to be with a group of people with a high level of intelligence and commitment to productive and purposeful lives. This made it easier for me to commit to the very early wake up calls and physical labor, which, although unpaid, still had considerable rewards.

Five days a week, we awoke before dawn and hurried to the dining hall for a 4:30 pre-breakfast snack of fresh juicy tomatoes, sliced bell peppers, and cheese. We were assigned to a particular work area for the day, primarily in the fields, depending on the need, and we loaded ourselves into the back of a truck to be driven to the site.

On the way, the truck radio often played music from Europe. On one of the beautiful fresh-air mornings, I first heard the wistful Beatles song "The Long and Winding Road." It seemed Paul McCartney had written it just for me.

Some days we climbed ladders and picked pears. On other days, we harvested tobacco leaves, and sometimes we trimmed banana trees, lopping off their outermost leaves with machetes. At nine, we hungrily filed into the field kitchen where other volunteers had made hearty breakfasts for us. Then it was back into the fields for a few more hours of work before quitting time at one.

It was hard work, but healthy. The routine was pleasant enough, and we were with good people. I loved spending so much time outdoors. We had excellent, nutritious dinners every day. The cook staff prepared special vegetarian dishes for Alex and me because we were converts to that way of eating since our ashram days. Late afternoons and evenings we spent with the other volunteers, a few of whom had guitars. Music always made for better times.

We were well taken care of, which for me was a welcome change. Our work clothes were provided to us and laundered, and the kibbutz gave us all the other necessities, even to toothpaste and shampoo. During our stay, we didn't use, and had no need for, money. This was a new experience for me and one I liked. I wasn't thinking long term then, probably not more than a year ahead, if that. I wasn't thinking about how commitment to this communal lifestyle and a lack of money would restrict our mobility and freedom to go where we wanted to go and do what we wanted to do. Freedom was in my bones and had been bred there through my ancestry. It was what so many people I had met during my travels had swooned for when they said the name *America.* Before my odyssey began I had no concept of life in a place where freedom wasn't as natural as breathing.

One could argue Alex and I had been operating for a few years now at the poverty level and it didn't stop us from traveling. But our travels were always by the lowest class or by hook or by crook. We slept everywhere from the cheapest inns to hillsides, train station platforms, and borrowed floors. Because we had precious little disposable income, we were often denied access to some of the world's culturally finer arts and experiences. Though travel was what we needed and wanted to do, it was frequently challenging, if not an outright struggle. Our greatest freedom then, was the freedom to control our lives by letting go. We had the freedom to allow Serendipity to sit in the driver's seat. For now, neither of us minded. We were young, foolishly fearless, and resilient. We didn't ask much of the planet.

One day, under the auspices of *Yehi'am*, Alex and I had the opportunity to get a broader perspective of this country called Israel. As small as it is, Israel has unique, stunning history and geography. When demands of the farm temporarily subsided, we took advantage of the time to experience some of that geography on a week-long field trip.

Traveling in a kibbutz bus with a couple of kibbutz members and other volunteers, we drove far south, pushing through the Negev Desert, and making several stops. We were constantly confronted by raw nature and reminders of intriguing history like the Pillars of Solomon. The towering red sandstone hills stood at the site of six thousand-year-old copper mines, located fifteen miles from the southernmost point of Israel.

The port city of Eilat sat on the Gulf of Eilat at the northern tip of the Red Sea. The Jordanian city of Aqaba was just to the east, and we were within sight of Saudi Arabia to the southeast. Saudi Arabia was never a real place to me. In my mind, it was a place peopled by dark, inscrutable, long-robed wealthy sheiks and their servants who went about mysterious missions in the desert. I had never troubled to study that nation's realities. Saudi Arabia was just another place people back home referred to as "over there." For people who did not travel, most of the world outside of the United States was in fact, "over there," but Saudi Arabia was more "over there" than most.

Sleeping on the sand within miles of a place that had only been fictitious to me was an indescribable feeling, but the most remarkable and thought-provoking place in all of Israel was Masada. The isolated, ancient mountain fortress in the southeast is perched on a cliff on the eastern edge of the Judean Desert, about eleven miles south of the oasis of Eingedi.

Masada spanned the entire eighteen-acre top of a mesa fourteen hundred feet high on its eastern cliff edge, and three hundred feet high on its western edge. Many types of beauty exist in the world. Masada's beauty is stark and haunting, but what staggered me was the story of what had happened here.

A kibbutz member recounted the story as we walked up the winding snake path on one side. Occasionally, we stopped to view the surrounding arid area, including the Dead Sea fourteen miles to the north. The sight took my breath away. At once I had a feeling of great dominion and of great humility.

King Herod the Great fortified Masada in the mid-thirties B.C., as a refuge for himself in anticipation of a possible revolt. He commanded the building of fortifications, towers, and a casemate wall forty-three hundred feet long and twelve feet thick that surrounded the top of the plateau. He built an elaborate "hanging palace" extending down the promontory of the mountain on three levels.

We saw remains of storehouses, barracks, an armory, bathhouses, and cisterns. The cisterns had been filled with rainwater, a feat accomplished when Herod built dams in the nearby valleys to first divert the winter rains into channels, and from there into the cisterns. Slaves carried water to the upper reservoir.

The year 66 A.D. saw the beginning of a great revolt against Rome. A group of Jewish Zealots captured Masada, overthrowing the Roman garrison stationed there. Eventually, Masada became a refuge for people fleeing Roman rule. By 70 A.D., after the fall of Jerusalem, the Zealots on Masada built a synagogue and public hall on the plateau, and lived there for three years.

The Romans, determined to re-possess Masada, began a siege in 72 A.D. that lasted several months. The Jewish rebels, just as determined to keep it, dug in their heels for the duration. The climb up the cliff trail was formidable, but the Romans used Jewish slaves to build an earthen ramp up the side of the mountain.

When the approximately one thousand stalwarts realized there was no escape for them, rather than surrendering or dying at the hands of the Romans, they decided to commit mass suicide. As the story goes, they burned all the buildings except the full storehouses, so the Romans wouldn't have the satisfaction of thinking they had been starved to death. They then drew lots to choose ten men to kill everyone else. One man of those ten chosen, killed the remaining nine, and then himself. A few women and children survived by hiding, and so the story was told.

I was overwhelmed by this heroic tableau and by what grit and determination these people demonstrated. The story both chilled and inspired me.

The site of Masada was only identified in the mid-eighteen-hundreds. Intensive excavations didn't take place until 1963 when an Israeli archeologist and hundreds of volunteers from Israel and other countries worked at excavating the site until 1965, only a few years before we arrived in this country. I felt fortunate I could be here.

The descent was not as arduous as the climb up had been, but was much more contemplative. Once down, we rode in the bus to the Dead Sea, which, at thirteen hundred feet below sea level, is the lowest point on earth. It is also the biggest natural spa in the world. This place too had a unique evolution beginning three million years ago during an earth upheaval that exposed layers of mineral-rich earth. Salt water springs erupted to form a valley.

It is called the Dead Sea because it is so salty nothing can live in it. We went in for a swim, of sorts. As exhilarating and moving as Masada was, the Dead Sea was comforting. Even as unimpressive a swimmer as I was, I had no worries about drowning. No matter what I did, I could not sink. When I tried to submerge my body, I bobbed right back up. This was fun. I felt like a kid again at play.

CHAPTER 26

Bomb

Nothing in life is to be feared. It is only to be understood.
—Marie Curie

On a breathless afternoon back at *Yehi'am*, after returning from the fields, I was relaxing under a tree, reading. In spite of the never-ending Middle Eastern hostilities, the unhurried nature of this communal farm offered at least an illusion of peace. But my own personal peace was interrupted when I had a peculiar sensation in my abdomen, like a tiny bubble moving inside me, a completely foreign sensation. Because it happened a few more times that evening, I went the next day to visit the kibbutz doctor to investigate.

Dr. Sharon, a kind-eyed, confidence-inspiring woman in her forties, first thanked me for being a volunteer. We chatted a little before she had me lie down on the examining table. My apprehension was probably visible, but just after she placed her intelligent hand on my abdomen, she relieved my fears with a smiling revelation.

"Oh Carroll, you're pregnant!" she said, almost laughing.

I almost laughed too. I wanted to be pregnant, but how could this be? The pregnancy test I had in India a few months ago had come back negative. At five feet six, I was still one hundred ten pounds, and I hadn't experienced any morning sickness.

"Yes," the doctor said. "You're definitely pregnant, maybe four months. That bubble you've been feeling is movement of the fetus."

Immediately, I was aglow, full of hope and inspiration for the future. We could have the baby here on the kibbutz and stay for a while, I thought, as my wheels spun wildly. *Perfect.* Alex was happy too, and we later talked as if staying at the kibbutz were already a done deal.

In fact, it wasn't. A year before our arrival at *Yehi'am*, a young volunteer Jewish couple, were expecting a child. Things hadn't gone well for them. During labor and delivery, the young mother had complications, which caused both logistical and financial problems for the kibbutz. *Yehi'am* didn't want to chance repeating that scenario, particularly for non-members. What's more, because we weren't Jewish, we couldn't become members if we wanted to.

Though Alex and I wanted a child, we had not considered what we would do if I became pregnant. Needing a place to nest made getting back on the road impossible, and other options were severely limited. Moving to Spain, a place we both loved, might be a possibility.

While we were contemplating our next move, our kibbutz volunteer friends, led by forever-smiling Lesley from London, threw us a small surprise baby shower. None of them had much to spare, but I was touched by the few tiny shirts and booties they gave us.

A few months remained before we would have to be safely ensconced somewhere. In the meantime, we continued our habit of living on a razor-sharp edge, and kept working on the farm.

Now though, I wouldn't be working in the fields. I was reassigned to the kitchen in the middle of the banana fields where workers took their morning breakfast break. Instead of lopping leaves with a machete, I was, with a few other women, flipping omelets with a spatula. I did miss the outside work, but I didn't mind except when I heard the thundering sound of a single-minded jet piercing both the sky and my serenity.

What if one jet wasn't friendly? In an instant, my world could dissolve. We could all be burned, crippled, or dead. Would the baby growing inside me never see the light of day? How could I protect him? With my imagination running wild, relaxing and enjoying the people around me became difficult. As the fetus grew, so did my maternal instinct, and my attitude toward risk wasn't as casual as it had been.

One Sunday we volunteers were offered a day at the beach near Nahariya. A few mature, teenage *kibbutzniks* were entrusted with a farm bus, and most of us piled into it with our swimsuits, towels, and picnic lunches. I needed to put my toes in the sand, bathe in the Mediterranean, and recharge my lungs with sea air, a little piece of bliss.

The wide public beach was buzzing with dozens of people with similar intent. We parked ourselves and our belongings on the sand under a small shelter. Soon I was beachcombing and dipping into the Mediterranean, shaking loose any nagging concerns, pretending I didn't soon have to face one of the biggest decisions of my life. For a while, it was a good day.

The old cliché that there are no perfect lives, only perfect moments, again rang true for me. I had had many perfect, fleeting moments. This was another one about to fly away.

After only a few hours at the beach, we were startled by a loud, though slightly sand-muffled explosion, coming from one of the nearby shelters. The bomb had been planted earlier, probably during the night. A few small shrieks rose from the crowd amid some minor commotion, but mercifully, no one was hurt.

What happened next though was what shocked me. No one panicked. No one screamed or ran. Instead everyone picked up their things and proceeded quietly and purposefully, walking off the beach to their vehicles. While returning to the kibbutz, I was horror-struck by what had just happened. The horror was not so much at the bomb explosion but more at the thought of these people being so used to such savage attacks and impending violence they appeared calm. They hadn't even run to get away from the beach. How did people become inured to violence and resistant to panic? I hoped to never find out.

One thing I did find out, many times over, was the Universe provided what we needed, as long as we provided the will, the right intent, and the faith. Although I knew I wouldn't be free from want and I would have to face challenges and suffering, I also knew I would find answers and ways to do what I needed to do.

Not long after the beach incident, the answer to our birthing-place-and-next-move question was delivered via three Swiss friend volunteers.

Hans, light-haired and the tallest of the three, who spoke the best English, made the proposal. "*Ve* have a solution to your problem," he said. "You can come back *vit* us to Switzerland and get a job there. There's a lot a *verk* right now. It's easy to get a permit. Yah, now, *ve* have so many immigrant people from Italy and Yugoslavia *verking*. It's not a problem."

"But what about a place to live?" I wanted to know. "We have to have a place."

"That's easy," Hans said. "See, my friend Peter has a friend, an old guy. His wife just left him."

"The old guy Arthur lives on a little farm and he needs some help. You could live there and you could help him and Alex could *alzo* get a job."

"Are you sure?" we both asked at the same time.

"Oh sure I'm sure," Hans insisted. "*Vy not*?"

Vy not, indeed? It sounded perfect.

CHAPTER 27

A New Life

Sons are the anchors of a mother's life.
—Sophocles, from "Phaedra"

Before leaves began to turn, we flew into the German-speaking region of Switzerland, and took a smooth, well-outfitted train to the small town of Leistal. Our Swiss friends picked us up and drove us farther out into the country to Arthur's place.

Although not the Alps area, the tall terrain still supported a few minor ski resort villages. Passing through hamlets, I was struck by the cleanliness and prettiness of everything. Bright red geraniums cheerily trimmed balconies and small gardens. White featherbeds, freshening in the sunshine, hung over balcony rails. This place seemed in a permanent postcard pose, with an everything-in-its-place attitude and an appreciation for the beautiful.

Thirty kilometers outside of Liestal, we turned onto a winding up and down tree-lined road leading to Arthur's homestead. At one point Hans stopped the car so we could get a birds-eye view of where we would be staying.

"That is Arthur's house," Hans said, pronouncing the name *Artoor*, and pointing through a stand of trees at an old stone farmhouse nestled in the green valley. I was delighted by the simple serene beauty.

This was the Switzerland of my childhood dreams, not a snow-covered, money-strewn ski-resort area, but a land of stout-hearted, robust, independent people. It was the landscape I had encountered in *Heidi*, a book that impressed me deeply as a child. The story was about a young girl reluctantly taken in by her gruff, hardy, reclusive grandfather to live a Spartan, though free life, on a mountain. Through those pages, I became Heidi, living hardily in these very hills and mountains. Now I would feel the same swelling ground under my feet.

Arthur was standing outside when we pulled up. He was a big and tall man with gray-brown hair and doleful, soulful eyes full of questions.

"*Guten tag. Wilkommen*," he only said. At this point we wouldn't have understood much more anyway. Hans translated all the preliminaries as Arthur showed us around the homestead. The two-story house had two bedrooms upstairs. Although it wasn't very big, everything was sturdy, basic, functional, and unassuming. I guessed it to be a hundred fifty or two hundred years old, young by European standards.

Arthur, a man in his early sixties, like the singing *patrona* of the Barcelona pension, seemed to be *abandonado*. Since his wife of thirty-five years had left him, Arthur was forlorn, looking for company, and needing help with chores around the place. Our understanding was that Alex and I would be this company and help, nothing more.

For the next couple of months that we stayed with Arthur, we felt our way around, unsure of what was expected of us. It was an awkward dance at times. The homestead, once a functioning farmstead, was now an unkempt, mostly unproductive vegetable garden plot, a few fruiting plum, apple, and cherry trees, and a barn with one cow, which Arthur dutifully milked every day.

Sometimes he shared with me the cream he skimmed off the top of the steamy milk he brought into the kitchen in the morning. It was absolute ambrosia to me. He employed Alex in some miscellaneous tasks, and we both picked the fruit that was left on the trees or had fallen to the ground. Arthur would dump this fruit into his schnapps-making process. Since alcohol didn't interest me, it seemed like a waste of good fruit, but Arthur liked to bend his elbow with a small glass of the clear schnapps occasionally. The upside was the schnapps seemed to lighten his mood.

A big box phone on the wall of his living room rang infrequently. The conversations Arthur had always started the same way, and I assumed it was the same person who called each time. After the initial hello, there was a pause where the caller must have asked how he was. Arthur always answered, with as much enthusiasm as he could muster, "*Immer lustig, immer lustig,*" as if to convince himself. Always happy, always happy.

Hardly. Because Alex and I had learned only the rudiments of *Schweitzer-Deutsche,* the Swiss brand of German, there wasn't much we could do to help him with his sadness. He needed someone to sit and listen so he could air out his suffering and feelings of loss.

Arthur rarely left the farm and had almost no visitors. One was his best friend, much younger than he, and the other his adult daughter, interestingly named Heidi. I wished she would come over more often. She was beautiful, tall, and bubbly, with enormous blue eyes and short-cropped strawberry blond hair. She spoke a little English and was concerned about me and my pregnancy.

Because many babies in Switzerland were still home-birthed, it was customary for a small town to have a nurse-midwife to care for the women in her district. "There is a midwife who lives a few kilometers away," Heidi kindly offered. "She is very good. If you like, I can take you to see her."

I was excited at the prospect and we drove over. In her early forties, Frau Thommen had short, dark hair, intelligent, sparkling brown eyes, and an efficient, amiable manner. She was just buxom enough to make me feel comfortable with her Germanic, motherly image. She seemed competent and confident in her role. I knew I would be in good hands with this woman in charge of our baby's coming out party. It was agreed then. A bonus was that even though *Schweitzer Deutsche* was her native tongue, she also spoke some French, a language I knew, so she and I would be able to communicate.

When Frau Thommen examined me on our first visit, she gave me an estimated birthing day. She kindly agreed when the time came she would drive over to the farm, pick us up and take us to her house where she had an accommodating and comfortable birthing room with nursery.

Like other midwives in the area, Frau Thommen had an arrangement with a doctor to come out and assist if he were needed. This was perfect. I couldn't have planned it any more to my liking.

I might have planned our temporary living quarters better though. Arthur's house had no indoor bathing facilities. When he bathed, it was mostly at the stone horse trough outside. I used water from the kitchen sink and improvised in the toilet room.

The kitchen was a delight for me. It had a wood burning stove and a five-foot long brick oven extending from its opening in the kitchen to a protruding living room wall. Wrapped in ceramic tile, the wall radiated the heat. A bench surrounded and was attached to this protrusion, creating a wonderful place to sit on and toast my whole backside. Arthur showed me how to use the oven. Also, on a couple of occasions, he made us *apfelkuchen,* sliced crisp apples, dipped into batter and deep fried—a scrumptious treat.

Part of my contribution to our "rent" was cooking. Unfortunately, because we were vegetarian and I had never learned much about cooking meat, the meals I prepared probably weren't very satisfying for him, although they were for me. In fact, I felt fine and healthy.

I absolutely loved being pregnant. I loved the feeling of the baby growing and moving inside me. I loved thinking about being a mother. I didn't worry about not having a home, about where we would live, or how we would support this new third part of our family. I was in storybook land where things just worked out.

When we arrived in Switzerland, I was nearly seven months pregnant, but that didn't slow me down much. Alex and I went for frequent hikes in the hills on weekends when he was there.

When our Swiss friends had invited us to come to this land of milk and honey, they said it would be easy for Alex to get work. The country was previously a haven for hundreds, maybe thousands of immigrant workers, particularly from Italy and Turkey. Our friends said Alex just had to request an "*arbeitsbiviligung,*" a work permit, and he could easily get a job.

We were misinformed, though unintentionally. During our friends' absence, the Swiss government had decided against admitting any more foreign workers, and the law was changed. Our friends had not kept up.

As Americans we had had no problem getting into the country, but, when Alex applied for a work permit, he was denied. Somehow, because of my pregnant condition, the gods or someone worked overtime to get around that law. Alex was hired to work in the packaging department of a watch factory in a town several miles away. Since we had no car, Alex rode with another worker, spending the week away, and returning to the farm on weekends.

Spending time alone was never a problem for me, and I was never bored. While Alex was away, apart from doing some daily tasks for Arthur, I occupied myself with reading, writing, and even drawing a little. I took long walks. I fantasized. I talked and sang to the little life growing inside me and I imagined being a mother. One day I found some scraps of fabric, a couple of old socks, and needles and thread in the attic, and made a rag doll, kind of goofy-looking, but sweet. I sent it to my sister Wendy for her baby who was to be born about six months after mine.

This Spartan "make do" attitude was an inheritance from my mother. She would stretch a single can of tuna with some boiled eggs and mayonnaise far enough to make lunch sandwiches for me, three sisters, and herself on summer Fridays, when Friday meat was forbidden to Catholics. Consequently, traveling third, or even abominable class, was nothing I couldn't handle. Although I aspired to better things, I was used to a certain level of poverty-consciousness. Frugality and sometimes deprivation had become the badges of our lifestyle.

Yet, I did want to have it all. I wanted a child badly, and Alex believed he did too. Wherever we went, he would find children to relate to and entertain. He always made them laugh. *Surely*, I thought, *he will be a good father, or at least a willing one.*

His father Robert, who was in Europe between ships, visited shortly before our baby was born. He didn't come out to the farm, but wanted us to meet him in town. We joined him on a train ride to Basel for dinner.

Robert was charming company, especially after a few Scotches. Well-read and bright, he had a quick, albeit cynical, wit. Throughout the evening father and son exchanged wry observations and sparred politically. We all laughed a lot. Clearly Robert was more comfortable in the role of pal to Alex than he was in the role of a father. On the train ride back, Robert dropped his guard, admitting he was poorly suited to fatherhood, and claimed he didn't know how to handle that responsibility. "I always thought it was best to stick by the *laissez faire* attitude with kids," he said with a sigh. I wanted to believe he was being honest.

His visit was brief. He went back to his travel agenda and we went back to our farm. Although I had gained some insights into my father-in-law's perspective, I hoped Alex's approach to fatherhood would be altogether different from what his father's had been.

At this point I felt myself fortunate to have more than what many pregnant women had, namely a supportive, caring father-to-be and a midwife who made me feel confident about the upcoming birth. Whether she inspired confidence or not, I would still have gone ahead with the midwife birthing. It was the way I had decided years ago it should be—naturally and not in a sterile, flood-lit room surrounded by strangers, but in a home setting under soft lights, surrounded by people who care about you. It made more sense that way.

My resolve had been strengthened at Ananda Ashram by Clara's *Childbirth Without Fear* book. The myth, that childbirth must be devastatingly painful and that the woman must be hospitalized and drugged, was exploded. Dr. Dick-Read's evidence was grounded in solid medical research and fact. If a woman could keep herself healthy, and release her fear, delivery was much easier. I could do that.

In my mind, the best part about natural delivery was that after it was all over, I would always have the supreme satisfaction of knowing I, not the doctor or midwife or anyone else, delivered this child. My baby wouldn't be dragged out by forceps clamped to the sides of his frail and impressionable skull. As his mother, I would feel and facilitate my child's passage into the world, holding his hand through the journey. If at no other time, I would feel like a queen, and one who's earned her throne.

On a crisp morning, at the end of November, at Frau Thommen's house, I had my first coronation. Alex hadn't left for the work week yet and was with me.

The day before was a mild and brilliantly gorgeous Sunday. Alex and I spent it doing nothing in particular until the late afternoon, when we decided to climb the hill just behind the house. Though not terribly steep, it was tall. Even at this late stage of pregnancy, climbing it was not too difficult for me. I was in great shape, and I had learned how to breathe.

Autumn was in full force now. Millions of leaves had fallen, making thick, lush, multi-colored carpets everywhere. Some places where the ground dipped and made hollows had turned into bathtubs filled with cushy leaves. Sitting in one, I picked up handfuls of leaves and threw them over my head, letting them shower me. A hefty wind announced itself, took the stage, and started blowing red, yellow, orange, and brown leaves in dances all around us. Alex, who liked creating fun out of simple things, made a game of trying to catch leaves as they flew by.

"If I catch one in my left hand, it's a girl," he called out. "In my right hand, it's a boy." With that, one landed squarely in his right hand. We walked down the hill, invigorated and laughing.

That night, after settling ourselves under woolly blankets, Alex went to sleep, but I didn't. I lay there with unusual stirrings in my head and body. In the wee hours I noticed something happening, beginning with a slight pressure in my lower back. After some time lying awake in the dark room, I felt the pressure return, and again a while later. By now I was excited to recognize the periodic pressure as contractions organizing themselves into a pattern. I awoke Alex.

"I think this is it," I told him. Once roused, he started timing the length of the contractions and the time in between. He went downstairs and called Frau Thommen to alert her, and at some time before dawn, she arrived to pick us up.

Although I was a little nervous, I had no doubt everything would be fine. I recalled my resolve to deliver the natural way and reminded myself women for centuries had been having babies this way, often in tents or under trees. *I'm healthy, and there's really no reason to worry*, I told myself.

As the contractions came faster and lasted longer, I was as comfortable as a woman in labor could be. Everything was going like clockwork, except that the Good Frau temporarily forgot her French and coached me in German. But as I was pushing, I fully understood her prompting. "*Noch ein bissien mer*," she urged, still a little more. I pushed with everything I had.

At 8 a.m. our son emerged, wailing. The midwife weighed him in—an eight-pounder. He was beautiful and luminous with hair so light it was almost non-existent, and he had nearly invisible eyebrows. He came flawless, with all of his parts intact. After Frau Thommen cleaned and swaddled him, she handed this precious new life back to me. My labor was truly the hardest work I had ever done, but my exhaustion quickly gave way to inexpressible joy. Alex and I were proud and happy parents.

Alex could not stay with me, of course, but he would take his pride with him to his job that week. Someone would pick him up shortly to take him there. Noticing a bit of blood on his shirt, Frau Thommen asked if he would like to borrow a clean shirt from her husband. "No," he beamed. "That's my woman's blood."

Within an hour, I asked to use my midwife's telephone. I walked to the next room and called my mother. "It's a boy!" I said. "Mama, we have a healthy, gorgeous, white-haired, blue-eyed boy… I wish you were here, too. … Yes, I did walk to the next room to call you… Yes, Mama, he's fine and I'm fine."

CHAPTER 28

No Forwarding Address

To live outside the law you must be honest.
— Bob Dylan, "Absolutely Sweet Marie"

"What are you going to name him?" Mama wanted to know.

One of our requirements for a name was that it couldn't be shortened into some pedestrian nickname. Jason, a name we both liked, met that requirement. It also happened to meet the requirements of the Swiss government, as stated in a booklet Frau Thommen handed me the day after our baby was born.

The booklet, published in the early 1900s, dictated rules Swiss parents were obliged to follow in naming their children. In essence, the rules described the kinds of names that were *verboten*. Naming children after abstract qualities like Faith, Hope, or Charity wasn't allowed, neither was saddling them with politically controversial ones like Lenin. Parents absolutely could not give a boy's name to a girl or vice versa, or burden the child with something that might be derogatory. Just in case there was any question, the booklet included a handy list of names that were acceptable. The name Jason was on it.

Choosing a middle name wasn't as easy, because several of the names either of us suggested during the next few days weren't on the list. Finally, because I was tired of the effort, I went along with Alex's choice, the name Simon, the first name of the South American liberator.

Since we were American citizens, and by extension, so was our baby, ultimately we were not subject to the naming regulations of Switzerland. Until we could get Jason's official American birth certificate, we chose to abide by Swiss rules to avoid any immediate problem with our baby's preliminary Swiss birth documentation.

Typically, a woman giving birth in a Swiss hospital or midwife's home stayed put for five days. For me this was a wonderful vacation. Frau Thommen was an excellent nurse, caregiver, and cook. My room, on the second floor of her home, was comfortable and mostly self-contained. I had a beautiful view of the pastoral landscape through thick, double-paned windows and a featherbed to keep me cozy. I never had to go downstairs at all. My midwife-hostess came in several times a day to change or bathe the baby and to give him to me to nurse. She also looked after me, serving me in bed outstanding meals she had prepared. Never had I been so pampered, except by my mother when I was a sick child.

Alex only managed a ride to come and see us twice during these days because we were dependent on others for transportation. Finally, Frau Thommen drove us back to Arthur's farm. We didn't have much in the way of baby things, not even a crib, but we did have a large, woven cane basket that temporarily served well as a bassinet.

The lightness of Jason's hair and barely perceptible eyebrows made his already large sky-blue eyes even more outstanding. It was such a joy to have him in our lives, to nurse him, hold him, play with him, and to experience this magically powerful mother-son bond that would forever change my life. No longer would my life belong only to me. Jason was flesh of my flesh and bone of my bone. I knew this was a tie that would never be broken.

Not very long after Jason joined us, we realized our living situation needed changing. The agreement we had with Arthur was no longer viable. We weren't able to be farm help anymore, not even with what little farm work remained to be done. It was winter and there were no gardens or orchards to be tended. Alex had to work at his job at a watch factory and I had to take care of our son. We weren't even much company for Arthur then, so he wasn't particularly interested in having us around. Besides, the house didn't have the facilities we needed to properly take care of our baby.

Through a man Alex met at the factory, we found a postage-stamp sized apartment upstairs in a house in a nearby town. It was a small village in the middle of an area popular with local ski enthusiasts, which we weren't. One uninspiring grocery store and a mobile store that came to town every Wednesday encompassed the entirety of the local shopping opportunities. The shortage didn't bother me because I had neither the inclination nor money for shopping. And most of the time it was really too cold to go out.

Occasionally when the sun shone I took Jason out for a walk on the hilly paths. He rode in an old-time cushy, heavily padded pram, a baby carriage with an accordion-style convertible lid. This sat on a heavy-duty frame with rugged springs that combined to give the baby a Cadillac of a ride. The carriage was given to us by an English-speaking preacher and his wife, a charming, cultured couple who sought us out to befriend us. They invited us for dinner on several occasions and showered us with beautiful baby clothes, including many delicate handmade and embroidered gowns and crocheted or knitted sweaters, caps and booties. The clothes had been donated to them by local residents who didn't need them anymore.

Used clothing stores didn't exist in Switzerland then, at least not in this part of the country, and nobody wanted hand-me-downs for their babies. The fact that the clothes had been hand-knitted or crocheted was immaterial, our friends clarified, because all Swiss girls learned those arts in school at a very young age. Consequently, this kind of handiwork was common and was not prized as it was in the United States. We accepted the baby clothes gratefully, knowing full well we now had much more than we could ever use.

Our days were predictable then and our lives almost orthodox. Alex and I even became "officially" married by a local magistrate in a civil ceremony with two witnesses. This nesting and nurturing time was a pleasant change for me. I loved my new role as a mother, just as I had loved being pregnant. Jason was a joy with a smile as big as the sun.

Some weekends Alex and I visited an interesting couple our age with two young daughters. Their home, only blocks away from ours, was a spacious old manse whose main attraction and envy for me was the huge sewing and craft room where Erika spent much of her time weaving on the mammoth loom or spinning wool on the wooden spinning wheel. Her husband Heinrich often played his classical guitar for us. Together they put us in touch again with a laid back and sane side of life.

Switzerland is populated by three different cultures, divided roughly into German, French, and Italian geographic areas. In the German Swiss region where we lived, I often found people to be somewhat cold, standoffish, and formal. Most of the people we met called us only by our last names and shook hands rather than hugged. I even saw our landlady and her grown son shake hands one morning as he was leaving the house.

But for the time being, we were safely ensconced. To break the monotony of being cooped up in the apartment, I took a weekly walk to the mobile grocery store. I soon discovered another reason for going. This store on wheels had an addictive delicacy I splurged on every week for myself. *Mille feuilles,* known in New Orleans as Napoleons, were bars of multi-leaved light pastry, layered in between with luscious custard and topped with a thin vanilla frosting. They came freshly prepared, five in a box. Each week I bought and squirreled away a box, having one or part of one every day until my next fix. Occasionally I shared one with Alex, but most of the time I kept my guilty pleasure hidden. I would wait until Jason was napping so I could sit back and indulge myself in an almost orgiastic ritual of eating my sinfully satisfying pastry, savoring each tiny bite slowly to make it last.

My other pleasure, besides enjoying my baby, was writing and exploring the pages of a beautiful old British dictionary, full of archaic words which Frau Siegen lent to me. We had rented a heavy, clunky manual typewriter so Alex could compose articles he wrote for his job as a stringer for the San Francisco Chronicle. But after he left for work in the morning, I squeezed in a little time for myself, taking full advantage of the typewriter and the dictionary to write, sometimes composing silly poetry using the treasure trove of archaic words I had found.

We didn't venture far from our nest during those days. New Year's Eve night we were huddled in our little kitchen, watching a silent movie through the window. The falling snow was quickly collecting on every rooftop like so many feather beds thrown to keep the inhabitants cozy. Just before the stroke of midnight I turned on our radio and heard the voice of George Harrison soulfully crooning, *My Sweet Lord.* It seemed excitement enough for now.

Honestly, we were enjoying being an almost conventional family. Alex went to work. When he came home, I would have dinner ready, and he would have fun giving the baby his bath at night. Jason was flourishing. Occasionally our landlady stopped in to see and play with him, calling him pet names and laughing with him. "*Wie gehts de shatsili?*" she would coo. How's the little dear doing?

But then our baby started to get fussy and we didn't know why. Eventually, his fussiness turned into screaming fits that went on and on. What was wrong? I was beside myself. One day I noticed a small lump in his lower abdomen. Being a new mother without my mother or close friends around for advice, I turned to my landlady. She took a look at Jason and the lump I pointed out and knew immediately what it was—an inguinal hernia, apparently a common occurrence in babies.

At a loss for what to do, I again called on Heidi, who was most helpful and resourceful. Through her investigations we learned there was an excellent children's hospital in Basel where we could take Jason for hernia surgery. Although his birth here would not admit him to Swiss citizenship or provide an easy path to it, fortunately, it did allow for his medical care. There would be no cost to us for the surgery. Heidi made the arrangements, and within a week she drove Jason and me to the hospital.

It was a modern, spotlessly clean, efficient hospital with a reputation for excellent care, although that did not assuage my feelings of anxiety. I dreaded leaving my infant son with strangers. I was not able to stay with him because there were no accommodations, and it was not allowed. I would be many miles away and had to trust that my son was in good hands. After the surgery, they would keep him for more than a week before releasing him to me. On my birthday, in the middle of the week I hitchhiked into town and took the train to the Basel for a hospital visit, but I was disappointed that their germ control policy dictated I could only see my baby through a glass. When I couldn't hold him, it broke my heart. He was barely three months old. I didn't think he even recognized me through the glass, or possibly his look registered that he thought I had abandoned him.

Finally, we brought Jason back home. We settled in once more, but not for long. This wasn't *our* home, we knew. The country was absolutely beautiful, meticulously clean and well-ordered, but it was staid, too staid, for us. Besides, we couldn't stay. Alex's work permit would run out soon, and it was almost spring, a time when we usually got itchy feet. Jason would be a traveler too.

While thinking about where we might let destiny lead us next, we were blindsided by a piece of mail that came for Alex. It was a note from a New York woman, a friend of his father, wrapped around an already months-old draft notice she was forwarding to him. "*Uncle Sam wants you now*" was its basic message.

This added an unsettling, frightening twist to our situation. Would this be the end of the odyssey? Would we have to go back to the States against our will or wishes before we were ready? Would Alex submit to serve in the Army? And what would Jason and I do? All of a sudden, I realized our vulnerability and felt tangled up in conflicting emotions.

We learned Alex's hometown draft board had been searching for him for some time and had traced a connection to the New York friend. Since quitting the University of Salamanca, Alex lost his student deferment, and somewhere along the line his number came up. Legally, Alex was supposed to keep in touch with the draft board, advising them of his whereabouts, just in case they needed him. He had not.

But now, he would write. He crafted a touching letter, explaining of course he would return and report, if he could, but he had a brand new son and no money to make the trip. Alex pleaded, what did they want him to do? He included our current address as the place to which they could send mail, and shortly afterwards we left, with no forwarding address. The draft board, we learned much later, did not bother to respond to his letter.

We were going back to Spain. Although we would not be traveling as light as we could before the baby, we still had to pare down. There were far too many baby clothes to take, including ones Jason had outgrown without even wearing. I tried giving clothes back to Frau Siegen, but she refused, saying they were out of storage room. She didn't even know anyone else who would want them.

"Why don't you just burn them?" she asked.

"Burn them?!" That was the most absurd thing I had ever heard. There was no way I could do that. It went completely against my grain. We shipped a small package to family back home and simply left the rest in the apartment. If someone was going to burn them, it wouldn't be me.

By the time we left Switzerland in May, patches of wildflowers had erupted over the hillsides and waved us on.

CHAPTER 29

Formentera and a New Yoga

I've looked at life from both sides now, from
win and lose, and still somehow
it's life's illusions I recall; I really don't know life at all.
—JONI MITCHELL, "Both Sides Now"

IT STARTED OFF INNOCENTLY ENOUGH. High on our beautiful baby son and on our recently-minted Yoga knowledge and practice, we boarded the train in Leistal for a ride from Switzerland back into the bosom of Spain. Obviously, our hitchhiking days were over.

Trains in Switzerland were quite comfortable, bordering on luxurious, and moderately priced. Being on a Swiss train made me lament that our American railroad system had declined so much from its glory days.

Unlike flying, traveling by train was an opportunity to see the countryside and feel the nerve center of the cities, without fighting traffic. It also meant that you naturally and gradually adjusted from one environment to another. Travel in real time with no jet lag.

My love for trains began the summer I was seven years old when my mother's Aunt Sarah and her family took me with them on a trip to San Francisco. The train was a magic carpet ride, and that city more magical, with specks of gold in the sidewalks. That trip was also the beginning of my dreams of travel.

Railroad magic was still happening for me on the Swiss train. The ride was pleasant and Jason handled it well, but by the time we arrived in Barcelona, we were all happy to get off the rails and into fresh air again.

We spent the day drinking in old memories that lingered in the familiar streets and buildings. We took Jason to visit the park at *Montjuich* and the wide-open port, hoping his little spirit might catch a whiff of the world-essence that motivated us.

Barcelona was not our final stop. We were going to Spain's Ballearic Islands, by ferry boat from Alicante, to Ibiza. From Ibiza we would travel in a much smaller vessel about five miles, to the peaceful little island of Formentera.

From the instant we docked at the sleepy harbor at the fishing village of *Es Calo,* I knew this sparsely populated, twelve-mile long island was the perfect place to simply *be* for a while, to collect ourselves, and to consider future moves. Formentera is mostly low and flat with stretches of rugged coastline, and is rimmed with white sandy beaches facing crystal clear turquoise waters. The air is warm and dry, but teasing breezes blow frequently across the land. Was this Utopia we had found?

La Mola, at the southern end of the island, is where the land rises up to form a rocky promontory. At its peak stands an age-old stone lighthouse. *Yes, this is my place,* I thought. Something about a lighthouse was comforting to me. Standing straight and tall, strong and secure against the elements, a lighthouse was a place to turn to when your direction was unclear. *How fitting.*

Formentera Island was a sparsely populated, undeveloped, unspoiled place. There weren't any hotels in San Francisco, its principal town, and only a few pensions where we might stay. The countryside suited us better, and we quickly found a small place to rent.

The thick-walled, two-room alabaster cottage had only a couple of foot-square windows. The builders of cottages like these which dotted the landscape, knew what they were doing. The three hundred days' worth of sunshine and heat didn't penetrate the stone, and the white exterior walls reflected the heat back to the atmosphere, away from the inhabitants.

The house had no electricity, but even without air conditioning or fans, it stayed fairly cool. We had no neighbors within at least forty yards, and it was heavenly for me to be living in this place. I think it was for all three of us, not to be cooped up in a little apartment, but to be able to stretch our bodies and our psyches. We drank in the sunshine and the delicious air. Jason seemed to thrive in this atmosphere.

Rosemary bushes and olive, fig, and carob trees grew wild all over the island. Formentera was in fact, my introduction to carob beans. I picked the long, dark brown, lightly sweet, leathery fruit and ate them straight from the tree. The scent of rosemary floated deliciously in the air, and I stuck my face straight into the bushes to inhale their healing fragrance every time I passed one.

Sometimes we walked into town to buy a few groceries from the *tienda* on the square. It became instantly obvious we weren't the only Americans and Europeans to have discovered this place. The same boat that ferried us from Ibiza brought handfuls of the counter-culture contingent twice a week. Like water, they sought their own level, congregating around the town square.

On one of our walks into town, Alex and I talked about what we might do to support ourselves, in the simple style to which we were now accustomed. We just wanted to be able to sustain our existence on the island for a while.

It was Alex's idea to teach Yoga, thinking a number of the counter-culture folks would be interested. Even though Yoga was relatively new to the West, and we wouldn't have much, if any, teaching competition there, we didn't expect or even desire to make a killing at it. The modest, understated notice Alex tacked to a pole outside of the grocery store said so. "Will trade Yoga lessons for beans," it read.

Someone soon took it down and confronted us as we sat relaxing in the sunshine. "Are you responsible for this?" the British-tongued stranger accused, waving the paper in front of Alex.

"Well, yeah, I am."

"What do you think you're doing?"

"Just trying to make a little living with my Yoga lessons," Alex returned in his recently-acquired softened tone.

"Well, how about I show you what *real* Yoga is," the stranger said. "I'm Ian, by the way." He paused briefly to let us introduce ourselves. Then after the shortest of small talk where he learned a smattering of our history, he said, "Look, why don't you come to our house tonight and have dinner with us, and we'll talk about it."

We took the bait. That night at seven we walked to Ian and his wife Jeannette's rental cottage, just outside of town. The hearty and robust vegetarian meal Jeannette cooked was a delicious feast for us. Her cooking was a far cry from the Spartan meals at the ashram, and from the thrifty ones in Switzerland where our focus had been more on excluding meat than with maintaining a nutritious balance. Jeannette cooked with an abundance of nuts, whole grains, and vegetables that my body devoured, recognizing the protein it had been lacking. That night though, we swallowed a lot more than dinner.

Ian not only convinced us our diets needed improving, but also opened our eyes to the possibility of knowledge we hadn't yet acquired through our study of Yoga. I didn't like his brash impertinent style, but his wizardry with words highly impressed Alex. Before we knew what was happening, we were cats following our curiosity. We wanted to know more of what Ian knew.

I'm certain before he met us, Ian didn't call what he promoted "Yoga." In fact, what he preached and practiced bore absolutely no resemblance to what we knew to be the centuries-old science of life. For him "Yoga" was apparently a convenient handle he could use to lure us in. We didn't question the fact that we never saw him socializing with anyone else on the square or that he and Jeannette didn't invite anyone else to dinner when they invited us. Maybe they did and no one else accepted their invitation. We had dinner with them several times. In retrospect, I realize with each meal we consumed more of the "philosophy" Ian was selling. Whatever he called it and for whatever motivation, it was essentially all about consciousness-altering through whatever means, especially the use of LSD and, to a lesser degree, weed.

Through my limited experience with LSD I believed it was like a sacrament to be used only rarely and for the purpose of gaining insight and personal and psychic growth. I would discover later Ian had other ideas.

On a couple of our visits, Ian gave Alex and me each a hit of acid delivered as quarter-inch blots on a piece of paper. Ian and Jeanette fed us a meal first so we would have enough glucose in our systems to handle the immense increase in brain activity. They made fruit, nuts, and honey available for the ride.

On one particular night, either the meal was not enough for me, or maybe the dose of LSD was too potent or it was adulterated, because what happened was extremely disturbing and frightening, unlike anything I had experienced before.

I let the dosed paper melt on my tongue as I sat on the floor, leaning against the wall. Quickly, the drug suffused my brain, and my body felt superfluous.

What I discovered about pure LSD was that it was generally not a physical thing, or I should say not a particularly sensual thing. In my experience, it didn't necessarily stimulate the libido, though it could, depending on the focus, because all the senses were enhanced. The body becomes merely a vehicle and a tool for the super-mind to carry out its needs. Consequently, there is no physical addiction to the drug. LSD affords the taker an opportunity for a detached inner body-mind exploration. Once the mind has been expanded in this way, I realized, that expansion remains and is recognized indefinitely, although it may be submerged under layers of mundane concerns.

The experience this night though, was not enlightening. As the LSD, and whatever other involved chemicals took over my mind, I became severely lacking in glucose, the brain food necessary to function. I couldn't say how long the trip lasted or how long I sat immobile. I was unable to get up and eat any of the food left for us, or to even recognize I needed some. I wasn't aware of the presence or absence of anyone else. I was in another world and totally alone. The "trip" was interminable.

Worst of all, I could not move my body. It wouldn't obey any commands, even to lift an arm, and I couldn't speak. Essentially, I was suffering catatonia. I thought about words I wanted to say and became frustrated when I couldn't say them, at first. Then after a time, as I sank deeper into this dark silent world, it occurred to me this was the way the world ended, "not with a bang but a whimper." Certainly it could be the way it ended for me. If I never spoke another word, verbally or nonverbally, I speculated, I would then just cease to exist.

By extension, my mind saw this as the way the whole world ended. Everybody would just stop speaking, even in their minds. They would stop thinking. "In the beginning was the Word," I considered. So then, what happened when there was no word? Were we not un-created?

To a sane and rational mind, this all must sound quite insane, which is exactly what it was. I went insane and catatonic for a while. When the drug, or drugs, wore off, I emerged from the experience with empathy for individuals who are trapped inside of what is termed insanity.

That trip was the last time Alex and I spent an evening with Ian and Jeanette in Formentera. From then on we used our time and energy in the brighter world of island living. Alex's sister sent us a very welcome care package of California snacks, a toy for Jason, a portable cassette player with batteries, and a cassette tape of the up and coming singer James Taylor. What a strong, friendly, mellow voice I heard singing *Rock-a-by Sweet Baby James*. We probably played it a hundred times both in our little cottage and outside in the sunshine. It is said, for those with musical souls, the first time you hear a piece of music or a song with significance for you will be indelibly imprinted in your psyche, inseparable from that place and time. And so it was.

Like Lewis Carroll's *Alice,* I must have fallen down my own rabbit hole at some previous time, as I continued to encounter Mad Hatters at tea parties and join Queens at croquet matches. I was about to have another *jabberwocky* day.

When we had been on the island for several weeks, Alex and I started thinking and talking about where we would go next. As lovely as the place was, we obviously couldn't stay here forever. We had a child to raise and a living to make. Besides, the wanderlust that ran in both of our bloodstreams was beginning to call attention to itself once more.

One day when we collected our mail at *Poste Restante*, we received a letter from our friends Don and Mary. They were preparing to leave their English teaching jobs in Japan. They wanted to know if we were interested in stepping into their positions in a month.

We were interested but couldn't afford the trip to the other side of the world. Maybe we should consider teaching possibilities in countries more within our reach.

In my mind meanderings, I consulted regularly with the Great Spirit. I once heard it said God looks out for children and drunks. In the strictest sense we were neither. Nonetheless, as long as we were open to the great experiment called life, God, or the Universe, provided for us, often in remarkable ways, like giving us the ten-dollar Taunus. We were on the verge of another dramatic happening.

Dreaming aloud one day, I asked Alex what he would do if, suddenly he had the means to travel wherever he wanted. He turned around and asked me the same question, so we fantasized about places we would visit or re-visit. We both agreed, among other things, we would take those jobs in Japan.

A day later as we were walking into town we were approached by a long-haired American stranger. After chatting for a few minutes, we found out he had something to sell.

"I've got two round-the-world airline tickets you can have for a hundred fifty dollars apiece," he said.

Disbelieving our ears, we asked him to repeat what he had just said.

"It's true. Somebody sold them to me, but I need the money more than the trip," he said, "so I'll sell them both for three hundred."

He had our attention, but how could this be possible? Where did the tickets actually come from? They might well have been stolen. And how did we know they would be usable? We didn't. Yet something in the stranger's demeanor and style led us to believe they were valid.

Considering the ethical side of the question, I wondered if we bought and used these tickets and they had been stolen, would that mean we were stealing? Somehow, I thought not. After all, we hadn't searched for ill-gotten goods. All we had done was to fantasize about what we would do if we suddenly had the means.

The ultimate justification was that this was providential. Just when we needed a next step and the resources to take it, these tickets fell into our laps.

We took the chance. A day later, we both held our breath as we delivered some of our hard-earned cash to this *Deus ex Machina* stranger.

We weren't quite ready to leave Formentera though, and still had to plan for the logistics involved in moving the three of us from here to Osaka and our new jobs.

Our choice would have been to travel together, stop for a visit in New Orleans to see family, and then move on to Japan. Our situation was complicated now, especially since Alex's delinquent draft notice had arrived in Switzerland. He couldn't go back to the States unless he wanted to present himself to the draft board for service in the Army.

We decided Jason and I would fly to New Orleans and spend a little time with my family, who hadn't even met their newest member yet. Alex would fly to Mexico and we would meet in Vancouver Canada for the trip to Japan. Before this happened, Alex's father, vacationing in Europe, visited us in Formentera. Jason and I left for the States while he was still there.

Until I passed through the boarding line at the airport, I truly didn't know whether or not the ticket would work. White-knuckled for a long time before the flight, I was immensely relieved when it did work. I was the test case, and Alex would leave several days later.

In the meantime, he and his father would have the chance to spend some buddy time together. Regrettably, Robert had brought along with him his current girlfriend, who was our age. She was bright and personable enough, but the situation felt strange to me.

What a joy it was to arrive home and to see my mother and father's faces. With siblings and aunts and uncles, we had a small family reunion. Jason was a huge hit with everybody. My parents couldn't have looked happier, and I basked in their glow. It had been three and a half years. So much had happened in all our lives, but in ways of the heart, no time had passed.

Then, when Alex arrived in Mexico, he asked if I could have my mother babysit Jason for a few days while I flew to meet him there for a second honeymoon. Of course I could. We met in Merida and took a fun day trip to *Chichinitza* to see the Mexican version of pyramids, and we sampled some of the tasty local cuisine. Blame it on the new place and the new adventure, but Alex and I renewed our romance yet again.

Back in New Orleans, I said another difficult good-bye to my family a few days later. When Jason and I caught up with Alex in Vancouver, we left North America for Japan, our home for the next ten months.

CHAPTER 30

Arigato—the Japanese Experience

This most valuable of arts, the art of living.
—Cicero, "Of the Education of Children"

Breathing the same recycled air over and again for eleven hours on the flight to Tokyo left me feeling like a dry desert landscape, and my bottom couldn't get comfortable in the rigid seat. Then we still had another leg to Osaka, where Alex and I would step into the teaching jobs vacated by our friends.

At first sight, industrial, crowded, concrete, and metallic Osaka wasn't a very attractive place to me. Everywhere I walked outside felt close, with hardly any sky view. But the apartment that was pre-arranged for us to live in was in a small complex on the mercifully green and welcoming grounds of a temple in *Tennoji-ku*.

The complex was run by a couple who lived in a house on the grounds. Evelyn, somewhat cold and distant, was a tall American with hard angles who had married Yoshi, a Japanese man several inches shorter with a much softer physical bearing. Evelyn, who was bi-lingual, introduced the three of us to our miniscule apartment.

The place consisted of one walk-in-closet-sized bedroom and one, equally small all purpose room which served as kitchen and living room combined. It had a small sink, an abbreviated counter top, and a tiny stove. Some sort of wood paneling lined the walls and a high, minimal window provided the place's only natural light.

The apartment had no bathroom. Both downstairs apartments used an enclosed toilet, a true water closet, situated at the end of an outside walkway.

Bathing was another matter. We couldn't just pop into a shower or tub as often as we wanted, as we could in the States. I had long ago stopped taking that luxury for granted. On occasion, in various places during the last couple of years, we two had joined the ranks of the great unwashed masses. Now, though we wouldn't be unwashed, getting clean wouldn't be the fast food version of bathing either. Japanese bathing became an interesting, social, even meditative experience which I came to love.

Some Japanese homes weren't equipped with bathing facilities. Instead, each neighborhood had its own communal bathhouse, or *sento*, where for a few yen you could enjoy bathing as royalty might have, except that it wasn't private and there were no frills.

Evelyn told us about one about a block away. "Don't worry," she said. "It's segregated into male and female sides." I was glad for that as I was sure I wouldn't enjoy the baths much with men's eyes scrutinizing my naked body and I didn't want to see theirs.

When we arrived at the bathhouse, Alex was shown to the male side and I was taken to mine. The one very large room held three different pools and a row of spigots several inches from the floor on each wall. In front of each spigot sat a metal, flat-bottomed bowl and a very short-legged wooden stool. A number of drains were planted in the ceramic tiled floor to collect all the run-off.

"You come sit here," the sweet, salt and pepper-haired hostess said to me. She directed me to one of the spigots. "You wash here. You go in pool *afta*."

The rule made sense to me. Everybody was required to wash and rinse off thoroughly before entering one of the pools. The water from the spigot was so chilly, it was jarring to get into the first hot pool, kept at a temperature of one hundred degrees. Several nude women and girls were quietly and serenely in the pool.

If tension were a visible element, I would have seen streams of it leaving my body as I sat there among the other women. Occasionally, a couple of them chatted. Sometimes I thought they were talking about me, as they tilted their chins down toward each other and fixed their eyes in my direction. I didn't begrudge them the talk. I stood out, with my blond hair and my height, a few inches taller than most of them. I was a curiosity, maybe even an intrusion in their little community place.

I found my own object of curiosity—a woman in her thirties whose entire back from her neck to her hips was tattooed in an intricately woven design of reds, blues, and blacks. Flowers and winding tendrils traced her muscles and curves. I was fascinated. She seemed so out of place here in this traditional bathhouse. I had never understood why someone would subject herself to so much pain with the puncturing. Neither did I understand such a commitment to the permanence of it. What of the additional ordeal involved in removal when the tattoo was no longer her statement to the world?

The custom was to soak in the hot pool for a time, then later, step into a much hotter pool to soak. The hotter one was almost unbearable for me, so I didn't dally long, and I did something I soon learned I shouldn't have. I stood up too quickly, the blood rushed from my head, and I nearly passed out. A couple of the women nearby helped me out of the pool and led me to the little spigot where I poured some cool water over my face and body.

I was not adventurous enough to get into the third pool, which was much smaller, and electrified! I didn't know how this worked, nor did I have enough curiosity to find out later, but I did summon some latent courage. I walked over to this pool in which only one elderly woman sat and quickly stuck the toes of my left foot into it. Just as quickly I retrieved them. It was, well, shocking. Since I didn't see what use it could ever have for me, I never tried again.

Alex and I became semi-regulars to this bathhouse, alternating our visits here with another one a few streets away. Bathing like this became a treasured ritual for me.

On a few occasions, when Evelyn was feeling especially generous, she invited us to use the bathing facility in their house. The *ofuro* was a deep, square tub, heated from underneath. Like the public bath pools, it was not designed for washing in but only for soaking. Made for only one person at a time, it had a built-in seat so the bather could sit neck deep in soothing hot water and unwind for half an hour, leaving the water for the next family member. What a concept. I loved the *ofuro* and thought, if ever I had a home of my own, I'd like to have a "bathtub" like this. Was this bath thing the reason so many Japanese people had serene, even inscrutable, expressions on their faces most of the time?

As I was on my way to my teaching job one morning, something happened in the subway station that reinforced this belief. To catch the train I needed, I had to go down a broad set of stairs leading to the platform. At seven-thirty, the wide corrugated metal door, shut nightly, should have been fully open. But this morning, for whatever reason, the door was still closed, barring everyone from getting to the trains. I knew in this situation, commuters in the United States would have immediately started yelling, flailing, and beating on the door, but nothing of the sort happened here. As commuters started down the steps and noticed the passage blocked, they simply stopped and waited quietly or read their newspapers until the door opened. I was baffled.

I felt somewhat chagrined because my tendency, like that of most of my countrymen, was to "do something" out of frustration or impatience. We would clamor aggressively for immediate action to remedy the situation. Here was a population with a different temperament. If they felt agitation they concealed it and either turned it into a meditation or the seedling of some future discontent.

There was probably a similar undercurrent which made it possible for the Japanese train-riders to allow themselves to be herded into the overcrowded trains and squeezed into every available standing spot. The herding was done by a man with a pole whose job it was to pack the bodies in, just enough so the doors would still close. Perhaps this worked because of human beings' immense power of adaptation. Adherence to certain cultural codes and conventions was necessary to avoid meltdown in overpopulated Japan.

Riding the trains to my classes and group sessions, I was faced daily with being crammed into the cars with people pressed in all around me, bodies touching bodies. I adapted and accepted it because no one, to my knowledge, took advantage of the situation. Many other cultures had much more rigid personal boundaries.

Within weeks of our arrival in Japan, Ekrem, Ozlem, and Ayla, a Turkish couple and their baby daughter, moved into the apartment next door, brought to Japan by Ekrem's job. Robust and friendly, he was a serious young businessman who dressed daily in a Western style suit for his work. On the other hand, his wife Ozlem wore the more traditional female Muslim garb, an ankle-length skirt, long-sleeved, high-necked blouse, and a scarf covering all but her face.

I met her outside one day when both of our husbands were away. Friendly and talkative, Oslem spoke enough English for us to communicate. Our children, about the same age, could be playmates.

Alex and I had coordinated our schedules so when I had students, he would stay home with Jason, and when he had students, I would do the same.

I was eager for Alex to get home so I could introduce him to our new neighbors, but my enthusiasm was dampened when he arrived. Ozlem and I were outside watching our kids play in the grassy area when she spotted Alex and did something I thought was strange. Dropping her eyes, she rushed to pick up her daughter, said a hasty good-bye to me, and disappeared into her apartment.

The next day, I made a point of knocking on her door. She let me in. Even though I didn't know what to say, she read my confusion and said, "I'm sorry. My religion does not permit me to speak to a man who is not my husband or my family."

"But you can't say hello?" I asked.

"No, I cannot look at another man. I also cannot be in the same room unless he is my brother or a close relative."

I was astounded. "But it is the way I have to do," she said, and the subject was closed.

Oddly, it was permissible for me to talk to and be in the same room with her husband, but she couldn't do the same. Many days Jason and I would be visiting in their apartment while the kids played and Oslem showed me how she cooked some of her dishes. Ekrem would come home and I'd stay just a little while longer to chat with both of them. On days that she and Ayla spent time at my apartment, Oslem made sure she left long before Alex was due back.

In all the months that we lived next door to them, Oslem never once even made eye contact with Alex. I had to respect her religious beliefs and practices, but I didn't understand them. There was a lot I didn't understand about many things, and the more I experienced, the more I realized how little I knew.

Teaching English in Japan was completely different from the teaching I had done in Spain and Thailand. Here, most of my students were business people who had learned English grammar in their elementary and secondary schools, but needed conversational skills in the worldwide language of commerce. Cost was not an issue although many of the individuals I taught made small salaries. They were willing to pay whatever was necessary to learn. The fees, much higher than I had been paid in other places, had already been established by our predecessors.

Some were private students, and some were teams of managers at a steel company with whom I met a few times a week at their corporate office. Those groups were both the most interesting and the most lucrative. There was no formal classroom structure. Generally, the managers chose a topic and we discussed it. I corrected their grammar and pronunciation where needed. Alex also taught there on a different schedule.

One day it became even more interesting. Mr. Yoshihashi, who was in charge of the company's program, invited us to an all-day Sunday event. "Please come," he said. "It will be a special day where we can practice our English. We will pay you, and I think it will be good for you."

"But what should we prepare for, and what will we be doing there? Do we need to make a presentation?" I wanted to know.

"Just come," he said. "You will not have to do anything."

Although we were confused, it was an opportunity for a new and possibly stimulating experience. We agreed to be there the following Sunday.

We arranged to leave Jason for the day with a friend who lived in our apartment building. Nobuko was a beautiful, young Japanese college student from Hiroshima. Her presence was as gentle and serene as a quiet forest brook. When she smiled, it was like muted sunshine through tall pine trees. I trusted her completely and had no reservations about leaving our son with her for the day.

"He will be fine," Nobuko assured me when we left about 8 a.m. for the subway trip. She had already started to entertain Jason, so he hardly noticed we were leaving.

My steel company student, Mr. Yoshihashi, had been right. From the moment we walked into the room with the sliding paper panels, we were made to feel welcome as guests of honor. In typical Japanese style, we were shown over-the-top graciousness and civility, bred into this nation's people for centuries. We joined the ten men already there and took our places, sitting on cushions around low tables, connected and arranged in a square.

There was no rigid agenda. It was an informal social seminar. Alex and I simply opened ourselves to conversation, and at times took the lead in directing it. The attendees contributed wherever they wanted. We covered a wide range of topics, both serious and comic, and it really wasn't work at all. We took breaks, walked around, drank sake and enjoyed one another's company. We were presented with a stunning array of delectable dishes throughout day. Not only were they delicious, but they were also lovely works of art.

The measure of artfulness seemed to be the criteria for almost everything the Japanese did. One of my private students was a tea ceremony instructor, who after one of our English lessons, taught me some of the ceremony's basics. As far as I could tell, there was no functional reason for preparing the finely powdered green tea this way and no practical reason for the order of serving it or for turning the cup just so. There was only the "reason" of beauty. Did tea taste better prepared and served this way? Did food taste better or have more health-sustaining value when it was art on the plate? It made sense to me that we were more nourished when we consumed consciously and slowly. Then, the food, drink, music, or artwork was appreciated and could more easily follow the path inside our bodies, minds, or spirits where it would do the work it was meant to do.

My food education in Japan included learning to love the different forms of sushi and the variety of soups and other dishes we could get easily and inexpensively in the neighborhood restaurants. We didn't have problems ordering what we wanted because many restaurants had exact plastic replicas of the dishes they served displayed in their windows. The replicas looked remarkably real, and all we needed to do was point. Eventually we learned the names of our favorites and stopped pointing. We also learned quickly how to use chopsticks. I learned the value of consuming less.

I was fascinated by an older gentleman I saw almost every day, walking briskly around the temple grounds where I took Jason to play. He was a man of about seventy-five or eighty, with a slight build, gray hair and wise, almost mischievous eyes. He walked with pep in his step, not breaking his stride as he nodded and spoke to people.

One day I chanced speaking English to him, and he understood. So, wanting to know his secret, I had to ask: "You seem so full of energy and life. What do you eat?"

The old gentleman just looked at me, smiling, and said, "Very little." That was it.

We tasted some excellent home cooking when our bright, energetic friend Midori invited us to her family's home in Nagoya for a weekend. Meeting us at the train station when we arrived, Midori was as excited at the prospect of our visit as we were.

I removed my shoes as we entered her home, and I was pleasantly struck by the simplicity of the place. The floors were all covered with tatami mats, and the walls were all but bare. The room, occupied by a low-to-the-floor dining table and cushions during the day, became sleeping quarters by night when futons were brought out from their hiding places. Refreshingly, there was no "stuff" around, no clutter whatsoever. Really, there wasn't much room for "stuff."

Until I was ten years old, my family and I didn't have much stuff either. In my shared bedroom, I had a single drawer at the bottom of a tall old armoire that was mine, and only mine. It housed ALL of my toys and treasures.

Things changed as I grew up. We moved to a house where I shared a bedroom with only one sister, but we had only a tiny four-foot wide closet for both of us. We didn't die from a lack of stuff, but over the years, it multiplied anyway.

Now, again I had an absence of stuff. Alex and I couldn't afford any of life's luxuries, even though at the time, the cost of living in Japan was quite low. We rarely bought anything more than what we needed, but at Christmas time, I felt compelled to have some kind of observation. Although Jason was just over a year old and didn't know he was supposed to get gifts, I went to the Kintetsu Department store and splurged on some wooden building blocks for him. My mother also sent us each a gift that we put under our symbolic Christmas tree—a small, leafless tree branch stuck upright in a boot.

The Japanese are masters of small spaces, squeezing every ounce of use out of every available place. Even their department stores doubled as minor entertainment venues.

The shopping experience in the Kintetsu store and other large stores was pleasant and sometimes surprising. On every visit we were formally greeted by a pretty young lady in a kimono at the bottom of the escalator. "Welcome to Kintetsu," she said, bowing slightly as we walked past her and stepped onto the moving stairs. All day long she bowed and greeted everyone who walked by. It was almost as if we were entering a concert hall, and in a sense, we were.

On occasion, the store hired musical groups to perform as shoppers watched or shopped around them. One day, we were on the second floor when I recognized the voices of the Beatles coming from another department. Was it possible the Beatles were performing live a few feet away? Their voices were unmistakable, but was it a recording? Walking over to check it out, we saw them, the shaggy-haired foursome. They were live all right, but they were Japanese imitators, and excellent imitators at that.

We played tourist, taking a couple of day trips to two of Japan's most beautiful areas, Kyoto and Nara. Kyoto, for eleven centuries the capital of Japan, is famous for its two thousand or so Buddhist temples and Shinto shrines. It is one of Japan's best preserved cities. I felt as if I were walking around in a *Shangri-la* come to life when we strolled around the grounds of the Temple of the Golden Pavilion.

The city of Nara, though, was closer to my heart. In 794, Nara was the nation's capital, long before Kyoto had that honor. Nara, considered to be the birthplace of Japanese civilization, maintains a feeling of age old serenity. The monumental bronze Buddha commanding the area around the *Todai* Temple is an awe-inspiring sight. Set against a backdrop of wooded hills, it made for me an unbroken connection to ancient times, where I was not just an observer, but a delighted part of it.

Another trip, with our friend Nobuko, was not as delightful. There I came face to face with the inhuman part of humanity that I didn't like to claim.

We were guests of Nobuko and her family in Hiroshima. The hosts were gracious and their home was lovely. Her father was a physician, and an atmosphere of artful elegance and dignity pervaded their home. The family couldn't have treated us more hospitably. After an outstanding meal, Nobuko, through her interpretive skills, facilitated a warm and lively conversation among us.

It was the next day that was troubling. Our friend took us to visit the Memorial Peace Park, widely recognized by its landmark, the *Genbaku* Dome. The Atomic Bomb Dome is a haunting, skeletal reminder of the horrors that happened at Hiroshima.

Walking through the museum was overwhelmingly sad and sobering. I saw grim remains of objects that bore the effects of the thousands-of-degree blast—melted glass bottles, a wristwatch stopped at the exact time of the explosion. Even more saddening were the photographs of so many burned bodies of adults and children.

My mind couldn't grasp the described intensity of the heat, the supersonic shock waves at the hypocenter, or the hurricane-force winds that followed the blast. But one photo in particular gave me some hint of the immense glare caused by the blast. It was a photo of the shadow of a man who had been incinerated. His shadow had been burned into the ground.

The intense shame and sadness I felt as I stood in front of exhibit after exhibit made it hard not to look away. But the shame I felt was not any more for being an American than it was for being a part of a species which has from time immemorial waged war on its own members. The people who died in Pearl Harbor or in the concentration camps at Auschwitz were no less dead than those who died in Japan, and their families no less grief-stricken.

Yet as brutal and insane as war was, I wondered if it were any less brutal or insane to live with the dishonor, enslavement, and spirit-death which were common consequences of failing to take up arms for what is right and noble and good. Sometimes, war is a necessary evil. At the same time, I felt great gratitude for all the brave and honorable men and women who sacrificed and died in my stead. What I didn't understand was why mankind had not figured out how to avoid wars altogether. Was it because we were not as intelligent as we thought we were?

CHAPTER 31
Anything Gelse?

Everything comes to pass, nothing comes to stay.
—Matthew Flickstein

During most of the time we were in Japan, Alex and Ian kept in touch, at first, only occasionally exchanging letters, then more frequently as we drew closer to the time we would leave the country.

Ian had an ulterior motive I didn't recognize at the time, but he was clever and calculating and something about him made me feel very wary. He had such an extraordinary gift for words that he could make them do circus acts, a talent that Alex, an accomplished wordsmith himself, admired and possibly even envied. While Alex might occasionally use his words to obscure the truth or to paint himself in a better light, Ian used his words most often to bully, intimidate and control. I had gotten a small taste of his extreme egotistical style when we were in Formentera, but I thought when we left there, we would be out of his force field. I did not and could not imagine a time when we would intentionally put ourselves back into it.

Had it been up to me, we would never have crossed paths again. Now though, in the frequent letters he wrote to Alex, it was clear he was putting on the hard sell, writing to impress Alex with his knowledge and convince him we should go to London to be his students. Although it wasn't clear what he had to teach, we would live with him and his wife and daughter, and, essentially, pay to sit at his feet. Alex was appropriately wowed or maybe, he only welcomed the opportunity to verbally spar with someone of Ian's ability. Although I had serious misgivings, we had no alternative plans.

Near the end of the Japanese chapter, as we searched for viable means to return to England, we found passage on a Soviet passenger ship going to Hong Kong. From Hong Kong we would travel both by air and by bus overland.

My great love for seagoing ships didn't necessarily include luxury liners. Given a choice between traveling on a vessel like a floating city, decked out with grand ballrooms and entertainment areas for thousands of people, and a vessel that didn't disguise and diminish the seagoing experience, I would take the latter any day. The Soviet ship met my low expectations.

The atmosphere aboard the ship did not speak "cruise liner." No attempt was made to disguise this no-frills steel hulk with its unadorned gray bulkheads, closet-sized, colorless cabins, and an obvious lack of games. White tablecloths did, however, adorn the tables. Because passengers were few, Alex and I received very personal attention from the dressed-in-drab, unsmiling server. She spoke little English, but managed a question at the end of our meals.

We smiled later at her pronunciation when she asked, "Anything *gelse*?" In fact, there was something *gelse*, but not anything she could help us with. We had a long way yet to travel.

The ship stayed in port in fabled Hong Kong for a few days and so did we. On the first morning, we rode a tram up the mountain to the end of its line. From this vantage point we had a stunning panoramic view of the grand harbor and the overstuffed city above it. Dwelling was stacked upon dwelling, shop upon shop of every description, squeezed and crowded between paths and roads ascending the mountainside, leaving no space without some kind of occupancy.

On another day, we explored the harbor via ferry boat that took us past dozens of clanging junks and fishing boats. We rode a bus to a point in the city where it met the Chinese border. It was 1972 and China wasn't yet open to the Western world. We could only stand at the border and gaze out into a "forbidden land."

Although the city of Hong Kong is as full of intrigue as any writer could imagine, with a young son in tow, I had little room and less desire in my life for intrigue. The West was calling.

Our stay in Bangkok visiting old friends, was pleasant. Things had not changed much. Many of the former crowd were still around. We said our hellos and goodbyes, and flew away on Thai Airways on a plane bound for Dacca, Bangladesh. There we would take Air India to New Delhi.

The first leg of this journey was beautiful. The airline, true to the best Thai tradition, made us more than welcome on board with hot, moist towels to wipe our hands before they served up a lovely meal on a flower-petal strewn tray. When we landed in Dacca's small, primitive airport, I actually felt refreshed. In view of what was in store for us next, the refreshment provided an invaluable reserve.

Taking advantage of the time we had between flights, we explored Dacca, or what remained of it since the war of the year before that had won Bangladesh its independence from West Pakistan. I had no way of knowing if the city's condition was a result of that war or if it had always been as poor and shoddy. I did know we found little in the streets or buildings to inspire, and a lingering, if subdued, sense of unease.

While it might not be fair to judge the place by its appearance or on only what we could observe in a couple of hours, first impressions tend to stick. In any case, my main concern was not the condition or people of Bangladesh, but of our son's safety. This kind of travel was hard on Jason. His eating and sleeping routines were disrupted, and at best, he was uncomfortable and cranky. The few hours couldn't pass quickly enough for me.

When the call finally came to board the Indian airliner, I was relieved. We settled into our seats and Jason was resting on my lap as the plane taxied. Within minutes though, the taxiing was interrupted. A mechanical problem forced us back to the gate. "Not to worry," we were told. We could stay put and they would have the problem taken care of shortly. After two hours passed with no clearance to fly, we were ordered to disembark and return to the terminal. More waiting. Finally, and reluctantly, airline officials announced they would put us up in a hotel in Dacca for the night while we waited for a substitute plane to arrive the next day.

Spending the night was better than flying on a plane that had problems, but the next day an unbelievable thing happened. When we boarded the new plane and it taxied, it too returned to its gate. This plane too had problems. As we sat on the tarmac, passengers grew restless and on edge. We comforted and entertained Jason as best we could, trying to amuse ourselves as well by making light of this absurd situation. I felt like the mother of the main character in *Grapes of Wrath.* Her son recalled that she made laughter out of inadequate materials.

Then, absurdity of absurdities, a young impatient Californian with a mechanical bent who was slouched a few seats in front of us, stood up, got off the plane and joined the small cluster of mechanics, armchair technicians, and airline officials at the belly of the plane.

Sometime later, the Californian re-boarded, and giving himself credit where possibly no credit was due—or scarier, where it *was* due—he announced they had found the problem and solved it.

By this time, night had fallen and a strong rainstorm had developed. Since there were no electric lights along the runway, smudge pots on either side of it were lit to guide our plane's way. The pilot started the engine. Alex and I looked at each other, each with the same questions on our faces. Should we get off this plane or should we trust that the gods would be with us and carry us safely out? Were we committing ourselves to death if we stayed on this flight? We were so frazzled and exhausted that our decision-making abilities were in a state of suspended animation. We couldn't stay, and we couldn't go on what would quite possibly be our last trip on planet Earth. Our moments of indecision led to the default.

The rain beat down hard on our plane, now taxiing down the runway. Quickly I took out my notebook and scribbled a few lines to my mother, in case we didn't make it, as if she would ever get the note. I hugged Jason close to me. Alex and I held hands and our breaths as we lifted off.

The gods and my mother's prayers must have been with us as we flew and landed safely in Delhi. From there, we made haste to move on through Pakistan and to Afghanistan without much trouble.

The brief stay in Afghanistan took its toll on Jason mainly because of the appalling water supply system. When Alex and I were first in Afghanistan, he had succumbed to a bout of dysentery, despite the fact that he was an adult with a strong immune system. We thought we were being extra careful with our son, but he developed diarrhea we couldn't stop. Through the U.S. consulate we found a hospital that saved Jason from dehydration, but the ordeal left him weaker and worse for wear. Now I was even more eager to return to Western civilization.

CHAPTER 32

Solo, So Low, in Soho

Life is easier to take than you'd think; all that
is necessary is to accept the impossible,
do without the indispensable, and bear the intolerable.
—KATHLEEN NORRIS

IAN AND JEANETTE PICKED US up at the London airport in an old-fashioned taxi, the kind you see in old movies, cushy and spacious with comfortable, fold-up seats between the front and rear seats.

The couple's three-year old daughter Daisy was with them. She had light hair that stood out, spiral-like, framing her face, light blue eyes, freckles and rosy cheeks. Daisy so much looked like an animated flower that I found myself wondering which came first, her given name or the resemblance to a flower. Was her psyche mimicking the name her parents gave her or did she look so much like a flower at birth that they gave her a name that fit?

We had no chance to catch our breath and decompress from the flight. Neither Ian nor Jeanette asked us about our trip, or anything else. I would soon learn that Ian usually didn't ask questions, especially about opinions, because in his mind, he already had all the answers.

For the entire taxi ride to the rented flat on Mercers Road, he talked his jazz, and I don't mean music. Apart from offhandedly pointing out a few of the city's landmarks as if they belonged to him, he mostly talked about himself. Honestly, I had trouble focusing on what he was saying because I was in serious jet lag and because of the way he spoke, which didn't invite open exchange. He was talking at us rather than with us, as if we were an audience. He and his over-the-top clever words were stage performers. "Look at me, look at me," was his message. Yet we would soon find out we were intended to be more than an audience for Ian. We were to be the first of his *devotees* and his meal ticket.

Before arriving at the close-quartered, dark and cheerless flat, already I was feeling uncomfortable, asking myself why I had agreed to this move.

Ian came from a poor working class family on the outskirts of London, but he had been blessed, or cursed, with a strong intellect, formidable mental agility, and an over-inflated ego. Some years earlier, when Ian had made his way to the big city, he became a heavy cocaine user. Because I had never known a junkie before, I couldn't tell if he was a user now or how he could have supported the habit. He was always up early in the morning, seemingly full of energy, albeit misplaced energy. Alex and I didn't realize what we had walked into.

In retrospect, if I had had any inkling of what was in store for us, I never would have agreed to this experiment. If Alex had insisted, as difficult as it would have been, I would have taken Jason away with me and ended our marriage. Painful hindsight.

Apparently, this was a life-learning experience I had to go through. Was it destiny? That all depends on your definition of the word. It was never my belief that at birth we were each dealt a hand of cards dictating our path and destination, but rather a hand that merely got us into the game. Although we are born with certain attributes and into certain circumstances, our destiny, like the outcome of a poker game, is to a much greater extent than we would like to believe, dependent on how we played the hand. Much of the "deciding" of our destiny is done on a subconscious level, and it only *seems* that our destiny is decided for us.

For as long as I could remember, I had always hungered for adventure, learning, and new experiences. I had also always wanted what many others want, namely a happy family life, friendship, respect, success, accomplishment of mission, and in my old age to be surrounded by people who love me and whom I love.

I realized the choices I made every day largely determined my path. However circuitous the path was that brought me to London, and however much uneasiness and apprehension I was feeling about being there, I had to accept a great degree of responsibility for the circumstances. Ian may have been a venomous spider weaving a dangerous web, but reluctantly or not, I walked into it with my family.

The one-bedroom flat was designed on the order of what in New Orleans was called a "shotgun" style house, with one room behind the next and little or no hallway. If someone fired a shotgun at one end, it would not hit anything on the way to the exit.

Privacy was scant. For a time Alex and I stayed in the space that was probably supposed to be the dining area located next to the kitchen, which was the last room. At any given time, anyone might walk through our sleeping space.

This easily accommodated Ian's regular practice of storming through our space early in the morning, like a drill sergeant, either shouting our orders for the day, or simply shouting. Along with him came a background of the nerve-jangling music of David Bowie or T. Rex, blaring from his stereo. He never apologized. I understood later it was part of a deliberate and calculated strategy to rankle us and keep us off balance. He was a lord and madman with a plan.

He was the "teacher" who intended to teach us the "real yoga." The lessons he wanted to teach us required adherence to whatever policies and practices he dictated. Ian was all about being on a permanent high, so to speak, which by his definition meant increasing the amount of blood flow to the brain, by whatever means necessary. His behavior and dictates were not colored by any traces of common courtesy, civility, sympathy, ethics, or morality. Unfortunately, except for his lack of common courtesy and civility, the absence of the other qualities only became apparent after we were already ensnared in an impossible situation.

He did know a great deal about nutrition and creating well-balanced meals. It was, however, Alex and I who paid for the food. We still had several dollars in the bank we had saved from our jobs in Japan. Ian didn't have a job.

His 'work' was on the street, he said, teaching the ignorant. And he didn't do any of the housekeeping or cooking or laundry.

Before we arrived on the scene, Ian had sent his wife out to work as an 'exotic dancer' in Soho, an entertainment district that had become a breeding area for sleazy pubs and clubs in the West end area of London. Jeannette was still working, but what little money we had would be added to the pot to support Ian's habits.

Aside from dining on the best quality foods, Ian's habits included nightly marijuana smoking and frequent LSD consumption.

During the day, I took care of Jason, cleaned, did laundry, helped with cooking, and did whatever else I was told to do. On occasion I had the chance to take walks in the neighborhood and stop in small shops to browse.

Obligatory nightly rituals included weed, and occasionally LSD. While the two children slept in the other room, we sat on the floor of the living room and played at playing music. Ian sometimes played a flute. Otherwise he joined the rest of us in making a semblance of music on tambourines, *tablas*, and tiny Indian brass cymbals. One day while shopping, I spotted and fell in love with a beautiful well-used black wooden xylophone. Daring to spend money on myself, I bought it and added it to our assortment of instruments. Music time was the only time of day when tensions were not at a fevered pitch and my own personal terror was abated. Although I'm sure we made an awful dissonant racket, we actually thought we sounded good.

Ian made sure we had plenty of honey and fresh fruit to consume during those evenings. His indoctrination was that hallucinogenic drugs had the ability to greatly increase the blood flow to the brain, but required a great increase in glucose in order to sustain the high and the energy level. The trick was to get on a high that actually fed the mind. In my experience of marijuana and LSD, I concluded that the crazy munchies, a sign of low blood sugar, resulted from the brain craving food.

This is where things began to get weird, or weirder. One day Ian introduced us to the idea of trepanation, a surgical procedure in which a circular piece of bone is removed from the skull by a special saw-like instrument called a trepan. Evidence exists that trepanation was used in ancient times in various cultures, including the Incan, as a treatment for psychotic disorders, epilepsy or chronic migraine headaches.

Neurosurgeons, in standard medical practice, occasionally performed trepanation to relieve pressure on the brain caused by trauma or to remove a brain blood clot. It was a legitimate practice for legitimate purpose in the right hands.

Along came a small group of 'alternative practitioners' who populated a Kafkaesque world and decided that trepanation would be a way to expand consciousness, permanently and literally. The hole in the head, they proposed, would increase blood flow to the brain, thus opening the "third eye" or inner eye, bringing mental freedom and an almost childlike expansion in perception.

I had learned about, and experienced the existence of the "third eye", physically located in the center of the forehead. I had accessed the third eye without any drilling, but through certain practices like *kundalini* yoga and meditation. Concentrating energy on the third eye and opening different dimensions of reality, was natural enough, reasonable enough, and worth pursuing. But when Ian talked about achieving this state of expanded consciousness through a surgical procedure, I was extremely uneasy and frightened. The thought of it made me nauseous.

Ian's information about trepanation came from the writings of a Dutchman named Bart Hughes who allegedly had been expelled from medical school a few years before, both for failing examinations and for using marijuana. Hughes was the person generally thought of as the founder of an alternative application for trepanation. He originated the theory of *brain-bloodvolume*, which called for the use of trepanation. Coincidentally and allegedly, the theory developed as Hughes was smoking pot at a party on the island of Ibiza, when he observed someone standing on his head in order to increase the intoxication of the marijuana.

Ian claimed some people had successfully undergone the procedure, but I didn't even like to hear about it. I had the distinct feeling he would have liked to see one of us volunteer as a guinea pig, but wasn't contemplating trepanation for himself. I had to believe Ian considered himself to be too valuable to be a subject for experimentation. I also believed he had the spine and guts of a clam. He was happy to let others do his bidding and take all the risks.

His complexion was pale and pasty, as I believed his character to be. At the same time, his surly, obnoxious attitude repulsed me. Ian defined the term bully. I never saw him confront anyone bigger or stronger than he was. Had he done so, he would have been exposed for the physical and moral weakling he was. He also didn't have any friends. For all the months we spent with him, he didn't introduce us to a single one. Why were these glaring faults and scary shortcomings not obvious to me or Alex? If they were, why and how did we allow ourselves to be trapped? How does anyone get trapped in a cult leader's domain?

Here we were though, day in and day out, allowing ourselves to be subject to this man's domination. We had to 'work' at keeping up our *brainbloodvolume*, so the night-time trips into pot and LSD became more frequent. The worst epithet Ian could hurl at anyone not on his level of "consciousness" was to call him a "sugarlacker." In other words, this person wasn't feeding his brain well enough, thus it was starved and the person was dim-witted and hopeless. In Ian's "yoga" nothing mattered but increasing and maintaining a high level of *brainbloodvolume*, while having others pay his way.

One day in late July he insisted I go with him to Portobello Road. The well-known flea market scene boasted a cultural soup of exotic, ethnic, and counter-culture shops and street vendors, hawking everything from Indian cotton clothing, teas, leather goods, rugs, jewelry, and musical instruments to junk.

I had heard so much about the place that I really wanted to go, but I didn't want to go with Ian. Why did he want to take me there? He wasn't doing it to show me a good time. That became obvious as soon as we walked there from the tube station. He wouldn't let me linger in any place, looking at things that caught my eye. Instead, he took me by the hand and pulled me up and down the street, in and out of shops, pointing out what he wanted me to notice, completely ignoring what *I* wanted.

Still, he caught me completely off guard when he pretended to know the clerks in one shop as he yelled some greeting to them and then dragged me into the closet-sized fitting room. Before I even realized what was happening, without words or looks, he shoved me against one wall and forced himself on me, relieving himself of his sexual venom. In a matter of minutes, I was turned into an object, no longer a woman or a human being. It was a rough and mechanical thing, with no pretenses at all. He wanted something and he took it.

I was suddenly thrust into a hellish underworld where nothing was real, or I hoped it wasn't. And as in a recurring nightmare I had had in years past, I was being physically attacked but was unable to scream. I opened my mouth, but nothing came out. I was so scared that I was overwhelmed, dumbstruck, and unable to grapple with the truth of what was happening.

I didn't dare fight him. First, I knew he was much stronger than I was, and secondly because I was terrified he would either kill me or somehow take my son.

I was already past the point of fearing he would take Alex from me. He had already done a good job of driving a strong wedge between us, and Alex was no longer my ally. I had no ally. I couldn't even go to the police. What could or would they do? We were living in Ian's house, not exactly living law-abiding, conventionally respectable lives. Ian would deny what had happened. They wouldn't believe me, and the incident would only serve to anger Ian. I was truly trapped.

Just as he had dragged me into the fitting room, Ian quickly dragged me out back onto Portobello Road. He dragged me as if I were his rag doll. I didn't see anything after that, and I don't have any recollection of the tube ride back to the flat.

The whole incident was beyond enraging or humiliating, beyond detestable, beyond anything that made sense. My internal processor shut down. I had no precedent for processing the thing that had just happened. For a long time afterward, I couldn't say it or even admit it, but yes, I was raped. I can't say I knew what Alex thought or felt about the incident because he was so distant. He certainly didn't dare confront Ian about it, whether out of fear of him or subjugation. He may have told himself I submitted, or that nothing had happened, and the days wore on as if nothing had. I later learned I had been at least a month pregnant when this *nothing* had happened.

I felt strongly that Ian wanted Jason for his own son, and every day I fought against this. Although everything in me cried, wanting to leave London with my family, I knew the only way to do it would be to snatch Jason and run away without Alex. But how could I do this? How could I make it on my own with my young son, a child in my womb, and no money or friends?

Ian harshly criticized how we fed and took care of our son. When Jason had some kind of intestinal bug problem, possibly the lingering effects of the Afghanistan experience, Ian demanded we make him fast. I couldn't do that, and I knew it wasn't wise. My heart was broken. I would sneak Jason food. When Ian found out, he would fly into a rage and try to turn Alex against me in this. He was a master at terrorizing.

What had happened to us? All I could think was that in India we had learned, or begun to learn, how to submerge the ego in favor of realizing balance and serenity. Our tough skins had been peeled and our psyches were exposed and extremely vulnerable to anyone who would take advantage.

What was it that kept Alex so much under Ian's sway? Why couldn't or wouldn't he stand up to Ian and take us away? I didn't know which was stronger in him, the fear factor, the desire to learn from this lunatic, or his infatuation with Ian's power, clever wit, and heady, bizarre theories. Was Alex's attachment to this man a result of his having had a detached, absentee father? Did Ian serve as the father figure he needed? Who could say? Sometimes in life, it's all we can do to figure out *what* happened, let alone *why* it happened.

As time passed, Ian was hatching a plan. We needed to leave London, he said. Great, I thought, a chance to get away from this dark place. He said we needed to find a house in southern Spain, a *Yoga* House. I shuddered at his mockery of the term. He would get more students, more paying students, and we would help him run the house.

He determined there wasn't enough money to last very long, so the best plan was for him and Alex to get a van, take the kids and head to Spain, where living was inexpensive. They would go to Torremolinos, find and set up a house. Jeannette and I would follow later, after we earned enough money to cover several months of rent and household expenses.

It was decided then. The only part of the plan I liked was getting out of this flat and out of London. I fought against the idea of my son being taken away. The thought of it tore holes in my heart, but Alex tried to assure me he would take care of Jason and that it was for the best. In any case, though I couldn't explain why, even to myself, we had no other options. I struggled to understand why I was so powerless to break away. I felt I was not only in a physical prison, but also a psychological one. My spirit was in shackles.

Ian had planned the practical side of the venture. He decided that I would join Jeanette as an exotic dancer in Soho. Astoundingly and regrettably it happened. Alex, Jason, Ian, and Daisy drove away on a Saturday morning in a Volkswagen van Alex had bought with a chunk of our dwindling funds, and I cried all day.

Under other circumstances I might have enjoyed being in this *grande dame* of a city where I could lose myself in the wonders of her living history, her parks, beautiful architecture, and her fine art, only a small part of which Alex and I had explored on our trip several years ago. But now, I hated London for all it represented to me.

For the remaining time here, Jeanette and I did very little in the way of entertainment or even distraction. We rode the tube to work together in the evenings, but we never did become friends. I couldn't confide in her, nor she in me. We had little in common and little to laugh about together—laughter being an essential component of friendship. And, Jeanette was the right hand of the enemy.

Although she was a strong-headed woman, she was also a slave to Ian with no apparent purpose of her own. For whatever prizes she gained, I believed she had sold her soul, and that she was a mere dark shadow of a woman. Yet, she still had an advantage over me. I was her hostage, just as my husband and son were the hostages of Ian. Neither of us could make a move without extreme sacrifice.

Several nights a week, we made the trek to Soho where the clubs were clustered within a few blocks of each other. The way it worked in this game was that the "girls" got hired by several of the clubs so we would perform at one club, then run over to the next one for a show, and still another, maybe even four in one night. It was grueling, not only from the physical strain but also the emotional and psychic strain. It is hard enough to work at a random job that you hate, but it is a hundred times worse to work at a job that is also demeaning and against everything you stand for, or stood for.

The clubs were dark and dingy, the men mostly drunk and repulsive. I wanted to cry or scream, but instead I was on stage in the underbelly of London, shaking, slinking, and posturing in front of lecherous swine, all the while trying to develop armadillo skin against the psychic assaults.

It was potentially dangerous too. The men were seated so close to the stage that at any moment a crazy might reach out and grab me. Fortunately, that didn't happen. Another danger was walking from club to club. I could have been followed and mugged, or worse. I didn't have anyone looking out for me. Neither did Jeanette of course, who was just as vulnerable. Some nights she wanted to stay after the gigs were over to hang out in the underworld and find parties or happenings. I was very stupid to stay, but we had an agreement that we would travel back to the flat together.

The most dominant emotion I felt was not fear. I was too foolish to be very much afraid. Even embarrassment wasn't much of a concern because I dissociated, and I was learning how to be a detached observer of the body I called mine. I put it through its paces while trying to find some place of comfort and sanity inside my head. At the same time, I kept bumping into a deeply suppressed and growing rage. My spirit ached and cried.

They say though, that anything is bearable as long as you can see some future end to it. That end finally arrived. Jeanette and I closed up the Mercers Road flat, bought tickets for the train-boat to France, and I said good-bye, or at least *hasta la vista,* to a nightmare.

CHAPTER 33

House in Torremolinos

If I'm going to be alone, I want to be by myself.
— Marilyn Monroe (Roslyn) in "The Misfits"

Torremolinos was a beautiful place, but what happened there was grotesque and colored the picture my mind would always hold of it. A deep and wide sadness and shame took up residence in me where my memories of that Spanish region should be. I was unable to do anything to prevent or halt the events that occurred there. I wasn't even able to quickly extricate myself and my son from the situation.

Surely there were lessons I learned from it all—lessons about compassion, facing fears, standing up for myself, and about doing what had to be done. But those lessons came with great soul-searing pain.

I learned too there is such a thing as psychic bankruptcy, an absence of resolve, or at least an inability to act on that resolve. It might best be described as a moral catatonia, when we have to be rescued from ourselves, as well as from those who control us. It is a moral obligation of those who love us to come to our rescue in situations from which we can't rescue ourselves. But, sometimes those who love us are nowhere near and have no idea we are slipping into a black pit. Such was the situation in which I found myself in Torremolinos.

Taking the train from London to Dover, Jeannette and I crossed the English Channel by ferryboat, and continued by train to Paris. Jeannette didn't seem to be in any great rush to get to Southern Spain, and I welcomed the opportunity to spend a little time in this City of Lights, the city of my dreams. Besides, even though I missed my son terribly, I wasn't sure I was prepared for a new episode in *la vida bizarra*. I had no idea what to expect.

After checking into an inexpensive hotel in the *Place Pigalle* neighborhood and depositing our luggage, we walked until we found a busy nightclub with a live burlesque performance. The elaborately staged show featured a couple of the performers transported on flying contraptions over our heads, while the smoke of black tobacco hung thickly in the air. People talked in muffled tones. The club and everything in it took on a surreal appearance, but the bottle of Bordeaux Jeanette and I shared with dinner made it feel almost normal.

Although the place had the look of faded glory, I believed the leggy dancers in their gaudy costumes were working just as earnestly to give the audience a good show as their counterparts must have done in the club's heyday. Great performers always put their heart and soul into their performances no matter what the venue. They can't help but do that. It's what's inside them and what has to come out.

The night in Paris was a good, if brief escape, though it hardly gave me the good times reserve I would need to carry me through what was to come in Southern Spain.

When we arrived at the one-story, spacious home located on a couple of acres of treed land just outside of Torremolinos, I was pleasantly surprised at its apparent normalcy. Jason and Daisy were playing in the yard under a tree. With tears in my eyes, I ran to pick up and hug my son. Maybe things would be different here, I thought. Maybe away from the big city and its meanness we could live here for a time and do some good work.

My optimism didn't last long. Ian called the rental *The Yoga House*. He knew he might lure young innocents to his den that way, those on a spiritual quest, or those simply questing to know more about themselves and the world.

My aim, and I believed Alex's too, was to further the word and practice of a simple lifestyle that was conscious and conscientious, holistic, healthful, and generous. Obviously, this was not at all Ian's goal. I had foolishly thought that Alex and the pastoral setting might have a modifying influence on Ian's attitude and motives, but I was wrong. He was all about himself. He especially disgusted me when we were all walking down the main street in town, passing by an American hippie hangout bar when a long-haired compatriot greeted Ian.

"What's happenin'?" he asked offhandedly.

In mid-strut, and without blinking an eye, Ian returned his simple friendly hail with an unbelievably egotistical, "I am. I'm happening." I had never before witnessed such complete arrogance in anyone I knew personally.

While arrogant people might be annoying to us, arrogance in and of itself doesn't pose a danger to anyone else. I came to learn that in Ian's case, the arrogance was evidence of some kind of god complex, a belief that he was superior and should be served. This was where he was dangerous.

On one of Ian's recruiting trips into town he managed to ensnare a young German couple with a ten-week-old infant. They were living at the *Yoga House*, presumably to learn at the master's feet while they did his bidding. In ancient days, it was common for young people to apprentice to masters of a given trade and essentially be servants at the same time.

No such equitable or amicable arrangement existed here. Ian's knowledge he sought to pass on to Marc and Inga was questionable at best, and what he extracted from them was infinitely more than their toil and subservience. In the end, Ian ravaged their spirits and stole their child.

The couple had been traveling since Inga learned she was pregnant and wanted to escape an unhappy home situation. She gave birth in a hotel in Amsterdam. They followed the sun south where they might rest and rejuvenate themselves and try to determine what the world wanted of them. Because they still had a little money in reserve, they were ripe for the picking. Ian saw them as gullible and a means of continued financial support for him.

Inga was only nineteen years old and had very little knowledge about the needs of a baby. She barely had knowledge of her own needs. She told me she had tried to nurse the baby, and did for a few weeks, but her poor diet and the stress of living on the road with no place to call home caused her milk to dry up. Inga seemed physically and emotionally older than her age. The life she and Marc were living had taken its toll, and their child wasn't in the best of health. By the time I first saw him, the baby looked pale and without vitality.

At some time before Jeanette and I arrived, Ian had insisted that Inga start nursing her baby again, and that she not give him anything by bottle, so he would start to suck again. It had been weeks since she had stopped nursing and there was no way she could make the milk flow again. There may have been rare instances when a woman's milk could have returned after such a hiatus, but it wasn't going to happen now. Even if there had been a chance, the extreme stress of living in Ian's household would have prevented it.

Inga tried futilely, again and again as Ian commanded her. The child must suck and the milk would come, Ian said. From time to time, in between breast-feeding attempts, Inga's motherly instincts took over and she tried to sneak a bottle to her baby. But the attempts were too few, too far between, and too late. The baby didn't have enough strength in his little body to suck very much. When Ian found out, he became irate and told Inga the reason the baby wasn't sucking on her breast was that she was giving him a bottle.

The baby grew weaker by the day and showed little inclination to attempt to feed at all. Inga cried and begged, but the situation grew more hopeless, and the struggle unbearable.

Finally, Marc and Inga managed to break the spell they were under. They told Ian they were leaving the next day. Ian wasn't happy, but probably realized that if they left, he would no longer have to deal with a sick baby he obviously couldn't cure. The couple's decision opened a window of opportunity for me.

Ian's treatment of the couple and their baby was more than I could stand, more terrifying to me because I was now five months pregnant. I prayed I could get away with my son. Alex and I had had heart-wrenching talks about it, and we concluded that my leaving with Jason was for the best. I made the decision to go. Marc and Inga agreed we could go with them. They didn't know yet where they were headed—possibly back to Germany—and I didn't either. Maybe I would go to Ibiza for a while. I could decide later. I just knew I had to get out of there.

Alex had been sick in bed for a couple of days, and he still was. He was feverish and miserable when I told him our plan to leave the next morning, but he still agreed with me about it. He would stay. We knew then, if not before, that our relationship was bankrupt.

I went to find Ian to tell him what I had decided to do. My legs were wobbly, my palms sweaty, and my heart was racing, but I summoned my courage. When I told him, as I was afraid of, he lost it. He bullied me and screamed at me, although I wasn't hearing what he said. Then, when I thought the worst was over, he violently shoved me against a wall. I was shaking and sobbing and I couldn't stop. Finally, when Ian's anger subsided, he demanded that we go. He had to. If he demanded we leave, he could believe it was his decision, and that he was still in control.

I slept little that night, and felt wretched in the morning. I was still shaking when I packed up my things. Somewhere around noon, Marc, Inga, their baby, Jason and I left in their Volkswagen van. It was a much calmer departure than I had imagined it would be. Somehow, Ian released us. He may have done so willingly because he had the victory of breaking up our family, and he knew he still had his disciple Alex. Maybe, just maybe, Alex's decision to stay was somewhat selfless, and was what made my leaving with our son possible.

Just before we left, Alex pulled me aside to tell me two things. First, he would be sure to see Jason somehow before his next birthday, and second, I should withdraw the rest of our money out of the Swiss bank account, as meager as it might be.

I took very little with me, just a few clothes for me and Jason and my notebooks. I had to leave the beautiful wooden xylophone I had bought because Ian wanted it. Other than my child, it was my only treasure. Its sound had brought me some comfort when there was none other to be had. But it was just a thing, and I couldn't have carried it anyway. I simply felt relief at leaving.

With Marc driving, we traveled for several hours along the southernmost road in Spain in silence. What was there to say? Even Jason was quiet. Inga was in the front seat and Jason and I in the second seat. Inga had put the baby to sleep in a portable crib in the back of the van. We stopped on a number of occasions so Inga could hold her child on her lap and try to feed him milk from a bottle. He barely drank anything.

We were parked at the side of the road as daylight gave way to shadow then dark sky. On this attempt, the baby wouldn't suck at all. He was noticeably weaker and had developed a grayish color. As Inga held him in her arms, I put some milk on my finger and touched it to his lips, hopelessly hoping he would at least lick it, so I could give him more and more this way until he was somehow miraculously nourished and able to survive. *Please baby, lick my finger. Please hang on.*

By now, tears were rolling down Inga's face as she realized what was happening. I could also feel tears welling up inside me. After trying and trying to save this little life, we all became aware of the futility of our efforts. The baby wasn't responding. This couldn't be happening, but it was. *What do we do? What do we do?*

We should try to find a doctor. It was late. We were in a small town that was already closed up for the evening. We didn't know anybody. We didn't know where to find a doctor.

Wait. There was a pharmacy, and above it, a residence.

Marc pulled the van over and we ran and beat on the door. A sleepy older doctor who lived upstairs, came to the door, rubbing his eyes, trying to understand what these strangers were saying.

He let us in and Marc held out the baby to him. He listened for a breath and a heartbeat. There was neither. He shook his head and gave the infant back to his father. "*El no vive*," the doctor sadly pronounced. "*El est muerto.*" His words needed no translation.

I supposed that the doctor assumed we had a home to go to, or a place where someone could help the baby's mother and father handle the details of the burial, if not the grief and devastation. But of course, this wasn't true. We were in a state of shock. No one and nothing in our lives previously had prepared any of us to handle this kind of situation. My mind balked. My heart hurt. And Inga, poor Inga. There was nothing I could say or do to comfort, console, or guide her and Marc. I only put my arms around them while we three cried.

In the van, Marc decided on a course of action. He drove far out into the countryside, picking a spot in a small clearing in the now dark night. With only a waning moon for light, Marc dug a hole in the soft ground. Then Inga, holding her child to her chest, and I, got out of the van. Jason stayed asleep inside.

The couple kissed their baby good-bye, put him into a pillow case along with the necklace Inga removed from her neck, and laid him in his grave and covered it. Marc said a few words over the burial spot. We stood silently for a few moments then drove off and headed northward on Spain's east coast.

No one spoke for hours until we pulled off the road again, this time to sleep. The next day the sun seemed dimmer and the air noticeably heavier. I decided Jason and I would indeed go to Ibiza because I knew I would find some fellow Americans there, and because I didn't know where else to go.

Marc and Inga dropped us off in Alicante. Still numbed, I went to the bank, withdrew the last of our savings, and Jason and I boarded a boat for the small Balearic island.

CHAPTER 34

Ibiza After the Fall

Once you've hit rock bottom, that's where you perfectly stand.
That's your chance of re-starting the right way.
—Justin Kanayurak

This time in Ibiza, I wandered as though in a daze, but with my young son in tow. No pension would accept me. "No room," the *patrona* of the house would say, looking down her nose at me, while I could hear the emptiness of the rooms in the cold stone building. No one wanted me. I was a free and flagrant hippie, who was diametrically opposed to all they stood for in their straight, somber Catholic world. I was without a husband, obviously pregnant, and with a two-year-old riding on my hip.

Stopping short of condemning these women who wouldn't let me in, it occurred to me that we all do this at times. We judge and avoid people who are not like us. Perhaps we see in them parts of ourselves we don't like or don't want to see, behind our smug exterior. *There is no room for you in my world. I don't want to have to examine my belief system, my code of conduct, or my lifestyle and see where they are lacking.*

Admittedly, I was possibly as unaccepting of these women and their belief system as they were of me and mine. Still, they had a roof over their heads, and I didn't.

So this is what the bottom feels like, I said to no one but myself. I had hit the rock bottom of my existence. This was not at all the way I ever imagined my life would be. I had always seen only a bright future, never believing in divorce, at least not for myself. I would be a happily married woman in a prosperous household with a husband who adored me and took care of me. I would never be a woman alone with two children, but I was. I was alone with no future I could see—no plans, no prospects, no job, no money, no home, and no friends or family nearby to help me. I had no one I could even talk to and tell about what had happened. Who would have been able to relate to what I had been through or was going through now? No one I knew, especially not my family.

Yet as I paced those merciless cobblestone streets, something inside me clung, if not to hope, at least to a disbelief in the reality of my situation. This could not be reality; it was all outside of me. Outwardly, materially, I had nothing. There was no false pride, maybe no pride at all.

My ego was a house of cards collapsed.

I went inside to what was real. Out of necessity I became an observer of my life. What I had learned from Swami in India, and what was revealed to me on Monkey Hill in Kathmandu was all there for me, and was my salvation. I caught myself at times being a disinterested observer, as if I were watching a sad movie, wondering what could happen next in the life of this poor woman. I didn't know what I was doing or what I *should* do except to take care of my son's immediate needs and mine, to find food and a place to stay.

I called on all I knew to be true. Because I had certain needs and because I was sincerely looking for answers, I knew if I listened quietly and opened myself to the possibilities, the answers would come. I knew that somehow I would find myself where I was supposed to be, doing "the work" I was called to do, and my children would be taken care of. Somehow there would be a resolution. Limbo doesn't last forever.

In spite of his young age, my son didn't make undue trouble for me as most two-year olds might. Maybe that was because he was an old soul. He had seen more than most toddlers see. He no doubt recognized that I had trouble enough.

It wasn't so bad then, when he and I hung out at a sidewalk café frequented by a number of other American and Western European travelers. I was able to buy a little food as we waited. I had a few dollars left from the small remains of our bank account, ninety dollars minus the cost of the boat ticket to this island. Fortunately, I knew how to stretch a peseta.

A couple sitting at the next table, who introduced themselves as Eileen and Michael, commented on what a beautiful child I had. We struck up a conversation. Eileen was pregnant and much nearer her due date than I was. They had been staying in a rented house on the island for the last couple of months. After we talked a while, Greg, an American friend of theirs, showed up, and they introduced us. A couple of years younger than I was, he seemed kind and sensitive. He had a broad, genuine smile and a gentle, completely unpretentious manner. Greg didn't waste much time zeroing in on the situation.

"I've got this little old house I'm renting out in the country a few kilometers from here," he said. "I'm by myself. Carroll, if you need a place to stay for a while you can stay with me."

"Are you sure? I mean, you don't mind kids?"

"No, I love kids," Greg said.

Immediately I liked and trusted him. Not that I had any other options at this point, but I agreed to move in. "It'll only be for a little while," I tried to assure him and myself at the same time.

"Sure that'll be great," he said, and that was that.

His house was small but adequate for our needs, except there was no electricity and not much for heat. Within a week of our arrival, he constructed a fireplace, using chicken wire as a foundation which he coated with some plaster of Paris type material. Otherwise, the place was pretty chilly, so we slept together snuggled up. The house had one bedroom, a small loft, a small kitchen, and a living area.

Greg's friends Michael and Eileen, from the heart of America, lived within hiking distance of his place. Both of them were sweethearts, but Eileen was a dear soul and vibrant spirit. She had a soft, hospitable nature and eyes that saw through to a person's core. Eileen was honest, but never brutally so, and she laughed easily. She was hardy and boldly self-reliant, and like me, had a great love and appreciation for the natural world. We became good friends instantly.

Eileen's baby was due in several weeks. She hadn't been to a doctor in some time and didn't have an exact date pinned down. I'm sure we were soul sisters, especially because she planned to deliver her baby at home with the help of a local midwife. Michael was fully supportive of her decision.

Until her time came, we spent many good days together, sharing meals, swapping stories, and walking in the countryside. She adored Jason, delighting in playing with him. She was like a child in her anticipation of being a mother too.

As for me, I very much needed to be part of this anticipation and the magic of another new life coming into the world, especially after being a witness to Marc and Inga's devastation with their poor child. Where do babies *really* come from? I wondered.

"So, what was it like, the labor and all? Was it really painful?" Eileen wanted to know.

"I can't say it was so bad. Mine started with a lower back ache," I said. "The contractions got pretty strong later, but I guess the reason they call it labor is because it really is. It was the hardest work I'd ever done in my life. After a while, you just want everything to stop so you can at least have a break and rest. But, really, the hard part for me was that final moment when my baby was crowning and I felt this intense burning sensation of my skin. Well, the skin of my perineum was being stretched beyond belief, but that only lasted a little while."

"I was exhausted after it was over, but just seeing Jason lying there, beautiful and healthy, made it all worthwhile."

"I can't wait," Eileen said.

"And another thing," I threw in, "I've found out there are a lot of things I can't do, but after I went through this birthing, I felt pretty victorious and proud. *I* did it. *Me.* Well, my midwife guided me and she caught the baby but *I'm the one* who did it."

Eileen said she would remember that. She told me about her midwife, Carmela, who lived nearby and who had had many years of experience. Carmela would come when she was called. "I feel good about her," Eileen told me. She also said she wanted me to be there too. She knew, of course, I would jump at the chance.

The days tumbled by peacefully. Eileen was in great shape for the delivery. Her skin glowed. She introduced me to an herbalist friend from Grenoble, France. Jeanne made wonderful mixtures of fragrant oils and put them in beautiful colored glass bottles. She had given Eileen some with instructions to rub it on her abdomen every day to prevent stretch marks from the pregnancy. She gave me a bottle too, which I gladly accepted and used. Jeanne promised she would also be at the birth. Everything was coming together beautifully.

Then the day came. As soon as we got word, Greg and I hurried to Eileen and Michael's house. Eileen was already well into labor. She was half lying, half sitting on her bed, laboring, but still able to smile a little between contractions.

The midwife was there, closely attentive to Eileen. She made sure we all stayed out of her way, with the exception of Michael who stood next to Eileen, wiping her forehead and encouraging her. The baby had dropped and was in position. Everything was a go.

After several hours passed, the midwife said Eileen could finally push, which she did. On the next strong contraction, she pushed again, and again, her face red and her whole body straining. Still there was no crowning. More time passed. More brave pushing and straining with hardly any cries from Eileen. We stood nearby.

Eileen was healthy, strong, and loving, with a remarkable attitude and will. What could be wrong? Why shouldn't she be able to snub her nose at convention and deliver her child naturally, the way she wanted to? We were so naïve. No, ignorant was probably a better word to describe us, considering the old adage that a little knowledge is a dangerous thing.

We had a little knowledge for sure, but not enough. We wanted badly to see Eileen deliver this baby, although of course not as badly as Eileen wanted it. She wanted it so badly and was so determined to make it happen that she failed to tell anyone a very important piece of information about her situation.

Hours passed. I lost track of the time. And then, almost abruptly, "*No puedo, no puedo,*" the old woman said. "I can't, I can't." As a midwife, she knew it was beyond anything she could handle alone. She gave up and soon left.

Wait a minute. What now? This was a frightening situation for all of us. None of us knew a doctor, how to find one quickly on this island, or how to transport Eileen in her condition even if we found one. We had no telephone, and we were several miles out in a very rural area.

Eileen pushed with everything she had. We stood by her side, taking turns wiping her face with a wet cloth, and giving her a hand to squeeze when the contractions came, stronger and stronger. She sometimes looked at me with a bewildered, mortally frightened look. She desperately searched my face for an answer she was looking for, and some reassurance that everything was going to be all right. For at least some time, with my spirit of perseverance, I was able to offer her that.

All of us looked to one another for guidance, and were determined that Eileen and we, were going to make this baby happen. How could it not? The baby was inside. It had to come out. My old friend in San Francisco had had two babies born this way, as nature had intended, and it was fine. I had had a baby too the same way, and it was fine. I was fine.

I remembered hearing the voice of my midwife in Switzerland, prompting me as I was on the brink of delivering my baby. "Just a little more," she urged a couple of times, and then, in a few more pushes, he was out. Hard work, but I did it. I had recounted this story to Eileen weeks before this day. She wanted to hear about it over and over. Maybe these glowing accounts of my triumphant delivery gave her foolhardy courage when she shouldn't have had it.

As the hours went by, Eileen's agony was more apparent, and she grew weaker. We were clearly over our heads, nearly petrified with fear. This was beyond belief. I wished I could have re-wound time to at least the beginning of her labor when we might have gotten Eileen to some medical facility, even if she had objected.

"Please try again, once more, Honey," Michael said, as the wave of a contraction reached its zenith. "Please."

But nothing. Nothing but more pain, frustration, and exhaustion.

Then as if we were all thinking with one mind, we decided on the only action we could take. Michael began to push downward on the top of Eileen's abdomen, at the fundus, as she would push. Again. Again.

"Oh, my God, help us," I almost demanded. Eileen's beautiful face was contorted now, her forehead glistening with beads of sweat, her eyes full of tears. She let out a few strident cries. I struggled to hold back my own tears for her sake. Michael pushed again. None of us was willing to accept that this child would not be born.

Beyond that, I finally realized if this child were not delivered soon, our lovely Eileen could die. No, that wouldn't be. We were all presumptuous enough or dangerously ignorant enough to think we had the power to dictate the outcome. What was worse, Michael sometimes looked wildly and expectantly to me, as if I had the answer. I had, after all, been a full participant in my baby's birth. I had no such answer.

But there was no time to question, no time to plead, only time for doing, and very little at that. We all knew it. Until then, we were each struggling on our own, in the isolation of our own heads and hearts and physical capabilities. But suddenly, something drew us together. What happened was an extraordinary merging and fusing of all of the spiritual energy of everyone in that room, entirely focused on this one life or death task. God was a palpable presence in that room, even in the varied forms and names he took in each of our lives, possibly just as it is on the battlefield. Clearly evaporated were whatever illusions we had of God, fostered by religious denominational distortions or even of our later rejection of those misrepresentations. This was pure universal energy. We were swimming in it and drawing from it. We knew this was it.

We all joined in one final strong push from within and without, one that drained us all, and it happened. A baby emerged.

But, "God help us," I prayed again. He had a grossly misshapen head that came almost to a point because of the very narrow opening it had been forced through. The baby was not alive.

A deep, dark silence engulfed us until the tears came. We surrounded and hugged Eileen and this tiny lifeless body until she began to breathe normally again.

I had many questions in my head but was too exhausted and too sad to grapple with them. I just wanted to be there with my friend awhile. Eileen finally spoke. With what must have been a torturously heavy heart, she revealed the information she had withheld. When she became pregnant, her doctor had told her that her bone structure was too narrow to have a baby without a Caesarian section. She chose not to believe that.

No words could say what devastation I felt at the time, and especially not what Eileen must have felt. It was a pity she couldn't even have felt the momentary rewarding wave of relief that comes immediately after delivering a child, which makes the mother forget all the pain she experienced. No, one agony was over for Eileen, but another had already begun.

CHAPTER 35

In My Own Skin

We shall not cease from exploration, and the
end of all our exploring will be
to arrive where we started and know the place for the first time.
—T.S. Eliot

Winters are usually mild on the sunny island of Ibiza, but now a definite chill was in the air in the hinterlands where I was staying with Greg. We found few ingredients to put together a good laugh.

Fortunately, we had toddler Jason in our midst who caused some smiles to break through our forlorn faces. I took him over to visit with Eileen as much as I could. She dearly loved my blond-haired boy, and the visits were bittersweet for her as she grieved for her lost child.

Not many weeks after Eileen's ordeal, I had an awakening, or perhaps it was a remembered longing. I realized I had to go home with my child and my child to be. I didn't know what else I had to do, but I had to go home to my own country, to my family, to a place that was normal, whatever that was. Greg practically begged me to stay. He was a dear sweet soul who was like a brother to me, and the prospect was tempting, but I couldn't. I needed a place where I could deliver my baby in the safety and comfort of a real home with running water and electricity.

After almost six years, I did miss some of the creature comforts and the relative ease of life that exists even among the poorer folks in America. I had learned that the poverty and hard times existing in the United States generally couldn't compare in depth or breadth to that in many other parts of the world. I missed many aspects of life in America, and I had a new appreciation for my country, the place so many people I met abroad thought of as the land of dreams. At that moment, even for all its faults, I knew that picture was true.

Uppermost in my mind was I needed a place where my children and I could be safe and where we could be taken care of. I could find a way to make my life work again and make some kind of sense. Tired of the vagabond life, I needed an emotional, if not physical rest. I was a mother, but I needed *my* mother, who had prayed me around the world, to put her arms around me and assure me that everything would be fine.

After that, where would I settle though? California seemed the logical choice. Alex's sister Miranda and I had maintained a long-distance friendship over the years, and she still lived there. Naturally, when she invited Jason and me to share an apartment with her and her son Gabe, the decision was made.

Providence directed me to find a cheap airfare on Icelandic Airlines from Luxembourg to New York. Providence also led me to Rolf, a young Luxembourger in Ibiza who agreed to have Jason and me as paying passengers on his drive back home. In the meantime, my parents wired money for the plane ticket.

After Greg and Eileen and I shared hugs and tearful good-byes on a January morning, we left the island. Jason and I packed ourselves into this stranger's pocket-sized car and drove north from Alicante. For better or worse, there were many things I had had to do on faith. This was another one of them.

I don't know how many hours we drove. I do know that the farther north we went, the colder it became. The headlights glanced off of patchy ice in the road. Because we didn't have money for lodging, we kept pushing on. Ultimately though, Rolf was too tired to drive and we had to pull over for a few hours to sleep. I pulled out from my bag practically all the clothes I had to cover the three of us. Jason was bundled into a multi-layered cocoon in the back seat. He seemed cozy enough, and he slept, but after a couple of hours passed, Rolf and I were still awake, extremely cold and miserably uncomfortable. There was nothing to do but drive on.

I was never so relieved and happy to get to an airport as I was in Luxembourg, even though we had to sit for hours in uncomfortable seats waiting for our plane. We were warm and not cramped.

As much as I loved ship and train travel, I also appreciated flying. The plane would provide an immediate escape from whatever circumstances I found myself in, take me above the clouds away from planet Earth, and give me godlike distance and perspective. The flight, which took about seven hours, also provided me with an opportunity to begin to make some assessments.

Looking down over the vast ocean below, I became a mere drop in it. As Jason mercifully slept, and the baby growing inside me stirred and shifted restlessly, I wondered, *when does our experience have real value?* When does it become fair payment for the price it has extracted from us? In this case, it certainly wasn't yet. It might not be for a while.

I had left the United States headed for a rendezvous with the man who would be my husband. Now I was returning home with our children, one yet unborn, but without him. On my own but not unencumbered, I wondered how I might make it in the world. Yet I was gathering strength in my independent state and releasing the ruinous rubbish that still clung to parts of my psyche, even as the plane swallowed the miles of sky and discharged its debris in a vaporous trail.

Arriving at JFK airport, I must have been a strange sight to behold. My too-long, wavy blond hair was tinged with red henna. I was wearing an ankle-length, age-worn and shiny, black crepe dress with red trim on its bodice, which had a large telltale bump protruding from my front. I carried a two-year old on one hip and had an enormous, long-handled, soft-sided basket slung over the other shoulder. It was crammed with an odd assortment of items which customs officials were more than a little interested in examining.

The first things they pulled out were several long sprigs of rosemary I had clipped from an Ibizan bush, and a couple of handfuls of dark brown, dry and edible carob bean pods. Looking at me quizzically, with his head cocked to one side, one of the officers asked the logical question, "What *is* this stuff?"

Trying to explain to him what it was and what I planned to do with it was almost as difficult as seeing it taken away from me. "You can't bring plants into this country," he said. "They might be disease carriers."

Well, at least that's all I've lost, I thought. Now maybe I could get on with the rest of my trip home. But before I could move on, I heard, "Wait just a minute, Miss," from another agent. "Please step over here." He pointed in the direction of a small side room.

When I went in, still carrying Jason on my hip and now totally exhausted, he called my attention to my open suitcase and something they had found inside it.

Unbelievably, it was a tiny bit of hashish, maybe a fingernail-sized piece that I had long ago forgotten in the bottom of a small Nepalese cloth purse.

So the bad drama isn't over yet. My heart sank. I don't know if they believed me that I didn't intentionally bring hash into the country or that I certainly had no intention of selling it, as small an amount as it was, but they made me sweat out the time they took thinking about it.

Suddenly I was thrown into another out of body experience in which I was objectively observing this young pathetic woman from a distance, both physically and emotionally. What would happen next to her and her babies? I wondered. What more could happen? Would she be thrown into jail and her children taken away? The thought of it might have left me paralyzed with fear or blubbering in tears. But it didn't. At that point, I was completely detached and unable to hope for or expect anything. Whatever would be would be. Just like the old song my mother used to sing, sometimes at the top of her lungs as she did her housework: "*Que sera, sera.* Whatever will be will be. The future's not ours to see. *Que sera sera.*"

A friendly but stern-faced customs agent brought me back to myself. "Listen, Miss, we're not going to keep you here. We're going to let you go," he said, as he eyed my big belly. "But you need to watch your step and take care of yourself and your kids. You can't be using drugs or carrying them around. You might not have such an easy time of it next time."

Those were kind words and he was absolutely right. I breathed a sigh of relief as I thanked him and picked up my bag.

After spending the night in the Manhattan apartment of an old friend of Alex's father, we flew in the morning to New Orleans. My mother and father met me and Jason at the airport to take us "home."

Someone said that home is where, when you have to go there, they have to take you in. I'm sure my parents didn't feel that they *had to* take us in. They *wanted* to. My mother, ever loving and hospitable, had fresh-smelling sun-dried sheets and cozy blankets on the bed that would be mine as long as I wanted it, and I felt truly welcomed and loved. She and my father were just that way. My father cooked breakfasts for us and my mother cooked my favorite dishes for nightly dinners—stuffed green peppers and baked macaroni, seafood gumbo, and pan-fried chicken and mashed potatoes.

We talked, reminisced, and laughed a lot. I got reacquainted with my sisters and my brother. And like old times, relatives came over to visit. Everyone held and laughed with and played with Jason. It was lovely to see my family getting to know my son and accepting him into the fold. It was strengthening to be with my parents again and feel their steadfastness. How good it was to feel so loved and cared for. My appreciation for them and their unconditional love swelled. I felt I had stepped out of the shadows of darkness into the light of love. It was a true healing.

Yet I knew I couldn't stay; it was impossible. After all I had been through and the life I had lived, I couldn't stay there in the suburbs and pretend it all hadn't happened. And there was so very much I couldn't talk about with my mother and father. The gap in experience was too immense to bridge. I still loved my family dearly and I would always maintain the soul connection between us, but since my initial leaving, someone had changed the locks on the door. It wasn't anyone in my family. *I* had changed the locks and my key no longer fit.

California was calling me. It was the only place where I thought I might find people who could understand this need of mine to push beyond the limits of conventional social mores to get at the meaty substance of life and then to suck out the marrow.

After a couple of weeks, we left. My father gave me an old Chevy which he had bought for a little taxi business he owned, and a friend of Miranda's came out from California to help me drive back across country to the Palo Alto area.

The two-bedroom apartment had a spacious kitchen where Miranda made many savory and hearty casseroles, which I especially appreciated in my oh-so-pregnant state.

Every day I made what I called my pregnant shake, an orange juice and yogurt-based smoothie, with added nutritional yeast and a variety of fruit. This shake strengthened and energized me. I felt myself to be a powerhouse and I knew I was building a strong, healthy baby.

Things were going well. I got a job working at home as a telephone surveyor. It wasn't bad work. Nobody even hung up on me. Miranda's son Gabe, who was a year older than Jason, made a fine playmate for his cousin.

I determined that the upcoming birth, now less than two months away, would be at home. Having already had one successful natural, non-hospitalized birthing under my belt, I felt absolutely confident the second too would be fine. Miranda agreed to help me when the time came. We read everything we could find on the subject, consulted with some midwives in Santa Cruz, washed sheets and sterilized them in the oven, and then went about our business.

Miranda's friends became my friends too. For the most part, they were caring, kind, well-intentioned people like me, but also like me, they were extremely naïve. We were politically misguided victims of Utopian thinking. We disparaged and rejected the government and all it stood for. Verbally and life-stylistically, we distanced ourselves from anything that smacked of establishment or institution. We went into quiet rages over war and violence. At the same time we happily benefitted from the fruits of our parents' and ancestors' wisdom, labor, sacrifice, and even wars, in building the free and bountiful society we enjoyed. We never made the connection. *Flower children indeed.*

Wisdom teaches us that neither Utopia nor perfect people exist, nor could they. For a while though, many of us kept childlike fantasies of Utopia in our dreams, where fantasies belong. Even as we carried on in our daily lives with the same personal conflicts and concerns that have bedeviled humankind from time immemorial, we were *California dreamin'*.

I was past my eighth month of pregnancy when my mother and her cousin came to visit. This was the same cousin whose family had taken me as a seven-year-old on a train for my first trip to San Francisco. I had been enchanted then.

Back in that city now I was enchanted once more, traipsing up and down the undulating sidewalks, still gold-specked to me, practically dancing on the way. My mother marveled aloud as I walked with my two-year old on my hip and a baby still inside my womb. How did I do it, she wanted to know. The secret was that I was now the strongest I had ever been, not only physically but mentally and emotionally as well. Finally I was walking comfortably in my own skin, not trying to fit into someone else's.

I didn't know my baby's exact due date, although I knew it must be close. One Saturday night I felt fine enough to go with Miranda and her friend Ben to a John McLaughlin concert in San Francisco. I was excited to be going to hear McLaughlin, an English jazz musician whose music I had learned to appreciate in London.

Ben drove the old Chevy taxi I still had. We squeezed into the parking lot at the concert hall, and then squeezed into apparently the only seats left, up front next to immense speakers already blaring with the sounds of the warm-up band.

About thirty minutes into their performance, I started having a strange sensation. The speakers were so loud and the booming bass so strong I couldn't tell if what I was feeling was the sound vibration or the beginning of labor. Miranda went with me to the ladies room where I had to stand in line for my turn in a stall. I didn't have to wait long because my water broke, and the sea of women parted to let me go in ahead of them.

Miranda ran to get Ben who ran to get the car, which, he said, was possibly the only car that wasn't blocked in. When we got on the road we had a thirty-mile drive to our apartment, a long thirty miles. I sat in the back seat with Miranda holding my hand as labor intensified. Contractions were about five minutes apart.

As Ben broke the speed limit on Highway 101, suddenly the trip became more complicated. A tread on the right front tire partially split apart from it, making a dishearteningly awful *thwap, thwap, thwap* as the wheel turned.

What next? I worried. *Please, please, I don't want to deliver this baby on the side of the highway.* The noise of the tread grew louder, or was it simply my imagination? Ben wasn't sure what he should do. There was no time to stop and change the tire, even if we did have a good spare in the trunk, which was doubtful. What was the alternative? I was crushed by the thought of possibly being stranded and having to hitch-hike. Then I would deliver this baby in the car of a stranger. *Please, no.* Ben drove on, more slowly now, but steadily, trying to hide his own panic. My contractions came faster and stronger. *Would we make it back home in time? Breathe. Focus. Breathe. Focus. Think about the strong, healthy baby inside me. Think about everything being fine. Breathe. Think about making it.*

And then finally we did! When we arrived at the apartment I walked to the bed, which was a mattress on the floor. Someone set up the piece of plywood and pillows on an angle against the wall so I had something to lean on as I delivered my child. Miranda brought out all the supplies and nervously washed and scrubbed and re-washed her hands.

Labor was progressing fast and predictably like a train headed for the station on its last run of the day. I was in control. I swear I could feel my body parts doing what they needed to do to accommodate a smooth passage.

A couple of friends who had been babysitting Jason in the apartment awoke him as I had asked, and brought him to sit next to me to be a part of this magical birth event. It was after midnight, but he was wide-eyed. Children know things we don't give them credit for knowing. Not much more than two years before, Jason had made the journey himself. I knew somewhere in his sub-conscious mind he was aware he was taking part in something greater than us all.

Pant, pant, pant. Ride the waves of contractions.

"Don't push yet… Just a little more... Okay, push," Miranda said, as if I could have held back any longer. The tiny head crowned, and quickly, my second son came sliding out.

"Fish!" said his big brother with an amazed look in his big blue eyes.

Miranda caught the precious package in her gloved hands and let out a huge sigh of relief and a smile. She had been a great help and support to me. My baby was perfect, with hardly a wrinkle or a red spot on him.

I was exhilarated. *I did it! I did it on my own, just like I knew I could. Just like I knew I would.* In about an hour I walked to the kitchen and called my mother. Victory was mine and my newborn son's. I was at home, claiming my place in the universe. No matter what else I might accomplish in the future, I didn't imagine that anything could ever top this.

This was the crowning glory and perfect closure to my odyssey. And yet, in the cycle of life, it marked a new beginning.

Had I gone where I was meant to go? How would I ever know? I am sure though, I ended up where I was supposed to be..

Would I ever travel again? Absolutely. I would never stop yearning for the world and hungering to experience life in all of its fullness. After all was said and done, my days of sleeping between the rails might not be over, because I would always be a traveler, even if I never went another place.

Afterword

Writing the account of this odyssey has been the fulfillment of my self-imposed pledge to share what insights have passed through my door, in hopes the reader would recognize a kindred spirit and welcome it within.

Still, I recognize that I am just a traveler. I am not an authority on anything but what I feel. Like John Keats, "I am certain of nothing but the holiness of the Heart's affections and the truth of the imagination."

The Author

The diversity of Carroll Devine's background rivals that of the thirty-two countries that she lived in or journeyed through for five and a half years.

With a degree in Education, she was a teacher of English in Spain, Thailand, and Japan. In the United States, she taught English in high schools, and English as a second language in multi-cultural, multi-lingual adult classrooms. She has been a teacher of Yoga and relaxation and a practitioner for decades.

Carroll is a freelance writer, journalist, public speaker, and voiceover artist. For a dozen years, she was a weekend radio announcer for WWNO, an NPR affiliate.

In another lifetime, she raised three awesome sons, and chickens, goats, and vegetables, on a farm.

Carroll believes that life is a dance, and she currently has two more books in the works.

Made in the USA
Charleston, SC
06 March 2016